FORMAL METHODS FOR INDUSTRIAL CRITICAL SYSTEMS

FORMAL METHODS FOR INDUSTRIAL CRITICAL SYSTEMS
A Survey of Applications

Edited by

STEFANIA GNESI
Istituto di Scienza e Tecnologie dell'Informazione, Consiglio Nazionale delle Ricerche, Pisa, Italy

TIZIANA MARGARIA
University of Potsdam, Potsdam, Germany

A JOHN WILEY & SONS, INC., PUBLICATION

Library of Congress Cataloging-in-Publication Data:

Formal methods for industrial critical systems : a survey of applications / edited by Stefania Gnesi, Tiziana Margaria.
    pages cm
  Includes index.
  ISBN 978-0-470-87618-3
  1. Formal methods (Computer science) I. Gnesi, Stefania, 1954– II. Margaria-Steffen, Tiziana, 1964–
  QA76.9.F67F654 2012
  004.01'51–dc23

2012016775

10 9 8 7 6 5 4 3 2 1

CONTENTS

PART III   TRANSPORTATION SYSTEMS 61

4   SOME TRENDS IN FORMAL METHODS APPLICATIONS TO RAILWAY SIGNALING 63

Alessandro Fantechi, Wan Fokkink, and Angelo Morzenti

5   SYMBOLIC MODEL CHECKING FOR AVIONICS 85

Radu I. Siminiceanu and Gianfranco Ciardo

PART IV   TELECOMMUNICATIONS   113

6   APPLYING FORMAL METHODS TO TELECOMMUNICATION SERVICES WITH ACTIVE NETWORKS   115

María del Mar Gallardo, Jesús Martínez, and Pedro Merino

9   AN APPLICATION OF STOCHASTIC MODEL CHECKING IN THE INDUSTRY: USER-CENTERED MODELING AND ANALYSIS OF COLLABORATION IN *THINKTEAM*®   179

Maurice H. ter Beek, Stefania Gnesi, Diego Latella, Mieke Massink, Maurizio Sebastianis, and Gianluca Trentanni

PART VI   RUNTIME: TESTING AND MODEL LEARNING 205

FOREWORD

BY MIKE HINCHEY

The motivation for what many credit as being the forerunner to the first computer, as we know it, was a significant problem in the shipping industry in the early-to-late nineteenth century. Logarithmic tables, critical to this industry, published around that time, often contained simple—but significant—errors that resulted in lost ships, cargos, and lives. Babbage's difference engine is generally regarded as embodying many of the concepts now standard in computer systems (including memory, programs, and even a design for a printer that would work on a principle similar to modern laser printers). The goal was to automate the printing of these tables used in the shipping industry, removing inaccuracies.

Correctness of the data being relied on for calculating position was crucial to the shipping industry. The very idea of "correctness" has plagued computer science from virtually its inception. Turing was concerned with the issue in the 1930s, before the first practical computers (as we now know them) were to come along. Computer pioneers such as Zuse and Wilkes recognized early that correctness would be an issue they would need to address.

Over the six decades or so during which we have had modern electronic computers, the related issues of *dependability* and *reliability* have arisen along with concerns over *safety*, *security*, *performance*, and many other issues. The field of *formal methods* (a term that, interestingly, itself predates the modern computer) has arisen to address correctness in software and hardware systems, along with the other related issues just referred to.

To those of us who are confirmed "formal methodists," this has been a very welcome development, and we are pleased to see the significant developments in the field and the contributions that formal methods have made to improve our critical applications. Yet, in reality, formal methods are still not used as much in practice as we would like, being believed by many not to scale, to be prohibitively expensive, and to be too difficult to understand and use.

The formal methods community has responded by focusing on education, developing more usable notation and better (integrated) tool support, emphasizing particular aspects of a system rather than the entire system (so-called formal methods light), building user communities, and trying to encourage the use of formal methods in real-life applications. It is in *critical* applications that industrial adoption of formal methods has been greater. Interestingly, our definition of "critical" has evolved, to mean not just loss of life or property, or breaches of security, as a consequence of failure, but also in a business sense, meaning failure results in financial loss, loss of competitiveness, or loss of reputation.

Formal Methods in Industrial Critical Systems (FMICS) is the longest running Working Group of the European Research Consortium for Informatics and Mathematics (ERCIM), having run now since 1992. The working group consists of more than a dozen ERCIM partners, and dozens of other associated research partners and groups throughout Europe. It has focused on research on improving technologies based on formal methods and encouraging the application of formal methods in critical industrial applications through technology transfer.

This book highlights some examples of the excellent research that has been undertaken by this working group and its application in a number of critical industrial examples, in such domains as avionics, aerospace, and railway signaling (itself an industry that has become a major driver for formal methods technology). While the book addresses all aspects of formal methods from specification through implementation and verification, there is a clear emphasis on model checking, reflecting the significant advances in this area and successful industrial applications over the past decade or so.

The applications illustrate the appropriateness of the use of *formal methods* in industrially critical systems. While the authors are all experts in their respective fields, and we should not downplay the often significant hurdle that there can be to introducing formal methods into an organization, the message is simple: for particular domain applications and particular critical industries, formal methods are here to stay.

MIKE HINCHEY

Lero, Limerick

FOREWORD

BY ALESSANDRO FANTECHI and PEDRO MERINO

This book has a long story, which is part of the story of the working group on Formal Methods for Industrial Critical Systems (FMICS) inside the European Research Consortium for Informatics and Mathematics (ERCIM), the oldest active working group in this consortium.

The FMICS WG focuses on the development of formal verification techniques and leads activities, such as joint international projects, related to verification and formal aspects of software, and the series of annual FMICS workshops, begun in 1996. Moreover, several special issues of international journals have been published and selected were the best papers presented at the workshop.

These activities have promoted an ongoing scientific discussion on identifying the most efficient formal development and verification techniques, with a keen eye on their industrial applicability. Most of the members of the FMICS community have strong links with the industry and have thus directly contributed to the slow but constant introduction of formal methods in the development cycle of industrial critical systems witnessed in the last decade.

The idea of this book was born in a workshop held in Aix les Bain in 2004. The continuous evolution of formal methods and, in particular, the growing importance of model-checking techniques due to their ever-increasing performance of tools, as well as the recent emergence of model-based design, have made it particularly difficult to present an up-to-date account of industrial application of formal methods in a book. So the idea of the book has kept shifting over the past years.

As the last coordinators of the FMICS working group, we are therefore grateful to this book's editors, who have succeeded in capturing a collection of snapshots that document the continuous evolution of this research field, as well as the increasing application in the industrial production of software and computer-controlled systems. As such, we believe that this gallery is a witness to the success that formal methods are experiencing in a number of different domains.

ALESSANDRO FANTECHI AND PEDRO MERINO

FMICS Working Group Chairs

PREFACE

Nowadays, the necessity of formal methods as an essential step in the design process of industrial safety critical systems is widely recognized. In its more general definition, the term "formal methods" encompasses all notations that have precise mathematical semantics, together with their associated analysis methods, which describe the behavior of a system in a formal manner.

Many formal methods have emerged during the last few decades: declarative methods, process calculi for concurrent and mobile systems, and their related languages, to mention a few. Although the benefits of using these formal methods are undeniable, practical experience shows that each method is particularly adapted for handling certain aspects of a system. Therefore, the design of a complex industrial system ideally requires an expertise in several formal methods in order to describe and analyze different views of the system.

This book aims at providing a comprehensive presentation of the mainstream formal methods that are currently used for designing industrial critical systems. The purpose of this book is threefold: to reduce the learning effort of formal methods, which is a major drawback for their industrial dissemination; to help designers adopt the formal methods that are most appropriate for their systems; and to offer state-of-the-art techniques and tools for analyzing critical systems.

The book is organized into six parts. Part I presents the introductory chapter. Part II is devoted to modeling paradigms. Chapter 2 is on development of the synchronous data-flow language LUSTRE and its industrial transfer inside the toolset SCADE; Chapter 3 is on the basic concepts of swarms, which are becoming prevalent in a variety of application domains: medical, bioinformatics, military/defense, surveillance, even Internet television broadcasting. The requirements of a formal method suitable for use with swarm-based systems are discussed.

Part III includes chapters on the use of formal methods and related tools in the development of applications in practical system domains. Chapter 4 is on transportation systems, where a survey about the current industrial usage of formal methods in railway signaling is presented, and Chapter 5 reports on the application of model-checking techniques to avionics applications.

Part IV, on telecommunication systems, begins with Chapter 6 on how to employ formal methods to increase reliability of active services, in particular when aspects such as code mobility, routing information, a high degree of reconfiguration, interaction between services, or security policies are considered, including Internet and online services. Chapter 7 is on the applications of probabilistic model checking, in particular using probabilistic timed automata, to communication protocols, with the emphasis on an industrially relevant case study: the IEEE 802.3 (CSMA/CD) protocol.

Part V covers the Internet and online services. Chapter 8 shows how to use models first to describe and verify the single components of an online distributed decision system that is designed as a large collection of cooperating models. Automata learning is applied to find out the collective emerging behavior of the real system after implementation. Chapter 9 shows the application of model checking to verifying user awareness in a groupware system with a publish/subscribe notification service.

Part VI introduces the application of formal methods at runtime. In Chapter 10, the Testing and Test Control Notation version 3 (TTCN-3) is introduced and applied to testing web services. Chapter 11 reviews the essence of practical automata learning, its major challenges, variants, possible solutions, and illustrative case studies, in order to show how the theoretically well-studied active learning technology can be an enhanced application to become a powerful tool for practical system development.

We realize that this book cannot be an exhaustive representation of the application of formal methods in industrial applications, but we believe and hope that the readers may find in it some interesting hints that may be useful in promoting and stimulating the application of formal methods in practice.

STEFANIA GNESI
TIZIANA MARGARIA

CONTRIBUTORS

GIANFRANCO CIARDO, Department of Computer Science and Engineering, University of California, Riverside, CA

MARÍA DEL MAR GALLARDO, Dpto. de Lenguajes y Ciencias de la Computacion, University of Málaga, Málaga, Spain

MARIE DUFLOT, LORIA, Equipe MOSEL/VERIDIS, Vandoeuvre-lès-Nancy, France

ALESSANDRO FANTECHI, Dipartimento di Sistemi e Informatica, Università degli Studi di Firenze, Florence, Italy; and Istituto di Scienza e Tecnologie dell'Informazione "A. Faedo," Consiglio Nazionale delle Ricerche, Pisa, Italy

WAN FOKKINK, Sectie Theoretische Informatica, Vrije Universiteit Amsterdam, Amsterdam, The Netherlands; and Specificatie en Verificatie van Embedded Systemen, CWI, Amsterdam, The Netherlands

STEFANIA GNESI, Istituto di Scienza e Tecnologie dell'Informazione "A. Faedo," Consiglio Nazionale delle Ricerche, Pisa, Italy

NICOLAS HALBWACHS, Vérimag, Grenoble, France

MIKE HINCHEY, Lero—the Irish Software Engineering Research Centre, University of Limerick, Limerick, Ireland

FALK HOWAR, Chair Programming Systems, TU Dortmund University, Dortmund, Germany

MARTA KWIATKOWSKA, Department of Computer Science, University of Oxford, Oxford, UK

DIEGO LATELLA, Istituto di Scienza e Tecnologie dell'Informazione "A. Faedo," Consiglio Nazionale delle Ricerche, Pisa, Italy

TIZIANA MARGARIA, Chair Service and Software Engineering, University of Potsdam, Potsdam, Germany

JESÚS MARTÍNEZ, Dpto. de Lenguajes y Ciencias de la Computacion, University of Málaga, Málaga, Spain

MIEKE MASSINK, Istituto di Scienza e Tecnologie dell'Informazione "A. Faedo," Consiglio Nazionale delle Ricerche, Pisa, Italy

PEDRO MERINO, Dpto. de Lenguajes y Ciencias de la Computacion, University of Málaga, Málaga, Spain

MAIK MERTEN, Chair Programming Systems, TU Dortmund University, Dortmund, Germany

ANGELO MORZENTI, Dipartimento di Elettronica e Informazione, Politecnico di Milano, Milan, Italy

JOHANNES NEUBAUER, Chair Programming Systems, TU Dortmund University, Dortmund, Germany

GETHIN NORMAN, Department of Computing Science, University of Glasgow, Glasgow, UK

DAVID PARKER, School of Computer Science, University of Birmingham, Birmingham, UK

SYLVAIN PEYRONNET, LRI, INRIA Université Paris-Sud, Orsay, France

CLAUDINE PICARONNY, LSV, CNRS & ENS de Cachan, Cachan, France

JAMES L. RASH, NASA Goddard Space Flight Center (Emeritus), Greenbelt, MD

CHRISTOPHER A. ROUFF, Near Infinity Corporation, Reston, VA

INA SCHIEFERDECKER, Fraunhofer FOKUS, Berlin, Germany

MAURIZIO SEBASTIANIS, Focus PLM srl, Ferrara, Italy

RADU I. SIMINICEANU, National Institute of Aerospace, Hampton, VA

JEREMY SPROSTON, Dipartimento di Informatica, Università degli Studi di Torino, Torino, Italy

BERNHARD STEFFEN, Chair Programming Systems, TU Dortmund University, Dortmund, Germany

MAURICE H. TER BEEK, Istituto di Scienza e Tecnologie dell'Informazione "A. Faedo," Consiglio Nazionale delle Ricerche, Pisa, Italy

GIANLUCA TRENTANNI, Istituto di Scienza e Tecnologie dell'Informazione "A. Faedo," Consiglio Nazionale delle Ricerche, Pisa, Italy

WALT F. TRUSZKOWSKI, NASA Goddard Space Flight Center (Emeritus), Greenbelt, MD

AMY K.C.S. VANDERBILT, Vanderbilt Consulting, Fairfax VA

ALAIN-GEORGES VOUFFO-FEUDJIO, Fraunhofer FOKUS, Berlin, Germany

PART I

INTRODUCTION AND STATE OF THE ART

CHAPTER 1

FORMAL METHODS: APPLYING {LOGICS IN, THEORETICAL} COMPUTER SCIENCE

DIEGO LATELLA
ISTI-CNR, Pisa, Italy

1.1 INTRODUCTION AND STATE OF THE ART

Giving a comprehensive definition of formal methods (FMs) is a hard and risky task, since they are still subject of ongoing research and several aspects of FMs, going from the foundational ones to those purely applicative, are in continuous change and evolution. Nevertheless, in order to fix the terms of discussion for the issues dealt with in this book, and only for the purpose of this book, by FMs we will mean all notations having a precise mathematical definition of both their syntax and semantics, together with their associated theory and analysis methods, that allow for describing and reasoning about the behavior of (computer) systems in a formal manner, assisted by automatic (software) tools. FMs play a major role in computer engineering and in the broader context of system engineering, where also the interaction of machines with humans is taken into consideration:

> All engineering disciplines make progress by employing mathematically based notations and methods. Research on 'formal methods' follows this model and attempts to identify and develop mathematical approaches that can contribute to the task of creating computer systems (both their hardware and software components). [26]

The very origins of FMs go back to mathematical logic—or, more precisely, to that branch of mathematical logic that gave rise to logics in computer science

Formal Methods for Industrial Critical Systems: A Survey of Applications, First Edition.
Edited by Stefania Gnesi and Tiziana Margaria.
© 2013 IEEE. Published 2013 by John Wiley & Sons, Inc.

(LICS) and theoretical computer science (TCS). An eminent example of these roots is the milestone work of Alan Turing [42] where key concepts and theoretical, intrinsic limitations of the algorithmic method—central to computer science in general and FMs in particular—are captured in precise terms. The above issues of computability have become one of the main subjects of scientific development in the field of automatic computation in the 30th's of the previous century. Central to the scientific discussion of that period was the clarification of the key notion of *formal system*, with a clear separation of syntax and semantics and with the notion of a formal proof calculus, defining *computational steps* [41]. Several fields of LICS and TCS have contributed to the development of the foundations of FMs, like language and automata theory, programming/specification language syntax and semantics, and program verification. More recently, solid contributions to the specification and analysis of systems—in particular concurrent/distributed systems—have been provided. These contributions range from the definition of specific notations, or classes of notations, to the development of solid mathematical and/or logic theories supporting such notations, to the development of techniques and efficient algorithms for the automatic or semiautomatic analysis of models of systems or of their requirements, and to the development of reliable automatic tools that implement such algorithms. In the following, we briefly describe some of the most relevant examples of (classes of) notations equipped with solid theories—process algebras; Petri nets; state-based approaches like VDM, Z, and B; and temporal logics—and analysis techniques—model checking and theorem proving. We will also recall abstract interpretation, which, although not bound to any particular notation, as a general theory of approximation of semantics constitutes another key contribution to FMs. We underline that what follows is *not* intended to be a comprehensive treatment of FMs, which would require much more space, and that it offers an overview of the field as of the time of writing:

- Notations and Supporting Theories
  - *Process Algebras.* Process algebra [30] is an algebraic approach to the study of concurrent processes. Its tools are algebraic languages for the specification of processes and the formulation of statements about them, together with congruence laws on which calculi are defined for the verification of these statements. Typical process algebraic operators are *sequential, nondeterministic*, and *parallel composition*. Some of the main process algebras are CCS, CSP, and ACP.
  - *Petri Nets.* Petri nets were originally proposed by Petri [33] for describing interacting finite-state machines and are constituted by a finite set of *places*, a finite set of *transitions*, a flow relation from places to transitions and from transitions to places, and weights associated to the flows. A Petri net can be given an appealing graphical representation, which makes specifications intuitively understandable. A state of a Petri net is given by marking its places, that is, associating a number of *tokens* to

places. Rules are defined to fire a transition by moving tokens, hence changing the state of the net. Many extensions and variations of Petri nets have been proposed, for example, adding values to tokens [18], time [19, 29], or probabilities to transitions [3].

○ *VDM, Z, B.* The first widely used formal specification languages resorted to the use of traditional mathematical concepts such as sets, functions, and first-order predicate logic. VDM [5] was proposed mainly for describing the denotational semantics of programming languages. Z [38] used the same concepts for defining types, which describe the entities and the state space of the system of interest. Properties of the state space are described in Z by means of *invariant* predicates. State transitions are expressed by relations between inputs and outputs of the operations of the models. The B method [1] adds behavioral specifications by means of *abstract machines*. The language is complemented with a refinement-based development method, which includes the use of theorem proving for maintaining the consistency of refinements. Reference 2 is a nice, informal introduction to the key concepts of system modeling in a mathematical framework as above.

○ *Temporal Logics.* Temporal logic [13] is a special type of modal logic, and it provides a formal system for qualitatively describing and reasoning about how the truth values of assertions change over system computations. Typical temporal logic operators include *sometimes P*, which is true now if there is a future moment in time in which *P* becomes true, and *always P*, which is true now if *P* is true at all future moments. Specific temporal logics differ for the model of time they use (e.g., linear time vs. branching time) and/or the specific set of temporal operators they provide.

• Analysis Techniques and Tools

○ *Model Checking.* Model checking is a verification technique in which efficient algorithms are used to check, in an automatic way, whether a desired property holds for a (usually finite) model of the system, typically a state-transition structure, like an automaton [4, 7]. Very powerful logics have been developed to express a great variety of system properties, and high-level languages have been designed to specify system models. Examples of the former are various variants of temporal logic, and notable examples of the latter are process algebras, imperative languages, and graphical notations. Prominent examples of model checkers are SMV [9], SPIN [22], and TLC [28].

○ *Automated Theorem Proving.* Automated theorem proving is the process of getting a computer to agree that a particular theorem is true. The theorems of interest may be in traditional mathematical domains, or they may be in other fields such as digital computer design [37, 44]. When used for system validation, the system *specification S* and its *realization R* are formulas of some appropriate logic. Checking whether the realization satisfies the specification amounts to verify the validity of the formula $S \Rightarrow R$, and this can be done—at least partially, and sometimes completely—automatically by a computer program, the theorem prover. Classical theorem provers are PVS [39], HOL [43], and Nqthm [6].

- *Abstract Interpretation.* Abstract interpretation is a theory of the approximation of semantics of (programming or specification) languages. It applies both to data and to control. It formalizes the idea that the semantics can be more or less precise according to the considered level of observation. If the approximation is coarse enough, the abstraction of a semantics yields a less precise but computable version. Because of the corresponding loss of information, not all questions can be answered, but all answers given by the effective computation of the approximate semantics are always correct [12].

A key difference between FMs and their mother disciplines of LICS and TCS is that the former attempt to provide the (software or systems) engineer with

concepts and techniques as thinking tools, which are clean, adequate, and convenient, to support him (or her) in describing, reasoning about, and constructing complex software and hardware systems. [41]

Emphasis is thus on construction rather than reduction and in pragmatics rather than classical issues like completeness. This shift in emphasis applies in general to what W. Thomas calls *logic for computer science* [41]—as opposed to more traditional logic *in* computer science—but it certainly applies to FMs in particular. Are FMs succeeding in their mission? Although a complete answer cannot be given yet—since we have not witnessed a complete and widespread uptake of FMs by an industry in computer engineering—there is a clear trend that justifies a tendency toward a positive answer to the above question, as it will be briefly elaborated below.

FMs have been used extensively in the past for security, fault tolerance, general consistency, object-oriented programs, compiler correctness, protocol development, hardware verification and computer-aided design, and human safety (see References 32 and 46 for extensive bibliographies on the use of FMs in the above areas). There are several IT industries, mainly larger ones like IBM, Intel, Lucent/Cadence, Motorola, and Siemens, which use FM techniques for quality assurance in their production processes [10, 31], and that FMs are making their way into software development practices is clear even from the words of Bill Gates:

Things like even software verification, this has been the Holy Grail of computer science for many decades but now in some very key areas, for example, driver verification we're building tools that can do actual proof about the software and how it works in order to guarantee the reliability. [17].

FMs and related tools are also used as a supporting technology in branches of fundamental sciences, like biology (see for instance Reference 40), physics, and others [24]. Moreover, FMs are used for the design and validation of safety critical systems, for example, in areas like aerospace* [34]. In the international standards for the engineering of safety critical systems, like those for space or transportation, more and more recommend or mandate the use of FMs. Examples of these engineering standards are the ECSS E-40-01 [15] and the CENELEC EN 50128 [14]. The need of FMs has been recognized also in other scientific communities, in particular the dependability one, as witnessed, for instance, by the organization of the specific workshop on Model Checking for Dependable Software-Intensive Systems in one edition of the International Conference on Dependable Systems and Networks, the most respectable conference in the field (for a discussion on the prominent role that FMs play—and will more and more play in the future—in the area of dependability, see also Reference 45). Finally, several commercial organizations nowadays provide FM-oriented services (some are listed in Reference 11). Unfortunately, the question on the success of FM cannot be fully answered yet also because many tools used in the industry are proprietary tools on which detailed information is very seldom publicly available; similarly, details on the specific methodologies and processes using such tools and the methodologies they support are difficult to be obtained for similar reasons†—a notable exception to this trend is Reference 21 where the AT&T Bell Laboratories NewCoRe project is described, which clearly shows how beneficial FMs can be in the software development process.

On the other hand, one can assess the success of a scientific/technological discipline also by the very advances that have been accomplished in the discipline itself, and, in the last few years, there have been tremendous advances in the field of FMs. First of all, their coverage has been broadened from purely functional aspects of behavior toward nonfunctional features of systems such as the following [27]:

- *Space and Mobility.* Several calculi and logics—and associated support tools—have been extended/developed in order to explicitly deal with notions like the (physical, discrete) *space* occupied by computing elements, their *migration* from one place to another, and its implication on *network connectivity* and the *communication structure*; thus, space and mobility—which are essential notions when developing or reasoning about large distributed networked applications—are first-class objects in these formal frameworks.

---

* A guide on the selection of appropriate FM can be found in the official site of *Formal Methods Europe* [16].
† Some advocates of FMs claim that this itself is a proof that FM and related tools are considered strategic in industrial contexts and this by itself can show their success.

- *Security.* Several calculi and logics—and associated support tools—have been extended/developed specifically for the modeling of *security* protocols and their desirable properties and for verifying or falsifying that the latter are satisfied by the former.
- *Bounded Resources.* Methods based on logics, types, and calculi—and associated support tools—have been developed for modeling and controlling *allocation* and *deallocation* of resources and for expressing the *trust* involved in resource allocation and its *propagation.*
- *Continuous Time (and Hybrid Systems in General).* In the last 15 years, several varieties of automata, process algebras, and logics—and associated support tools—have been extended with elements of *continuous* nature, like for instance *time*, and functions of continuous variables with their *derivatives.*
- *Stochastic Behavior.* Elements of stochastic behavior, like *probabilistic choices* and *stochastic durations*, have been introduced in models like automata and process algebra, and corresponding operators have been added to proper logics, thus providing conceptual *formal*, language-based tools for the modeling and reasoning about of *performance* and *dependability* attributes and requirements. Automatic software tools for (process algebras/automata) *discrete simulation* and for Markov chains and Markov decision processes *model checking* constitute their practical support counterpart.

An account of advances in the above-mentioned fields together with a rich bibliography can be found in Reference 31. Moreover, the field of application of FMs has been broadened too, including novel disciplines, like computational biology, to mention just one. Finally, the capabilities of the tools supporting FMs have been dramatically improved. For instance, some model checking techniques

> work especially well for concurrent software, which, as luck will have it, is the most difficult to debug and test with traditional means [22],

and nowadays, model checkers are able to deal with system models of up to 10^{100} states and, in some cases, even up to 10^{100} [4, 20]. Nevertheless, there are still several open problems in the area of FM, among which are the following:

- Most specification—and especially automatic verification—techniques do not easily *scale up* due to the infamous *state explosion* problem, which arises when the system to be modeled and verified has many independent actions that can occur in parallel.
- Although significant progress has taken place in the field of compositional specification of concurrent systems (notably by the introduction of process algebras), the same cannot be claimed for verification. In particular,

compositionality is not currently fully exploited in model checking techniques.

- Many specification paradigms and verification techniques developed independently from one another, often giving rise to maybe technically unjustified dichotomies. Lack of *full integration* between different paradigms—like state-oriented ones of some specification languages versus *action/event-oriented* ones of others—or between different verification techniques—like automated theorem proving versus model checking—is likely to be detrimental for each of such paradigms or techniques.
- FMs should find their way toward full acceptance and use in system—and particularly software—engineering. They should be smoothly embedded into more traditional industrial production processes.

1.2 FUTURE DIRECTIONS

In the medium/long-term future, the grand challenge for FMs will be large-scale industrialization and intensification of fundamental research efforts. This is necessary for tackling the challenge of computer—and in particular software—reliability. The latter will be a major grand challenge in computer science and practice [11].

On a more technical level, several research directions will require particular effort. In the following list, some of them are briefly presented. The list is necessarily incomplete and its items necessarily interrelated; the order of appearance of the items in the list does not imply any relative priority or level of importance:

- In the context of *abstract interpretation*, "general purpose, expressive and cost-effective abstractions have to be developed e.g. to handle floating point numbers, data dependencies (e.g. for parallelization), liveness properties with fairness [...], timing properties for embedded software [and] probabilistic properties, etc. Present-day tools will have to be enhanced to handle higher-order compositional modular analysis and to cope with new programming paradigms involving complex data and control concepts (such as objects, concurrent threads, distributed/mobile programming, etc.), to automatically combine and locally refine abstractions in particular to cope with 'unknown' answers" [11]. Moreover, new ways for exploiting abstraction for (extended) static analysis, including the use of theorem proving, will need to be investigated [35].
- In the context of *model checking* [7, 8, 24], *abstraction* will be a major pillar. It will be of vital help especially for winning over the state explosion problem. Moreover, it will allow the extension of model checking to infinite models. Finally, it will make model checking of software *programs*

(and not only their specifications) a reality [23]. Research is needed in order to embed abstraction techniques within model checking ones. The following are some of the issues that need to be further investigated: (1) how to build—possibly automatically—an abstract model from a concrete one; (2) how to identify spurious abstract counterexamples provided by the model checking algorithms when checking an abstract model reports an error—spurious counterexamples originate from the very fact that an abstract model necessarily contains less information than the concrete one; (3) how to refine an abstract model when a spurious counterexample is detected in order to eliminate it; (4) how to derive concrete counterexamples from abstract (nonspurious) ones; and (5) how to develop methods for verifying *parameterized* systems, that is, systems with arbitrarily many identical components. Another major pillar will be *compositionality*. There is no hope to be able to model check—and in general, analyze— complex real-life systems of the future, like global ubiquitous systems, without having the possibility of exploiting their structure and architecture—that is, them being composed of simpler components. Compositional reasoning and compositional model checking will play a major role in the area of automated verification of concurrent systems. Finally, a smooth *integration* of model checking and theorem proving will result in a quantum leap in verification for example, by facilitating the modeling and verification of infinite-state systems, for which powerful induction principles will be available together with efficient proof of base cases.

- In the area of *FMs for security*, *access to resources*, and *trust*, we expect the development of security-oriented languages, directly derived from the theories and calculi for mobility and security mentioned in Section 1.1. Moreover, specific protocols for mobile agents to acquire and to manage resources need to be developed, which will base access negotiation on an evaluation of *trust*, the level of which will in turn depend on *knowledge* and *belief* about agents and on how trust is *propagated*. Such protocols will undergo serious and intense investigation and assessment including automatic verification [27].

- In the area of *hybrid* systems, the basic ideas used in the current tools for representing state sets generated by complex continuous functions in hybrid automata (including timed automata) will be further developed, and related efficient algorithms will be developed, which will facilitate automated reasoning on hybrid system models. More emphasis will be put on efforts for unification with control theory [27].

- Model checking techniques for *stochastic* and *probabilistic* models and logics will be further developed in order to scale up to real-life system sizes. Particular emphasis will be put on the problem of counterexample generation and on the tailoring of numerical analysis algorithms and techniques required for such kinds of model checking. Moreover, integration with mobile and hybrid models as above will be required in order to model and verify essential aspects of future global ubiquitous computing [27].

- *Game semantics* is a promising approach to the formal semantics of specification/programming languages and logics, which has developed from mathematical games, logics, and combinatorial game theory and category theory. Although it lays more on the side of foundations for FMs, it will provide solid basis for advances in model checking—especially with respect to compositionality—partial specification and modeling, integration of qualitative and quantitative approaches, and developments in physics-based models of computation—for example, quantum computing [27].
- Finally, in order to properly face the "engineering challenge" of FMs, a proper *merging* of the languages of formulas and diagrams must be devised. Attempts have been made in the software engineering community, and especially in the industry, most notably with the UML—although not particularly impressive from the mathematical foundations' point of view. On the other hand, there are other, historical examples like the equivalence of Boolean formulas and ordered binary decision diagrams, or regular expressions and finite automata, which have been quite successful and which resulted in useful engineering tools. This should push research on "[t]heories which support merging diagram-based languages with term- or formula-based ones" since this "would help in designing better specification languages" [41].

Although the above list is far to be complete, we can definitely claim that all the above lines of research are essential for properly facing the grand research challenges in information systems [25], in TCS and its applications [36], and for making the potentials of LICS and TCS fully exploited in computer science and engineering as well as in other branches of science and engineering [24].

ACKNOWLEDGMENTS

The author wishes to thank Peter Neumann (SRI Int., USA), Rocco de Nicola (University of Florence, Italy), and Scott Smolka (SUNY, USA) for precious suggestions; Stefania Gnesi and Alessandro Fantechi, for their help on a number of issues; and Mieke Massink and Angelo Morzenti for reviewing the present report.

REFERENCES

1. J. R. Abrial. *The B-Book*. Cambridge University Press, 1996.
2. J. R. Abrial. Faultless systems: Yes we can. *IEEE Computer Society*, 42(9):30–36, 2009.

3. M. Ajmone Marsan, G. Conte, and G. Balbo. A class of generalized stochastic Petri nets for the performance evaluation of multiprocessor systems. *ACM Transactions on Computer Systems*, ACM Press, 2(2):93–122, 1984.

4. C. Baier and J.-P. Katoen. *Principles of Model Checking*. The MIT Press, 2008.

5. D. Bjorner and C. Jones. *Formal Specification and Software Development*. Prentice Hall International, 1982.

6. R. Boyer. Nqthm, the Boyer-Moore prover, 2003. Available at: http://www.cs.utexas. edu/users/boyer/ftp/nqthm/index.html.

7. E. Clarke, E. Emerson, and J. Sifakis. Model checking: Algorithmic verification and debugging. Turing lecture. *Communications of the ACM*, 52(11):75–84, 2009.

8. E. Clarke, O. Grumberg, S. Jha, Y. Lu, and H. Veith. Progress in the state explosion problem in model checking. In R. Wilhelm, ed., *Informatics 10 Years Back 10 Years Ahead, Volume 2000 of Lectures Notes in Computer Science*, pp. 176–194. Springer-Verlag, 2000.

9. E. Clarke, O. Grumberg, and D. Peled. *Model Checking*. MIT Press, 1999.

10. E. Clarke, J. Wing, et al. Formal methods: State of the art and future directions. *ACM Computing Surveys*, ACM Press, 28(4):626–643, 1996.

11. P. Cousot. Abstract interpretation based formal methods and future challenges. In R. Wilhelm, ed., *Informatics 10 Years Back 10 Years Ahead, Volume 2000 of Lectures Notes in Computer Science*, pp. 138–156, 2000.

12. P. Cousot. Abstract Interpretation and Semantics, September 30, 2003. Available at: http://www.di.ens.fr/~cousot/Equipeabsint-eg.shtml.

13. A. Emerson. Temporal and modal logics. In J. van Leeuwen, ed., *Handbook of Theoretical Computer Science—Vol. B: Formal Models and Semantics*, pp. 995–1072. Elsevier, 1990.

14. European Committee for Electrotechnical Standardization. CENELEC. Railway application—Communications, signalling and processing systems—Software for railway control and protection systems. CENELEC EN 50128. 2011.

15. European Cooperation for Space Standardization ECSS. Space segment software. ECSS E-40-01. 1999.

16. Formal Methods Europe. FME Home Page, September 30, 2003. Available at: http://www.fmeurope.org.

17. B. Gates. Remarks by Bill Gates. WinHEC 2002 Seattle—Washington April 18, 2002. Available at: http://www.microsoft.com/billgates/speeches/2002/04-18winhec. asp [Accessed October 6, 2003].

18. H. Genrich. Predicate/transition nets. In G. Rozenberg, ed., *Advances in Petri Nets 1986, Volume 254 of Lectures Notes in Computer Science*, pp. 207–247. Springer-Verlag, 1986.

19. C. Ghezzi, D. Mandrioli, S. Morasca, and M. Pezzè. A unified high-level Petri net formalism for time-critical systems. *IEEE Transactions on Software Engineering*, 17(2):160–172, 1991.

20. L. Hoffman. Talking model-checking technology. A conversation with the 2007 ACM A. M. Turing Award winners. *Communications of the ACM*, 51(7):110–112, 2008.

21. G. Holzmann. The theory and practice of a formal method: NewCoRe. In *Proceedings of the 13th IFIP World Congress*, pp. 35–44. IFIP, 1994.

22. G. Holzmann. *The SPIN Model Checker. Primer and Reference Manual.* Addison-Wesley, 2003.

23. R. Jhala and R. Majumdar. Software model checking. *ACM Computing Surveys*, 41(4):21:2–21:54, 2009.

24. D. Johnson. Challenges for Theoretical Computer Science, 2000. Draft Report from the Workshop on Challenges for Theoretical Computer Science held in Portland on May 19, 2000. Available at: http://www2.research.att.com/~dsj/nsflist.html.

25. A. Jones, ed. Grand research challenges in information systems. Computer Research Association, 2003.

26. C. Jones. Thinking tools for the future of computing science. In R. Wilhelm, ed., *Informatics 10 Years Back 10 Years Ahead, Volume 2000 of Lectures Notes in Computer Science*, pp. 112–130, 2000.

27. M. Kwiatkowska and V. Sassone (moderators). Science for Global Ubiquitous Computing, 2003. Proposal for discussion nr. 2 in the context of the Grand Challenges for Computing Research initiative sponsored by the UK Computing Research Committee with support from EPSRC and NeSC.

28. L. Lamport. *Specifying Systems: The TLA+ Language and Tools for Hardware and Software Engineers.* Addison-Wesley, 2002.

29. P. Merlin and D. Farber. Recoverability of communication protocols. *IEEE Transactions on Communications*, 24(9):1036–1043, 1976.

30. R. Milner. Operational and algebraic semantics of concurrent processes. In J. van Leeuwen, ed., *Handbook of Theoretical Computer Science—Vol. B: Formal Models and Semantics*, pp. 1201–1242. Elsevier, 1990.

31. R. Milner, A. Gordon, V. Sassone, P. Buneman, F. Gardner, S. Abramsky, and M. Kwiatkowska. Theories for ubiquitous processes and data. Platform for a 15-year grand challenge, 2003. This paper is written as a background for Reference [27].

32. P. Neumann. Practical architectures for survivable systems and networks. Technical Report Cont. 1-732-427-5099—Final Report, SRI International, 2000. Available at: http://www.csl.sri.com/users/neumann/ [Accessed September 30, 2003].

33. W. Reisig. *Petri Nets—An Introduction, Volume 4 of EATCS Monographs on Theoretical Computer Science.* Springer-Verlag, 1985.

34. J. Rushby. Formal methods and the certification of critical systems. Technical Report CSL-93-7, SRI International, 1993. Also issues under the title *Formal Methods and Digital Systems Validation for Airborne Systems* as NASA CR 4551.

35. K. Rustan and M. Leino. Extended static checking: a ten-year perspective. In R. Wilhelm, ed., *Informatics 10 Years Back 10 Years Ahead, Volume 2000 of Lectures Notes in Computer Science*, pp. 157–175, 2000.

36. A. Selman. Challenges for Theory of Computing, 1999. Report of an NSF-Sponsored Workshop on Research in Theoretical Computer Science held in Chicago on March 11–12, 1999. Available at: http://http://www.cse.buffalo.edu/~selman/report/.

37. N. Shankar. Automated deduction for verification. *ACM Computing Surveys*, 41(4):20:2–20:56, 2009.

38. J. Spivey. *The Z Notation—A Reference Manual.* Prentice Hall International, 1989.

39. SRI International—Computer Science Laboratory. The PVS Specification and Verification System, September 30, 2003. Available at: http://pvs.csl.sri.com/.

40. The BioSPI Project. The BioSPI Project Home Page, October 27, 2003. Available at: http:// www.wisdom.weizmann.ac.il/~biopsi.

41. W. Thomas. Logic for computer science: The engineering challenge. In R. Wilhelm, ed., *Informatics 10 Years Back 10 Years Ahead, Volume 2000 of Lectures Notes in Computer Science*, pp. 257–267, 2000.

42. A. M. Turing. On computable numbers with an application to the entscheidung-sproblem. *Proceedings of the London Mathematical Society*, 2(42):230–265, 1936.

43. University of Cambridge—Computer Laboratory. Automated Reasoning Group HOL page. Available at: http://www.cl.cam.ac.uk/research/hvg/HOL/.

44. Various Authors. Wikipedia, September 30, 2003. Available at: http://www.wikipedia.org

45. J. Woodcock (moderator). Dependable Systems Evolution. A Grand Challenge for Computer Science, 2003. Proposal for discussion nr. 6 in the context of the Grand Challenges for Computing Research initiative sponsored by the UK Computing Research Committee with support from EPSRC and NeSC.

46. J. Woodcock, P. G. Larsen, J. Bicarregui, and J. Fitzgerald. Formal methods: Practice and experience. *ACM Computing Surveys*, 41(4):19:2–19:36, 2009.

MODELING PARADIGMS

CHAPTER 2

A SYNCHRONOUS LANGUAGE AT WORK: THE STORY OF LUSTRE

NICOLAS HALBWACHS

Vérimag, Grenoble, France

2.1 INTRODUCTION

The design of the synchronous language LUSTRE started more than 20 years ago, and resulted in an industrial software development tool, SCADE, which is now in use in many major companies developing embedded software (avionics, transportation, energy, etc.). It seemed to us that this success story deserves to be reported and analyzed, from the point of view of the problems raised by the industrial transfer of a new technology: Why did it succeed? How could it succeed better?

So-called embedded systems are much more fashionable nowadays than in the 1980s, when they first appeared in large industrial applications. It is now admitted that this domain concerns systems presenting one or several of the following features: (1) they have to run in strong interaction with their—possibly physical—environment (real-time systems, industrial control, etc.), (2) their development combines software and hardware aspects, (3) they are subjected to strong nonfunctional constraints (execution time, memory limitations, fault tolerance, power consumption, etc.), and (4) they are safety critical—often because of (1), since they influence physical processes and devices. Because of (1) and (2), the domain of embedded systems is strongly related to both control theory and hardware design, and this is why the inspiration of synchronous languages comes both from control engineering formalisms and from hardware description languages.

One can wonder why the main three synchronous languages—ESTEREL [4], SIGNAL [27], and LUSTRE [18]—were all born in France, approximately at the

Formal Methods for Industrial Critical Systems: A Survey of Applications, First Edition.
Edited by Stefania Gnesi and Tiziana Margaria.
© 2013 IEEE. Published 2013 by John Wiley & Sons, Inc.

same time and quite independently. Of course, at the beginning of the 1980s, the idea of synchrony was already in the air, be it in theoretical works by Milner [30], or in "almost synchronous" formalisms, like Grafcet (or IEC 1131 Sequential Function Charts) [3, 13] or Statecharts [23]. But the conditions were particularly favorable, both for academic and industrial reasons.

On the academic side, the three involved teams mixed researchers from control theory and computer science: Jean-Paul Rigault, Jean-Paul Marmorat, and Gérard Berry for ESTEREL; Albert Benveniste and Paul Le Guernic for SIGNAL; and Paul Caspi and the author of this chapter for LUSTRE. This double competence seems to have played an important role in the design of the languages.

On the other hand, strong industrial needs were appearing: the European and French industry of embedded software was faced with some big challenges:

- For the very first time, in the new family of French nuclear reactors, called N4, the most critical functions (in particular, the emergency stop) were realized by a computer system, the SPIN (for "integrated nuclear protection system").
- At the same time, the Airbus A320 was designed, which was the very first fully "fly-by-wire" aircraft.
- In the railways industry, various automatic subways were designed (e.g., the VAL [15]), and the successive versions of the French TGV (high-speed train) were more and more computerized.

Started in 1984, the development of LUSTRE beneficiated from these very good circumstances. After briefly recalling the principles of the language (Section 2.2), we will detail in Section 2.3 the main stages of its development, both from academic and industrial points of view. Section 2.4 analyzes the feedback from industrial usages of the language. Finally, Section 2.5 outlines the current evolutions of the language and its associated tools.

A preliminary version of this chapter was published in Reference 16.

2.2   A FLAVOR OF THE LANGUAGE

Let us first recall, in a simplified way, the principles of LUSTRE: A LUSTRE program operates on *flows* of values. Any variable (or expression) x represents a flow, that is, an infinite sequence $(x_0, x_1, \ldots, x_n, \ldots)$ of values. A program is intended to have a cyclic behavior, and x_n is the value of x at the nth cycle of the execution. A program computes output flows from input flows. Output (and possibly local) flows are defined by means of equations (in the mathematical sense), an equation "x = e" meaning "$\forall n, x_n = e_n$." So, an equation can be understood as a temporal invariant. LUSTRE operators operate globally on flows: For instance, "x + y" is the flow $(x_0 + y_0, x_1 + y_1, \ldots, x_n + y_n, \ldots)$. In addition to usual arithmetic, Boolean, conditional operators—extended point-wise to flows as just shown—we will consider only two temporal operators:

- The operator "pre" ("previous") gives access to the previous value of its argument: "pre(x)" is the flow $(nil, x_0, \ldots, x_{n-1}, \ldots)$, where the very first value nil is an undefined ("noninitialized") value.
- The operator "->" ("followed by") is used to define initial values: "x -> y" is the flow $(x_0, y_1, \ldots, y_n, \ldots)$, initially equal to x, and then equal to y forever.

As a very simple and classical example, the program shown below is a counter of "events": It takes as inputs two Boolean flows "evt" (true whenever the counted "event" occurs) and "reset" (true whenever the counter should be reinitialized), and returns the number of occurrences of "events" that occurred since the last "reset":

```
node Count(evt, reset: bool)returns(count: int);
let
    count = if (true -> reset) then 0
             else if evt then pre(count) + 1
             else pre(count);
tel
```

Intuitively, "true -> reset" is a Boolean flow, which is true at initial instant and whenever "reset" is true; when it is true, the value of "count" is 0; otherwise, when "event" is true, "count" is incremented. Otherwise, it keeps its previous value.

Once declared, such a "node" can be used anywhere in a program, as a user-defined operator. For instance, our counter can be used to generate an event "minute" every 60 "second," by counting "second" modulo 60:

```
mod60 = Count(second, pre(mod60) = 59);
minute = (mod60 = 0);
```

Here, "mod60" is the output of a "Count" node, counting "second," and reset whenever the previous value of "mod60" is 59; "minute" is true whenever "mod60" equals 0.

So, through the notion of node, LUSTRE naturally offers hierarchical description and component reuse. Data traveling along the "wires" of an operator network can be complex, structured information.

From a temporal point of view, industrial applications show that several processing chains, evolving at different rates, can appear in a single system. LUSTRE offers a notion of Boolean clock, allowing the activation of nodes at different rates.

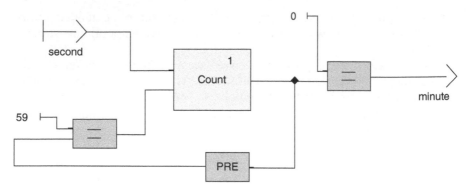

FIGURE 2.1   A graphical view in SCADE.

The graphical counterpart of LUSTRE textual syntax is obvious; for instance, Figure 2.1 is a SCADE view of the "minute detector" described before.

2.3   THE DESIGN AND DEVELOPMENT OF LUSTRE AND SCADE

The initial idea of LUSTRE came from our previous works [9] about modeling real-time systems by means of time functions. Such a global handling of variable "histories," together with the inspirating proposal of the Lucid* language [2], suggested us to design a programming language describing variables as timed sequences of values. Moreover, from his background in control theory, Paul Caspi knew that this kind of description—we would say, today, "MATLAB/ Simulink-like"—was the natural one for control engineers: From their experience with previous technologies, they were used to declarative or data-flow formalisms, that is, at high levels, differential or finite-difference equations, and at lower levels, various kinds of graphical network (block diagrams, analog networks, switches schemas, etc.).

2.3.1   The Industrial Story

Caspi's intuition was promptly confirmed: We found, in many companies, many in-house development tools based on these kinds of formalisms. The goal of such tools ranged from simple graphical description (without any idea of mechanical exploitation) to some attempts in consistency checking, simulation, and even automatic code generation. In particular, the Merlin Gerin company (now Schneider Electric), located in Grenoble, was in charge of the development of a large part of the SPIN ("integrated nuclear protection system").

---

* As a matter of fact, the name "LUSTRE" is a French acronym for "synchronous Lucid for real time."

Being aware that they were confronted with radically new problems, because of the software criticality, the management people decided to develop their own development environment, and they naturally chose a data-flow formalism. Our great chance was to collaborate with them from the very beginning of the design of this environment, which was called SAGA (for "assisted specification and automatic generation"): SAGA was based on Lustre, provided with a mixed graphical/textual syntax, and offered a simple, but efficient, code generator. Two members of the Lustre team, Eric Pilaud and Jean-Louis Bergerand, were hired by Merlin Gerin to supervise the development of the tool. The use of SAGA was very successful for the design of the SPIN and several other systems.

But after a few years, people at Merlin Gerin understood that the maintenance and development of such a software toolset was not their job, so a software company, Verilog, was contacted for commercializing the SAGA product. Merlin Gerin being already an important reference for SAGA, Verilog accepted the challenge: Developing such a tool, with critical constraints of correctness, robustness, life duration, and so on, was completely new for such a small company. Being located in Toulouse, Verilog contacted Aerospatiale (now part of Airbus), which was confronted with a problem very similar to that of Merlin Gerin: For the design of the onboard software of the Airbus A320, Aerospatiale designed an in-house tool, called SAO (for "computer-assisted specification"), based on principles very similar to those of SAGA, but which was not intended, at the beginning, to perform the automatic generation of embeddable code. A kind of consortium was constituted between Aerospatiale, Merlin Gerin, and Verilog to design a new tool, inspired by both SAO and SAGA. This new tool was called Scade (for "Safety Critical Applications Development Environment"). At this time, VERIMAG was created as a common laboratory between Verilog and our academic institutions, in particular to make easier the cooperation about the design of Scade. A member of the Lustre team, Daniel Pilaud, was hired by Verilog to head the Scade team.

The new big challenge with Scade was to comply with the requirements of the avionics certification authorities. In particular, the avionic norm DO-178B requires that any tool used for the development of a critical equipment be itself qualified at the same level of criticality as the considered equipment. As a consequence, for the code generated by Scade to be embeddable, the Scade code generator had to be qualified at the same level as the most critical software (flight software, level A). Let us say at once that such a qualification has nothing to do with a formal proof of the compiler, but is rather a matter of design process, test coverage, quality of the documentation, requirements traceability, and so on. The Scade code generator, KCG, is probably the first commercial compiler to be qualified for producing embedded software for civil avionics. KCG was a prominent argument for Scade: As any code generator, it suppresses not only the manual coding from data-flow specifications, but, more importantly, since it is qualified, also the need for expensive *unit testing* for checking the correctness of this translation. This is what process people call the change from the "V" cycle to the "Y" cycle: The lowest part of the "V," which consist of coding and unit testing, becomes free and instantaneous.

In the 1990s, the Swedish company Prover Technology connected its SAT-based model checker PROVER with SCADE, thus providing the tool with an integrated verification capability. In doing so, they adopted our technique for specifying properties and assumptions by means of *synchronous observers*.

Then, the industrial story became complicated: Verilog was bought by the CS group, then sold to Telelogic, which finally sold SCADE to Esterel Technologies, a company founded in 1999, mainly to develop an industrial tool around the ESTEREL language. The main application domain of the ESTEREL language is circuit CAD, while the one of SCADE is embedded software, so the two languages do not compete with each other. They are quite different externally, but they share the same synchronous semantic model. So it makes sense to develop both tools together, and even to try to combine them (see Section 2.5). The purchase of SCADE by Esterel Technologies was followed by a resumption of its development (in particular, a gateway from Simulink/Stateflow [7] was developed in the framework of the project IST-RISE) and a strong extension of its commercial promotion: SCADE is now used all over the world.

2.3.2 The Research Stages

The research about LUSTRE and its associated tools was driven in the very stimulating context of collaboration/competition with teams working on other synchronous languages, structured by successive French and European projects, called C2A, Eureka-SYNCHRON, Esprit/LTR-SYRF,* and SafeAir-II.†
This research was also punctuated with a series of theses, unfortunately written in French.

2.3.2.1 Compilation The first research topic, after the design of the language (Jean-Louis Bergerand's thesis), was of course its compilation. LUSTRE can be quite naturally and easily translated into sequential imperative code, as a single endless loop:

```
initializations
loop
  acquire inputs;
  compute outputs;
  update memories
end
```

One has just to determine a correct order for computing outputs and memories, in order to minimize the number of memories (very often, there is no need of two memories to deal with x and pre(x)).

---

* See http://www-verimag.imag.fr/SYNCHRONE/SYRF/syrf.html.
† See http://www.safeair2.org/.

However, in the middle of the 1980s, the only way of compiling ESTEREL was to produce an explicit automaton. We experienced a similar way of compiling LUSTRE (John Plaice's thesis). The idea was to specialize the code according to the known *previous* values of Boolean expressions: When "b" is true at some cycle, one knows that "pre(b)" will be true at the next cycle, and the code can be simplified accordingly. Of course, the initial cycle can also be specialized according to the semantics of the "->" operator. So, a state of the automaton corresponds to a configuration of the Boolean memories, and the code specialized according to a state represents the outgoing transitions, carrying conditions and actions on non-Boolean variables. In cooperation with the ESTEREL team, the common format OC was defined [34] as a target code for automata generators, in order to share common tools on this format, like generators to various target languages (C, Ada, etc.), minimizers, optimizers, and graphical visualizers.

It promptly appeared that, in contrast with ESTEREL, our generator produced automata with many redundant states, thus involving an explosion of the code even for simple programs. This is why we proposed the first algorithm of "symbolic bisimulation" [6, 22], aiming at performing bisimulation reduction together with the generation of the automaton. This optimization, implemented by means of binary decision diagram (BDD) technology, was the subject of Pascal Raymond's thesis.

Explicit automaton code can be much more efficient than the single-loop code; however, it is also generally much bigger, and the size of the code is often a more important criterion than its efficiency. The size of the automaton may even be exponential with respect to the size of the source program, so the explicit automaton can rarely be used for real size programs. However, the different ways of generating control automata were very useful for designing verification tools. Another influence from ESTEREL and the automaton generation was the introduction of *assertions* in the language: In ESTEREL, simple *relations* of exclusion or implication between input signals were introduced to allow the compiler to simplify the automaton accordingly. In LUSTRE, the relations were naturally generalized ("assert *<expression>*") to indicate the invariance of arbitrary Boolean expressions.

2.3.2.2 *Specification and Verification*   LUSTRE program verification was the topic of two theses by Anne-Cécile Glory and Christophe Ratel. As soon as we had a generator of control automata, we also had an automatic verification tool for Boolean programs. For instance, to verify that two nodes involving only Boolean variables and operators behave the same, one just has to connect them as in Figure 2.2, compile the resulting program into an explicit automaton, and check on the resulting code that the output "ok" is never assigned false. This works also for comparing general nodes, but in a conservative way: If "ok" is never assigned false, the two nodes are equivalent; otherwise, the verification is inconclusive. A more general verification scheme is given by Figure 2.3: In general, we want to prove that, as long as the environment

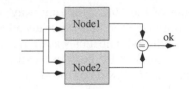

FIGURE 2.2 Comparing two nodes.

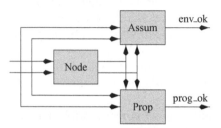

FIGURE 2.3 Specification with observers.

behaves properly (i.e., satisfies some *assumption*), the program satisfies some *property*. Now, if we restrict ourselves to the verification of *safety properties*, both the assumption and the property can be expressed by some programs, called *synchronous observers* [20], which receive as input all the relevant variables, and compute a single Boolean output, which is true as long as the inputs fulfill the considered property or assumption. The node to be verified is connected to the observers as in Figure 2.3, and the verification consists of showing (by model checking over the control automaton) that the output "prog_ok" can only be set to false if "env_ok" was set to false before. Of course, because of the state explosion, it is better to use specialized verification tools than the compiler. A specific model checker, called LESAR, was developed for LUSTRE [19]: It proceeds either by enumerative exploration of the automaton, or by symbolic forward or backward techniques. The model-checking techniques are classical, but the specification by observers is especially natural in a synchronous declarative language. The same technique was adopted by Prover Technology when integrating its industrial verification tool with SCADE. We also developed a verification tool, called NBAC [21, 25], based on linear relation analysis and capable to handle simple (linear) behaviors of numerical variables (Bertrand Jeannet's thesis).

2.3.2.3 Automatic Testing The same technique of specification with observers was used to perform automatic testing [14, 24, 33, 35]: The assumption observer is used to generate only realistic test sequences, while the property is used as an "oracle" to determine whether each test passes or fails.

2.3.2.4 Hardware Description and Arrays An experience was driven in 1989–1992, in cooperation with the Paris Research Laboratory of Digital

Equipment, to use LUSTRE for configuring large FPGAs, which were emerging at these times (Frédéric Rocheteau's thesis). For this, the language was extended with a mechanism of arrays (obviously needed to represent registers and regular architectures), which remained in the version 4 of the language [36].

2.3.2.5 Distributed Code Generation: Dynamic Scheduling Code generation from synchronous programs to distributed architectures is a very challenging topic. We addressed the problem when the distribution is imposed by the user, for example, by assigning a computation site with each variable. A first solution was proposed in Alain Girault's thesis [8], which consists of (1) replicating the whole sequential code for each site, (2) slicing the code on each site according to the variables to be computed locally, and (3) adding communication and synchronization code, assuming a very simple communication mechanism (fixed-size FIFOs). Another solution, inspired by control theory and industrial uses, was proposed in Rym Salem's thesis [10]: This proposal does not pretend to implement exactly the synchronous semantics of the centralized program, but takes advantage of the remaining nondeterminism at the interface between synchronous and asynchronous worlds (mainly asynchronous input sampling). More recently, the problem of really multicycle programs was addressed: Through the mechanism of *clocks*, LUSTRE allows variables to evolve at different rates; however, even if a variable is "slow," its computation must take place in the same "short" cycle than other variables. Reference 37 proposes a way of generating truly multicycle code, where slow tasks are preempted by fast urgent ones, *while strictly respecting the synchronous semantics.*

2.4 SOME LESSONS FROM INDUSTRIAL USE

Let us now report the feedback we perceived from more than 10 years of industrial use of LUSTRE/SCADE. Some of our expectations were confirmed, some were not; unexpected qualities appeared, together with unexpected needs.

2.4.1 About Our Expectations

2.4.1.1 Synchronous Data Flow First, as said before, Caspi's initial idea about the convenience of the formalism for control engineer was completely confirmed. In particular, the graphical syntax was completely natural for SCADE users. This may look strange for programmers—who will generally prefer the textual LUSTRE syntax, and the capabilities of a text editor—but the graphical syntax is compulsory for reaching system designers; as a matter of fact, a graphical syntax, the SYNCCHARTS [1], had also been defined for ESTEREL.

2.4.1.2 Formal Semantics   The fact that, in contrast with many control engineering formalisms, LUSTRE is equipped with a formal, simple, clean, and *abstract* semantics, is a more hidden advantage:

- It probably increases the quality of the programs, because it improves the quality of understanding of the language by the users; however, this impact is difficult to measure.
- It makes formal reasoning about programs easier, but it is not clear that formal reasoning is an important issue nowadays in the industry.
- However, it has a tremendous importance for ease of compilation and for the quality of the generated code. Languages that—like Grafcet, Statecharts, or Simulink—are defined by means of a simulation algorithm leave very little freedom for code generation and optimization.
- Our hope was that, using the formal semantics, a LUSTRE compiler could be formally *proven*. In spite of a successful attempt by Eduardo Gimenez with the proof assistant Coq [5], the industrial compiler was never proved. The main problem is probably that, for the time being, such a proof would not be accepted by certification authorities.

2.4.1.3 From Clocks to Activation Conditions   In LUSTRE, the concept of clock is very similar to the one that plays a prominent role in SIGNAL: It allows a flow to have values only at some cycles and then to trigger operators only at these cycles. This quite abstract concept was seldom used by SCADE users, because it was considered too complicated. As a consequence, it was replaced by a simpler primitive, called "activation condition": A Boolean flow can be attached to a node call as an activation condition: The node is active only when the condition is true; otherwise, its output keep their previous values (instead of being "absent" with the clock mechanism).

2.4.1.4 Formal Verification and Automatic Testing   For the time being, the conclusion concerning formal verification is mitigated. We know of some experiences of property verification, using either the industrial Prover-plugin tool, or our academic prototypes. The technique of observers was appreciated, because it uses the same language for writing programs and properties. However, formal verification is far from being a routine task in software design. Even requiring that people express high-level properties and assumptions is difficult. Moreover, it is difficult to quantify the benefits of using verification: People often deny that it improves the reliability of final programs ("anyway, my programs are zero default!"), and concerning the reduction of costs, it is not yet admitted that it could reduce the amount of testing required for code certification. Our hope is to use automatic testing as a kind of "Trojan horse": Since automatic testing is well accepted (since it makes easier an already existing task), and since the effort needed for automatic testing (i.e., writing observers for the assumption and the property) is essentially the same than the one for verification, people can get used with verification tasks.

2.4.2 Unexpected Features and Needs

On the other hand, we discovered other advantages of LUSTRE/SCADE over existing tools, the importance of which was neglected before, mainly because they are classical in modern languages:

- *Program Structure.* In contrast with many control engineering languages, LUSTRE enables a structuring of programs to an arbitrary depth, through the concept of node, which can be constructed by means of very few predefined operators. Tools like SAO only offered a partitioning of programs into *sheets*, the nesting of which was not possible; otherwise, the tool was based on a huge (and continuously increasing) library of predefined operators.
- *Compiler Efficiency.* We expected the code efficiency to be the major gain with respect to previous tools. In fact, some users were also impressed by the efficiency of the compiler as some existing tools take hours to compile even simple programs!
- *Detection of Instant Loops.* In LUSTRE, it is forbidden for a variable to instantly depend on itself (without a "pre" in the loop): It is called a *causality error.* It was noticed that the detection by the compiler of such instant loops may highlight specification inconsistencies, which would be left hidden when programming with a sequential imperative language: Since such a language forces the user to specify the evaluation order, some problematic loops existing in the specification can be ignored, since they are cut at some arbitrary points just because of the order of statements.

2.4.2.1 *The Question of Causality: Modular and Separate Compilation* As said before, synchronous languages raise the problem of causality errors (instantaneous self-dependence). The exact detection of causality errors is undecidable, since it can depend on arbitrary data properties. So it is necessarily approximated: Some executable programs are rejected by the compiler. In LUSTRE, this approximation is especially rough, since the detection is done syntactically. However, it appeared that this rough detection was not disturbing for users, and even too sophisticated: In SCADE, the criterion is even stronger,* since it is forbidden that an input of a node instantaneously depend on an output of this node (i.e., not only there should be a "pre" in the loop, but it should also appear outside the node; see Fig. 2.4). This restriction has a huge consequence: Nodes can be compiled separately (in contrast with all other synchronous languages), since the correct order of computations inside the node cannot depend on the way it is called. Of course, separate compilation is an important topic for real-life applications. It is also important for code

---

* According to some SCADE compiling options, which are used for separate compilation and code traceability. Other options allow the same criterion than in LUSTRE.

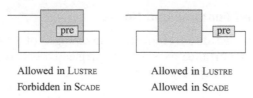

Allowed in LUSTRE   Allowed in LUSTRE
Forbidden in SCADE   Allowed in SCADE

FIGURE 2.4   Causality in LUSTRE and SCADE.

traceability (i.e., the ability to relate the generated code to the source program), which is often required for certification: The code generated for a node, or a node call, is clearly identified as a contiguous block in the whole object code.

2.5   AND NOW . . .

Let us conclude by an overview of ongoing research and development around LUSTRE and SCADE.

First, some important evolutions of the language are still going on. These evolutions are often prototyped thanks to Marc Pouzet's "Lucid synchrone" [11, 12], which is a higher-order extension of LUSTRE (or a kind of merge of LUSTRE and ML):

- *Arrays.* The array mechanism introduced in LUSTRE-V4 [36] aimed at describing regular circuits. It appeared that it is not convenient for software implementation, because V4 arrays cannot be compiled into arrays (updated with loops) in the target code: Presently, they are expanded into as many variables as array elements. In Reference 31, a new mechanism of arrays is proposed, provided with a small number of *iterators*, similar to those of functional programming. Experiments show that this new mechanism is powerful enough for most practical applications and can lead, of course, to tremendous reduction of the code size. Moreover, this mechanism also permits an original technique [28] for generic verification of programs containing arrays.

- *State Machines.* It is known for long that the data-flow style is sometimes inconvenient in some situations, where the system to be described is naturally sequential, or automaton-like. Several attempts have been made to mix imperative and data-flow descriptions [26, 29]. Presently, a weakened version of the SYNCCHARTS, called "safe state machines" (SSM), is being introduced into SCADE.

- *Packaging and Genericity.* LUSTRE is still quite poor concerning such classical topics as encapsulation, packaging, and genericity, which are essential for large designs, libraries definition, and reuse. We are currently introducing mechanisms for defining generic packages; encapsulating definitions of constants, types, functions, and nodes; and possibly taking as static parameters constants, types functions, and nodes. This could lead, some day, to an "object-oriented LUSTRE."

The new ways of compiling LUSTRE toward distributed architectures and event-triggered tasking (cf. Section 2.3.2.5) remain to be transferred in the industrial tool. Another topic about code generation is intra-instant scheduling: In some applications, the basic cycle is considered too long with respect to some input–output required delays. In such cases, one would like to influence the static scheduler inside the compiler, so that some input acquisitions can be scheduled "close to" some output computations and emissions. Such a feature is possible in the SAXO compiler [38] for ESTEREL. It is under investigation for LUSTRE [7].

Finally, we are also using LUSTRE for modeling, simulating, and verifying nonsynchronous systems: For instance, the so-called globally asynchronous, locally synchronous (GALS) systems can be modeled [17] by introducing controlled nondeterminism through the use of additional inputs (oracles), possibly restricted by assertions. Some experiences are also conducted concerning the simulation of circuits descriptions at transaction level in SystemC [32].

REFERENCES

1. C. André. Representation and analysis of reactive behaviors: A synchronous approach. In *IEEE-SMC'96, Computational Engineering in Systems Applications*, Lille, France, July 1996.

2. E. A. Ashcroft and W. W. Wadge. LUCID, *The Data-Flow Programming Language*. Academic Press, San Diego, CA, 1985.

3. A. D. Baker, T. L. Johnson, D. I. Kerpelman, and H. A. Sutherland. Grafcet and SFC as factory automation standards. In *American Control Conference*, pp. 1725–1730, 1987.

4. G. Berry and G. Gonthier. The Esterel synchronous programming language: Design, semantics, implementation. *Science of Computer Programming*, 19(2):87–152, 1992.

5. Y. Bertot and P. Castéran. *Interactive Theorem Proving and Program Development— Coq'Art: The Calculus of Inductive Constructions*. Texts in Theoretical Computer Science. An EATCS Series, Springer Verlag, Berlin, 2004.

6. A. Bouajjani, J.-C. Fernandez, and N. Halbwachs. Minimal model generation. In R. Kurshan, ed., *International Workshop on Computer Aided Verification*, Rutgers, New Brunswick, NJ, 1990.

7. P. Caspi, A. Curic, A. Maignan, C. Sofronis, S. Tripakis, and P. Niebert. From Simulink to Scade/Lustre to TTA: A layered approach for distributed embedded applications. In *LCTES 2003*, San Diego, CA, June 2003.

8. P. Caspi, A. Girault, and D. Pilaud. Automatic distribution of reactive systems for asynchronous networks of processors. *IEEE Transactions on Software Engineering*, 25(3):416–427, 1999. Research report INRIA 3491.

9. P. Caspi and N. Halbwachs. A functional model for describing and reasoning about time behaviour of computing systems. *Acta Informatica*, 22:595–697, 1986.

10. P. Caspi, C. Mazuet, R. Salem, and D. Weber. Formal design of distributed control systems with Lustre. In *Proceedings of Safecomp'99, Volume 1698 of Lecture Notes in Computer Science*, Springer Verlag, September 1999.

11. P. Caspi and M. Pouzet. A functional extension to Lustre. In *Eighth International Symposium on Languages for Intensional Programming, ISLIP'95*, Sidney, May 1995.

12. P. Caspi and M. Pouzet. A co-iterative characterization of synchronous stream functions. In *Coalgebraic Methods in Computer Science (CMCS'98)*, Electronic Notes in Theoretical Computer Science, March 28–29, 1998.

13. R. David and H. Alla. *Petri Nets and Grafcet: Tools for Modelling Discrete Event Systems*. Prentice Hall, New York, 1992.

14. L. du Bousquet, F. Ouabdesselam, J.-L. Richier, and N. Zuanon. Lutess: Testing environment for synchronous software. In B.W. Boehm, D. Garlan, and J. Kramer, ed., *Proceedings of the 1999 International Conference on Software Engineering, ICSE '99*. Los Angeles, CA, May, 1999.

15. D. Ferbeck. The VAL product line. In *APM'91 Conference*, Yokohama, 1991.

16. N. Halbwachs. A synchronous language at work: The story of Lustre. In *Third ACM/ IEEE International Conference on Formal Methods and Models for Codesign, MEMOCODE'2005*, Verona, Italy, July 2005.

17. N. Halbwachs and S. Baghdadi. Synchronous modeling of asynchronous systems. In *EMSOFT'02*, LNCS 2491, Springer Verlag, October 2002.

18. N. Halbwachs, P. Caspi, P. Raymond, and D. Pilaud. The synchronous dataflow programming language LUSTRE. *Proceedings of the IEEE*, 79(9):1305–1320, 1991.

19. N. Halbwachs, F. Lagnier, and C. Ratel. Programming and verifying real-time systems by means of the synchronous data-flow programming language LUSTRE. In *IEEE Transactions on Software Engineering, Special Issue on the Specification and Analysis of Real-Time Systems*, pp. 785–793, September 1992.

20. N. Halbwachs, F. Lagnier, and P. Raymond. Synchronous observers and the verification of reactive systems. In M. Nivat, C. Rattray, T. Rus, and G. Scollo, eds., *Third International Conference on Algebraic Methodology and Software Technology, AMAST'93*, Workshops in Computing, Springer Verlag, June 20, 1993.

21. N. Halbwachs, Y. E. Proy, and P. Roumanoff. Verification of real-time systems using linear relation analysis. *Formal Methods in System Design*, 11(2):157–185, 1997.

22. N. Halbwachs, P. Raymond, and C. Ratel. Generating efficient code from data-flow programs. In *Third International Symposium on Programming Language Implementation and Logic Programming*, LNCS 528, Springer Verlag, Passau, Germany, August 1991.

23. D. Harel. Statecharts: A visual approach to complex systems. *Science of Computer Programming*, 8(3):231–274, 1987.

24. E. Jahier, P. Raymond, and P. Baufreton. Case studies with Lurette V2. In *First International Symposium on Leveraging Applications of Formal Method, ISoLa 2004*, Paphos, Cyprus, October 2004.

25. B. Jeannet, N. Halbwachs, and P. Raymond. Dynamic partitioning in analyses of numerical properties. In A. Cortesi and G. Filé, eds., *Static Analysis Symposium, SAS'99*, LNCS 1694, Springer Verlag, Venice, Italy, September 1999.

26. M. Jourdan, F. Lagnier, P. Raymond, and F. Maraninchi. A multiparadigm language for reactive systems. In *5th IEEE International Conference on Computer Languages*, IEEE Computer Society Press, Toulouse, May 1994.

27. P. Le Guernic, T. Gautier, M. Le Borgne, and C. Le Maire. Programming real time applications with SIGNAL. *Proceedings of the IEEE*, 79(9):1321–1336, 1991.

28. F. Maraninchi and L. Morel. Arrays and contracts for the specification and analysis of regular systems. In *Fourth International Conference on Application of Concurrency to System Design (ACSD)*, Hamilton, Ontario, Canada, June 2004.

29. F. Maraninchi and Y. Rémond. Mode-automata: About modes and states for reactive systems. In *European Symposium on Programming*, Springer Verlag, Lisbon, Portugal, March 1998.

30. R. Milner. Calculi for synchrony and asynchrony. *Theoretical Computer Science*, 25(3):267–310, 1983.

31. L. Morel. Efficient compilation of array iterators for Lustre. In *First Workshop on Synchronous Languages, Applications, and Programming, SLAP02*, Grenoble, April 2002.

32. M. Moy, F. Maraninchi, and L. Maillet-Contoz. LusSy: A toolbox for the analysis of systems-on-a-chip at the transactional level. In *Fifth International Conference on Application of Concurrency to System Design (ACSD)*, 2005.

33. F. Ouabdesselam and I. Parissis. Testing synchronous critical software. In *5th International Symposium on Software Reliability Engineering (ISSRE'94)*, Monterey, November 1994.

34. J. A. Plaice and J.-B. Saint. The LUSTRE-ESTEREL portable format. Unpublished report, INRIA, Sophia Antipolis, 1987.

35. P. Raymond, D. Weber, X. Nicollin, and N. Halbwachs. Automatic testing of reactive systems. In *19th IEEE Real-Time Systems Symposium*, Madrid, Spain, December 1998.

36. F. Rocheteau and N. Halbwachs. Implementing reactive programs on circuits, a hardware implementation of Lustre. In *REX Workshop on Real-Time: Theory in Practice, DePlasmolen (Netherlands)*, pp. 195–208. LNCS 600, Springer Verlag, June 1991.

37. N. Scaife and P. Caspi. Integrating model-based design and preemptive scheduling in mixed time- and event-triggered systems. In *Euromicro Conference on Real-Time Systems (ECRTS'04)*, Catania, Italy, June 2004.

38. D. Weil, V. Bertin, E. Closse, M. Poisse, P. Venier, and J. Pulou. Efficient compilation of Esterel for real-time embedded systems. In *International Conference on Compilers, Architecture, and Synthesis for Embedded Systems (CASES)*, San Jose, 2000.

CHAPTER 3

REQUIREMENTS OF AN INTEGRATED FORMAL METHOD FOR INTELLIGENT SWARMS

MIKE HINCHEY
Lero—the Irish Software Engineering Research Centre, University of Limerick, Limerick, Ireland

JAMES L. RASH
NASA Goddard Space Flight Center (Emeritus), Greenbelt, MD

CHRISTOPHER A. ROUFF
Near Infinity Corporation, Reston, VA

WALT F. TRUSZKOWSKI
NASA Goddard Space Flight Center (Emeritus), Greenbelt, MD

AMY K.C.S. VANDERBILT
Vanderbilt Consulting, Fairfax, VA

3.1 INTRODUCTION

NASA is investigating new paradigms for future space exploration, heavily focused on the (still) emerging technologies of autonomous and autonomic systems [46–48]. Missions that rely on multiple, smaller, collaborating spacecraft, analogous to swarms in nature, are being investigated to supplement and complement traditional missions that rely on one large spacecraft [16]. The small spacecraft in such missions would each be able to operate on their own to accomplish a part of a mission, but would need to interact and exchange information with the other spacecraft to successfully execute the mission.

Formal Methods for Industrial Critical Systems: A Survey of Applications, First Edition.
Edited by Stefania Gnesi and Tiziana Margaria.
© 2013 IEEE. Published 2013 by John Wiley & Sons, Inc.

This new systems paradigm offers several advantages:

- the ability to explore environments and regions in space where traditional craft would be impractical,
- greater mission redundancy (and, consequently, greater protection of assets), and
- reduced costs and risk, to name but a few. Examples of concept swarm missions include
  - the use of autonomous unmanned air vehicles (UAVs) flying approximately 1 m above the surface of Mars, which will cover as much of the surface of Mars in seconds as the now-famous Mars rovers did in their entire time on the planet;
  - the use of armies of tetrahedral walkers to explore the surface of Mars and the Moon [15];
  - constellations of satellites flying in formation; and
  - the use of miniaturized pico-class spacecraft to explore the asteroid belt, where heretofore, it has been impossible to send exploration craft without the unacceptably high likelihood of loss [16].

However, these new approaches to exploration simultaneously pose many challenges. These missions will be unmanned and highly autonomous. Many of them will be sent to parts of the solar system where manned missions are simply not possible within the foreseeable limits of technology, and to destinations where the round-trip delay for communications to spacecraft exceeds 40 minutes, meaning that the decisions on responses to exploration opportunities as well as problems and undesirable situations must be made *in situ* rather than from ground control on Earth.

The degree of autonomy and intelligence necessary for such missions would require an unprecedented amount of testing of any developed (software and hardware) systems. Furthermore, with learning and autonomic properties—such as self-optimizing and self-healing—emergent behavior patterns simply cannot be fully predicted. Consequently, these missions will be orders of magnitudes more complex than traditional single-spacecraft missions, and verifying these new types of missions will be infeasible using traditional techniques. The authors believe that formal specification techniques and formal verification will play important roles in the future development of NASA space exploration missions. Formal methods would enable software assurance and proof of correctness of the behavior of swarms, even when (within certain bounds) this behavior is emergent (as a result of composing a large number of interacting entities, producing behavior that, absent extraordinary design and verification measures, was not foreseen). Formal models derived may also be used as the basis for automating the generation of much of the code for the mission [25].

To address the challenge in verifying these types of missions, a NASA project, Formal Approaches to Swarm Technology (FAST), investigated formal methods for use in such missions [33–37, 40, 41]. A NASA concept mission, Autonomous Nano-Technology Swarm (ANTS), was used as an example mission to be specified and verified [15–17]. An effective formal method for use on the ANTS mission would have to be able to predict the emergent behavior of 1000 agents operating as a swarm, as well as the behavior of the individual agents. Crucial to the mission would be autonomic properties and the ability to modify operations autonomously to reflect the changing conditions and goals of the mission.

This chapter gives an overview of swarm technologies, and the ANTS swarm-based mission concept presents the results of an evaluation of a number of formal methods for verifying swarm-based missions, and proposes an integrated formal method for verifying swarm-based systems.

3.2 SWARM TECHNOLOGIES

Swarms [3, 4] consist of a large number of simple agents that have local interactions with each other and the environment. There is no central controller directing the swarm and no one agent has a global view; the simple interactions give rise to "emergent behaviors" and dynamic self-organization of the swarm. Emergent behavior is observed in insects and flocks of birds. Bonabeau et al. [8], who studied self-organization in social insects, stated that "complex collective behaviors may emerge from interactions among individuals that exhibit simple behaviors" and described emergent behavior as "a set of dynamical mechanisms whereby structures appear at the global level of a system from interactions among its lower-level components." The emergent behavior is sometimes referred to as the macroscopic behavior and the individual behavior and local interactions as the microscopic behavior.

Agent swarms are often used as a modeling technique and as a tool to study complex systems [22]. In swarm simulations, a group of interacting agents [50] (often homogeneous or near homogeneous) is studied relative to their emergent behavior. Swarm simulations have supported the study of flocks of birds [11, 32], business and economics [28], and ecological systems [42]. In swarm simulations, each of the agents is given certain parameters that it tries to maximize. In terms of bird swarms, each bird tries to find another bird to fly with, and then will fly off to one side and slightly higher to reduce its drag, and eventually the birds form flocks. Swarms are also being investigated for use in applications such as telephone switching, network routing, data categorizing, and shortest path optimizations [7].

In intelligent swarms, the individual members of a swarm exhibit intelligence [6, 7]. With intelligent swarms, members may be heterogeneous or homogeneous. Due to their differing environments, swarm members, even if initially they are homogeneous, may learn different things and develop different goals, and thereby, the swarm may become heterogeneous. A swarm that is homogeneous from the start (such as the NASA concept mission described below) will possess different capabilities as well as a possible social structure. This makes verifying such systems even more difficult, since the swarms are no longer made up of homogeneous members with limited intelligence and communications.

The emergent behavior of swarms can be unpredictable. Though swarm behaviors are the combination of often simple individual behaviors, they can, when aggregated, form complex and often unexpected behaviors. Verifying *intelligent* swarms will be even more difficult, not only due to the greater complexity of each member, but also due to the complex interaction of a large number of intelligent elements. Intelligent swarms possess a huge state space, and since the elements may be in "learning mode," the behavior of the individual elements and the emergent behavior of the swarm may be constantly changing and difficult to predict. Accurately predicting these behaviors, however, will be very important to mission developers in assuring that these missions operate safely and as planned.

The remainder of this section gives an overview of the NASA ANTS concept swarm-based mission and the difficulty in specifying such a mission. We are using the ANTS mission as an example test bed and case study, for the purpose of evaluating multiple formal methods in the specification, validation, and verification of swarm-based missions.

3.2.1 ANTS Mission Overview

The ANTS concept mission [15–17] would involve the launch of a swarm of autonomous pico-class (approximately 1 kg) spacecraft that would explore the asteroid belt for asteroids with certain scientific characteristics. Figure 3.1 gives an overview of the ANTS mission [46]. In this mission, a transport ship, launched from Earth, would travel to a point in space where net gravitational forces on small objects (such as pico-class spacecraft) are negligible (a solar system Lagrangian point). From this point, 1000 spacecraft, that have been manufactured en route from Earth, would be launched into the asteroid belt. Because of their small size, each spacecraft would carry just one specialized instrument for collecting a specific type of data from asteroids in the belt.

To implement this mission, a heuristic approach is being considered that provides a social structure to the swarm, with hierarchical behavior analogous to colonies or swarms of insects, and with some spacecraft directing others. Artificial intelligence technologies such as genetic algorithms, neural nets, fuzzy logic, and on-board planners are being investigated to assist the mission to maintain a high level of autonomy. Crucial to the mission will be the ability to modify its operations autonomously to reflect the changing nature of the mission and the distance and low bandwidth of communications back to Earth.

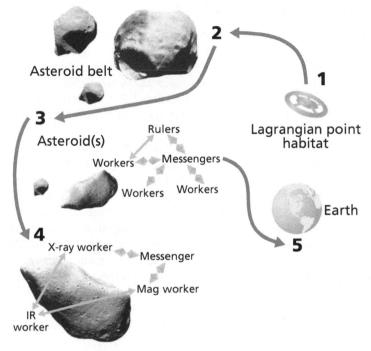

FIGURE 3.1   ANTS mission concept.

Approximately 80% of the spacecraft will be workers that will carry the specialized instruments (e.g., a magnetometer, a sensor in the X-ray, gamma ray, or visible/IR band, or a neutral mass spectrometer) and that will obtain specific types of data. Some will be coordinators (called rulers or leaders) that have rules that will decide the types of asteroids and data the mission is interested in and that will coordinate the efforts of the workers. The messengers are the third type of spacecraft that will coordinate communication between the rulers and workers, and communications with the mission control center on Earth (also known as "ground control").

Many things can happen when an ANTS team encounters an asteroid. A spacecraft can do a flyby and do opportunistic observations. The flyby can be used to first determine whether the asteroid is of interest before sending an entire team to the asteroid, and whether, due to the nature of the instrument on the spacecraft, only a flyby is necessary. If the asteroid is of interest, an imaging spacecraft will be sent to the asteroid to ascertain its exact dimensions and features and to create a rough model to be used by other spacecraft for maneuvering around the asteroid. Other teams of the spacecraft will then coordinate to finish studying and mapping the asteroid to form a complete model.

3.2.2 Specifying and Verifying ANTS

The above is a very simplified description of the ANTS mission. For a more detailed description, the interested reader is directed to References 39 and 46, or to the ANTS website. As can be seen from the brief exposition above, ANTS would be a highly complex system that poses many significant challenges. Not least among these are the complex interactions between heterogeneous components; the need for continuous replanning, reconfiguration, and reoptimization; the need for autonomous operation without intervention from Earth; and the need for assurance of the correct operation of the mission.

In missions such as ANTS that will be highly autonomous and out of contact with ground control for extended periods of time, errors in the software may not be observable or correctable after launch. Consequently, a high level of assurance is necessary for these missions before they are launched. Testing of space exploration systems is done through simulations, since it would be impractical or impossible to test them in their end environment. Although these simulations are of very high quality, often very small errors get through and can result in the loss of an entire mission, as is thought to have happened with the Mars Polar Lander mission [5], where the absence of one line of code in the flight software may have resulted in the loss of the entire mission. In the report on the loss of the Mars Polar Lander [12], it is stated that

> it is important to recognize that space missions are a "one strike and you are out" activity. Thousands of functions can be correctly performed and one mistake can be mission catastrophic

and

> a thorough test and verification program is essential for mission success.

Complex missions such as ANTS exacerbate the difficulty of finding errors, and will require new mission verification methods to provide the level of software assurance that NASA requires to reduce risks to an acceptable level. Many of the ANTS behaviors, including those that produce race conditions, for example, are time-based and only occur when processes send or receive data at particular times or in a particular sequence, or after learning occurs. Errors under such conditions can rarely be found by inputting sample data and checking for correct results. To find these errors through testing, the software processes involved would have to be executed in all possible combinations of states (state space) that the processes could collectively be in. Because the state space is exponential (and sometimes factorial) to the number of states, it becomes essentially untestable with a relatively small number of processes. Traditionally, to get around the state explosion problem, testers have artificially reduced the number of states of the system and approximated the underlying software using models. This reduces the fidelity of the model and can mask potential errors.

A significant issue for specifying (and verifying) swarm behavior is support for analysis of and identification of emergent behavior. The idea of emergence is well known from biology, economics, and other scientific areas. It is also prominent in computer science and engineering, but the concept is not so well understood by computer scientists and engineers, although they encounter it regularly. Emergent behavior has been described as "system behavior that is more complex than the behavior of the individual components . . . often in ways not intended by the original designers [49]." This means that when interacting components of a system whose individual behavior is well understood are combined within a single environment, they can demonstrate behavior that can be unforeseen or not explained from the behavior of the individual components. The corollary of this is that making changes to components of a system of systems, or replacing a subsystem within a system of systems, may often have unforeseen, unexpected, and completely unexplained ramifications for both overall system behavior and the behavior of other subsystems.

A formal specification for swarm-based missions will need to be able to track the goals of the mission as they change and be able to modify the model of the universe as new data come in. The formal specification will also need to allow for specification of the decision-making process to aid in the decision as to which instruments will be needed, at what location, with what goals, and so on. Once written, the formal specification must be usable to prove the properties of the system and check for particular types of errors, and be usable as input to a model checker. The formal method must also be able to track the models of the leaders, and it must allow for decisions to be made as to when the data collected have met the goals. To accomplish all of this, an integration of four identified formal methods [34, 36, 37, 40, 41] seems to be the best approach for verifying cooperating swarm-based systems.

3.3 NASA FAST PROJECT

The FAST project identified several important attributes needed in a formal approach for verifying swarm-based systems [35, 37] and surveyed a wide range of formal methods and formal techniques [34, 40, 41] to determine whether existing formal methods, or a combination of existing methods, could be suitable for specifying and verifying swarm-based missions and their emergent behavior. Various methods were surveyed based on a small number of criteria that were determined to be important in their application to intelligent swarms. These included

- support for concurrency and real-time constraints,
- formal basis,
- (existing) tool support,

- past experience in application to agent-based or swarm-based systems, and
- algorithm support.

A large number of formal methods that support the specification of one of, but not both, concurrent behavior and algorithmic behavior were identified. In addition, there were a large number of integrated formal methods that have been developed over recent years with the goal of supporting the specification of both concurrency and algorithms. Based on the results of the survey, four formal methods were selected to be used for a sample specification of part of the ANTS mission. These methods were

- Communicating Sequential Processes (CSP) [24, 26, 27],
- Weighted Synchronous Calculus of Communicating Systems (WSCCS) [45],
- X-Machines [29–31], and
- Unity Logic [13].

CSP was chosen as a baseline specification method because the team had significant experience and success [23, 38] in specifying agent-based systems with CSP. WSCCS and X-Machines were chosen because they had already been used for specifying emergent behavior by others, with some success. Unity Logic was also chosen because it had been successfully used for specifying concurrent systems and was logic based, in contrast with the other methods. Integrating the memory and transition function aspects of X-Machines with the priority and probability aspects of WSCCS and other methods may produce a specification method that will allow all the necessary aspects for specifying emergent behavior in the ANTS mission and other swarm-based systems. In addition, available tools supported these formal methods [37].

The approach being taken to integrate the formal methods was the viewpoint integration [18, 44] method. In this type of formal methods integration, the base formalisms of the methods are maintained, and relationships between the formalisms are developed to reflect the new formal method. This approach preserves the strength of the underlying methods, allows a seamless specification of the ANTS mission, and allows the development of support tools using existing semantics of the methods.

Specification by viewpoints is also widely advocated as a useful method for dealing with the complexity of specifying large systems. Each view specification describes an aspect (rather than a component or module) of the system, using a language most suited to that view. A consequence of using this approach is that specifications of the same or related elements often appear in different views and must adequately cross reference each other.

3.4 INTEGRATED SWARM FORMAL METHOD

The majority of formal notations currently available were developed in the 1970s and 1980s, and reflect the types of distributed systems being developed at that time. Current distributed systems are evolving and may not be specifiable the same way past systems have been specified [14]. Consequently, many researchers and practitioners are combining formal methods into integrated (hybrid) approaches to address the new features of distributed systems (e.g., mobile agents, swarms, and emergent behavior).

Integrated approaches have been very popular in specifying concurrent and agent-based systems. Integrated approaches often combine a process algebra or logic-based approach with a model-based approach. The process algebra or logic-based approach allows for easy specification of concurrent systems, while the model-based approach provides strength in specifying the algorithmic part of a system. The following is a partial list of integrated approaches that have been used for specifying concurrent and agent-based systems:

- Communicating X-Machines [2],
- CSP-OZ (a combination of CSP and Object-Z [19]),
- Object-Z and Statecharts [10],
- Timed Communicating Object-Z [20],
- Temporal B [9],
- Timed CSP [43],
- Temporal Petri Nets (Temporal Logic and Petri Nets) [1], and
- ZCCS (a combination of Z and CCS [21]).

To illustrate the integration of CSP, WSCCS, X-Machines, and Unity Logic, examples of different views of the ANTS mission are given below. These views show how they can cross reference each other and how each can provide a different view of the ANTS mission. CSP provides the interprocess communication view, X-Machines provide the state machine and memory views, WSCCS provides the probability and priority views, and Unity Logic provides the logic views. Variables that each of them references, such as goals and models, will have additional notation or highlighting to indicate cross references to specifications by other views. For a longer specification, color coding could be used. Since this is only a sample specification for illustration purposes, only bold highlighting will be used. The following sections give examples of these views based on the specifications presented in References 36, 37, and 41.

3.4.1 CSP View

The following is the top-level specification of the ANTS mission in CSP:

$$ANTS_{\text{goals}} = Leader_{i,\text{l\_goals}} \parallel Messenger_{j,\text{m\_goals}} \parallel Worker_{k,\text{w\_goals}},$$
$$1 \le i \le m, 1 \le j \le n, 1 \le k \le p,$$

where m is the number of leader spacecraft, n is the number of messenger spacecraft, and p is the number of worker spacecraft. This specification shows that the ANTS mission starts, or is initialized, with a set of goals given to it by the principal investigator, and some of these goals are given to the leader (while some of these goals may not be given to the leader because the goals are ground based or not applicable to the leader). In addition to goals, each of the spacecraft is given a name (in this case, in the form of a number) so that it can identify itself when communicating with other ANTS spacecraft and the Earth.

For the viewpoint integration, the goals of ANTS will also be specified by the X-Machine view of ANTS. The goals are highlighted here to indicate they are also referenced in other views. The following gives the specifications for the communications of a leader with indications of where the specification and the variables are used in other views.

3.4.1.1   Leader Specification   The leader spacecraft specification consists of the communications process and the intelligence process:

$$Leader_i = LEADER\_COM_i, \{\} \| LEADER\_INTELLIGENCE_{i,\text{goals,model}}.$$

The communications process, $LEADER\_COM$, specifies the behavior of the spacecraft as it relates to communicating with the other spacecraft and Earth, and specifies a protocol between the spacecraft. The second process, $LEADER\_INTELLIGENCE$, constitutes the intelligence of the leader; it maintains the goals and the models of the spacecraft and its environment, and specifies how they are modified during operations. For each of the above processes, one of its parameters is a spacecraft group identifier, and other parameters represent sets that store conversations (empty at startup), goals, and models. The models and goals are specified in the X-Machine specifications, and the reasoning part of the $LEADER\_INTELLIGENCE$ process is specified in the WSCCS specifications.

The following gives the specifications for the communication process of the leader.

3.4.1.2   Leader Communication Specification   A leader spacecraft may receive messages from another leader, a worker, a messenger, or Earth. A message from any other sender constitutes an error condition and the message is returned (it is assumed that there is a mechanism that keeps an error message from being returned as an error message, thus causing an endless loop). It is assumed that messages that are relayed through a messenger from another spacecraft are marked as being sent from the original sender and not the messenger. Leaders also maintain a set (*conv*) of persistent messages to keep track of the current state of the conversations. Requests may be made to other spacecraft for status, to move to a new location, change goals, or return specific data. Requests may also be sent to other spacecraft for similar actions.

Leader communication is specified via WSCCS, X-Machines, and Unity Logic, and when a communication occurs, a change of state is executed from either the reasoning state or the processing state. Also, if, while communicating, any of the actions listed in the WSCCS, X-Machine, or Unity Logic specification occur, then a change is executed from the communicating state to either the reasoning state or the processing state. Again, highlighting is used to indicate specifications in other views. The rendezvous for each of the below CSP specifications also acts as a transition to the WSCCS, X-Machine, or Unity Logic finite-state machine.

The following is the top-level specification of the leader communication:

$LEADER\_COM_{i,conv} = leader.in?msg \rightarrow$
   case **LEADER_MESSAGE**$_{i,conv,msg}$
      if $sender(msg) = LEADER$
   MESSENGER_MESSAGE$_{i,conv,msg}$
      if $sender(msg) = MESSENGER$
   WORKER_MESSAGE$_{i,conv,msg}$
      if $sender(msg) = WORKER$
   EARTH_MESSAGE$_{i,conv,msg}$
      if $sender(msg) = EARTH$
   ERROR_MESSAGE$_{i,conv,msg}$
      otherwise

The above shows the messages from other spacecraft types that a leader may receive. The WSCCS, X-Machine, and Unity Logic views define the above "LEADER_MESSAGE," "MESSENGER_MESSAGE," "WORKER_MESSAGE," "EARTH_MESSAGE," and "ERROR_MESSAGE" as actions that change the state of the leader from either reasoning or processing to communicating. The specification in Unity Logic also has predicates that express the conditions for passing messages. The above statements are highlighted to indicate a link to another view.

The following processes further describe the messages that may be received from other leaders. Messages sent from another leader may be one of two types: request or informational. Requests may be issued for, among other things, information on the leader's model or goals, for resources (e.g., more workers), or for status. Messages may also be informational and may contain data concerning new goals or new information for the agent's model (pertaining, e.g., to a new discovery or a message from Earth). This information needs to be examined by the intelligence process and the model process to determine whether any updates to the goals or model need to be made. Since X-Machines also specify the goals and models, references to each of them have links to the X-Machine specification:

LEADER_MESSAGE$_{i,conv} =$
   case $LEADER\_INFORMATION_{i,conv,msg}$
      if $content(msg) = information$

$LEADER\_REQUESTS_{i,conv,msg}$
  if $content(msg) = request$
$LEADER\_RECEIVE_{i,conv,msg}$
  if $content(msg) = reply\_to\_request$
$ERROR\_MESSAGE_{i,conv,msg}$
  otherwise

Further specification of each of the above subprocesses follows:

$LEADER\_INFORMATION_{i,conv} =$
  leader_model$_i$ $!(NEW\_INFO, msg)$
  $\rightarrow$ **goals_channel**$_i$ $!(NEW\_INFO, msg)$
  $\rightarrow LEADER\_COM_{i,conv}$

If the message is new information, then that information has to be sent to the deliberative part of the agent to check whether the goals should be updated, as well as to the model part to check whether any of the information requires updates to the model. Again, since the model and goals are defined in other views (X-Machines) and the communications causes state changes in the WSCCS, X-Machine, and Unity Logic specifications, the channels above are highlighted:

$LEADER\_REQUESTS_{i,conv,msg} =$
  case $LEADER\_STATUS\_REQ$
    if $content(msg) = status\_request$
    $LEADER\_INFO\_REQ_{i,conv,msg}$
    if $content(msg) = info\_request$
    $LEADER\_RESOURCE\_REQ_{i,conv,msg}$
    if $content(msg) = resource\_request$
    $ERROR\_MESSAGE_{i,conv,msg}$
    otherwise

If the message is a request, then, depending on the type of request, different processes are executed. An agent (e.g., a worker) may issue requests for the status of the spacecraft, requests for information on the leader's goals or model, or requests for resources (e.g., a request that some workers under the leader's direction should form a subteam to investigate a particular asteroid, or that a messenger should be relocated to perform communication functions). Since this specification is an abstraction of lower-level specifications, it does not affect specifications in other views:

$LEADER\_STATUS\_REQ_{i,conv,msg} =$
  leader$_i$**!reply**$(msg, current\_status())$
  $\rightarrow LEADER\_COM_{i,conv}$

As shown above, if the request is for status, then the current spacecraft status is sent back to the sender using a standard function that retrieves the status. The *leader!reply* part of the specification is a communication that causes a change of state in the WSCCS, X-Machine, and Unity Logic specifications:

$LEADER\_INFO\_REQ_{i,conv,msg} =$
    case **goals_channel$_i$**!$(REQUEST, msg) \rightarrow LEADER\_COM_{i,conv}$
        if $content(msg) = goals\_request$
    leader_model$_i$!$(REQUEST, msg) \rightarrow LEADER\_COM_{i,conv}$
        if $content(msg) = model\_request$
    $ERROR\_MESSAGE_{i,conv}$
        otherwise

For the *LEADER_INFO_REQ* process, if the request for information is for the leader's goals, a message is sent to the leader's intelligence process to retrieve the information, which is then sent to the requestor. If the request is for part of the leader's model, then a request is sent to the leader's model process, which then sends the model information to the requestor. The goals and the model are specified as part of the X-Machine specification, and the communication causes a change of state in the WSCCS, X-Machine, and Unity Logic specifications:

$LEADER\_RESOURCE\_REQ_{i,conv,msg} =$
    goals_channel$_i$!$(RESOURCE, msg)$
    $\rightarrow LEADER\_COM_{i,conv}$

For resource requests, the goals of the leader must be checked to determine whether giving up the resource would affect the leader's current goals. The message is therefore sent to the intelligence process to check against the current goals, to update its goals and model (in case it can give up the resources), and to reply to the requestor as appropriate. The highlighted channel indicates that the goals are also specified in the X-Machine view and that the communication causes a change of state in the WSCCS, X-Machine, and Unity Logic specifications:

$LEADER\_RECEIVE_{i,conv,msg} =$
    case **LEADER_STATUS_RECEIVED**$_{i,conv,msg}$
        if $content(msg) = status\_returned$
    LEADER_INFO_RECEIVED$_{i,conv,msg}$
        if $content(msg) = info\_returned$
    LEADER_RESOURCE_RECEIVED$_{i,conv,msg}$
        if $content(msg) = resource\_request\_return$
    ERROR_MESSAGE$_{i,conv,msg}$
        otherwise

After sending a request to other entities, a leader will receive messages back that give requested status, information, or resources. The above *LEADER_ RECEIVE* is the process that handles the messages that have been sent back. These messages have to be sent to the deliberative part of the leader so the leader's goals and models can be updated. The communication changes the state machines in the other views, and the Unity Logic specification also defines the conditions for receiving messages from other spacecraft:

$$LEADER\_STATUS\_RECEIVED_{i,conv,msg} =$$
goals_channel$_i$!$(STATUS\_RECEIVED, msg)$
$$\rightarrow LEADER\_COM_{i,conv}$$

The *LEADER_STATUS_RECEIVED* process is executed when the leader receives a status message from another leader. When this happens, a message is sent to the goals channel containing the message so that the goals and model can be updated. The goals may need updating if the status indicates the worker is no longer able to perform some of its functions. This channel is highlighted to indicate a specification in the X-Machine view:

$$LEADER\_INFO\_RECEIVED_{i,conv,msg} =$$
goals_channel$_i$!$(INFO\_RECEIVED, msg)$
$$\rightarrow LEADER\_COM_{i,conv}$$

The *LEADER_INFO_RECEIVED* process is executed when the leader receives an informational message from another leader. As above, the message is sent to the goals process for possible updates of the goals and leader's model. This channel, again, is highlighted to indicate a specification in a different view (X-Machines):

$$LEADER\_RESOURCE\_RECEIVED_{i,conv,msg} =$$
goals_channel$_i$!$(RESOURCE\_RECEIVED, msg)$
$$\rightarrow LEADER\_COM_{i,conv}$$

As with the above processes, when the *LEADER_RESOURCE_RECEIVED* process is executed, a message is sent to the goals process of the leader for updating of the goals and model, and for taking action if necessary. This channel is highlighted to indicate a specification in a different view (X-Machines):

$$ERROR\_MESSAGE_{i,conv,msg} =$$
messenger$_i$!**return**$(msg, error)$
$$\rightarrow LEADER\_COM_{i,conv}$$

If a message does not match any of the other interactions, then an error message is returned to the sending spacecraft. The error message is highlighted because a communication occurs, which causes a state change in the WSCCS, X-Machine, and Unity Logic views.

Messages to a leader from messengers, and messages to a leader from workers, have specifications similar to the above: sec References 34, 40, and 41.

3.4.2 WSCCS View

To model the ANTS leader spacecraft, WSCCS, a process algebra, takes into account

- the possible states (agents) of the leader,
- actions in each agent state that would qualify an agent to be "in" those states,
- relative frequency of each action defined for an agent, and
- the priority of each action defined for an agent.

3.4.2.1 Actions Table 3.1 gives the actions, agent states, and view of priority on the actions of a leader. All of these actions are reflected in other specification views.

Since the state part of the specification is similar to the X-Machine and Unity Logic specifications, all changes in states in WSCCS would also affect the memory and state changes both in the X-Machine specification and in the state machine of Unity Logic, and would be subject to the predicates of Unity

TABLE 3.1 Agent State and Actions

Agent State	Actions Leading to the Agent State	f	p
Communicating	Identity		
	SendMessageWorker	50	2
	SendMessageLeader	50	2
	SendMessageError	1	1
	ReceiveMessageWorker	50	2
	ReceiveMessageLeader	50	2
	ReceiveMessageError	1	1
Reasoning	ReasoningDeliberative	50	2
	ReasoningReactive	50	2
Processing	ProcessingSortingAndStorage	17	2
	ProcessingGeneration	17	2
	ProcessingPrediction	17	2
	ProcessingDiagnosis	16	2
	ProcessingRecovery	16	2
	ProcessingRemediation	17	2

Logic. The above highlighted actions cause transitions into the communicating state, are specified as part of the CSP view, and indicate when the CSP specification would cause data to be passed on a CSP channel. In addition, the predicates of Unity Logic specify their own applicable preconditions. The reasoning and processing portions are also related to the CSP specification in the *LEADER_INTELLIGENCE* part of the specification (which is not included in this report but given in References 34, 40, and 41.

Continuing with the WSCCS specification, given the information from Table 3.1, we define the various agent states as

$$AgentD \equiv n_a : a.AgentA + n_b : b.AgentB + n_c : c.AgentC.$$

Here, n_a is a weight of the form $n\omega^k$ where n is the relative frequency of the action a, and k denotes the priority of action a, which would then turn agent D into agent A. The addition seen here represents a type of choice between possible actions. Thus, agent D may choose to perform action a, which would turn agent D into agent A. Agent D makes this choice with frequency n and priority k. Or agent D may choose to perform action b and so on. Using this notation, the leader has agent states defined by the following statements:

Communicating $\equiv$

$50\omega^3$: *ReasoningDeliberative.Reasoning*
$+50\omega^3$: *ReasoningReactive.Reasoning*
$+50\omega^2$: *ReasoningDeliberative.Reasoning*
$+17\omega^3$: *ProcessingSortingAndStorage.Processing*
$+17\omega^3$: *ProcessingGeneration.Processing*
$+17\omega^3$: *ProcessingPrediction.Processing*
$+16\omega^4$: *ProcessingDiagnosis.Processing*
$+16\omega^4$: *ProcessingRecovery.Processing*
$+17\omega^4$: *ProcessingRemediation.Processing*

According to this statement, a leader, when in a communicating state, has the option (is allowed) to perform any action from the set

{*ReasoningDeliberative, ReasoningReactive,*
ProcessingSortingAndStorage, ProcessingGeneration,
ProcessingPrediction, ProcessingDiagnosis, ProcessingRecovery,
ProcessingRemediation}

and that the communicating leader will perform *ReasoningDeliberative* with a probability of 50 out of 200 (25%) (the total of all above listed frequencies) and will give that action a priority of 3. The second term in the statements tells us that the communicating leader will perform *ReasoningReactive* with the same 25% probability and priority of 3. The symbol + in this notation denotes that the communicating leader will make a choice between the various allowed actions, and that that choice will be made based on the frequencies and priorities of each allowable action. WSCCS is the only one of the views that takes into account probabilities and priority of the state changes. The probabilities and priorities allow for the calculation of the steady state of the system and therefore what the emergent behavior would be.

A transitional semantics defines what series of actions are valid for a given agent, and allows us to interpret agents as finite-state automata represented by a transition graph where nodes represent the agents, and the edges between represent the weights and actions.

The agent's transition is defined as

$$D\lceil \{a, b, c\} \xrightarrow{a\left[\frac{n_a}{n}\right]} A\lceil \{a, b, c\},$$

where $a[n_a/n]$ is the probability of action a occurring and n is the sum of the relative frequencies of the possible actions $a, b,$ and c. Consider the transition written above. This transition definition expresses that agent D can perform only action $a, b,$ or c. The probability of agent D performing action a is $[n_a/n]$, and the outcome of that action is that agent D becomes agent A, who can perform only action $a, b,$ or c.

The following is a portion of the specification for the communicating part of the swarm. The rest of the communicating part and the processing and reasoning parts are similar:

Communicating⌈*{ReasoningDeliberative, ReasoningReactive,*
ProcessingSortingAndStorage, ProcessingGeneration,
ProcessingPrediction, ProcessingDiagnosis, ProcessingRecovery,

$$\textit{ReasoningReliverative} \left[\frac{50\omega^3}{200}\right]$$

ProcessingRemediation}   →
Reasoning⌈*{SendMessageWorker, SendMessageWorkerVIAMessenger,*
SendMessageLeader, SendMessageLeaderVIAMessenger,
SendMessageError, ReceiveMessageWorker,
ReceiveMessageWorkerVIAMessenger, ReceiveMessageLeader,
ReceiveMessageLeaderVIAMessenger, ReceiveMessageError,
ProcessingSortingAndStorage, ProcessingGeneration,
ProcessingPrediction, ProcessingDiagnosis, ProcessingRecover,
ProcessingRemediation}

The above statement about the communicating leader specifies that the communicating leader, when allowed the set of actions

{*ReasoningDeliberative, ReasoningReactive,*
ProcessingSortingAndStorage, ProcessingGeneration,
ProcessingPrediction, ProcessingDiagnosis, ProcessingRecovery,
ProcessingRemediation}

will choose the action *ReasoningDeliberative* with a probability of 50% and a priority of 3, and that, when the action is performed, the communicating leader will transition to a reasoning leader who is allowed to choose from the set of actions given below to then be able to transition to another state:

{*SendMessageWorker, SendMessageWorkerVIAMessenger,*
SendMessageLeader, SendMessageLeaderVIAMessenger,
SendMessageError, ReceiveMessageWorker,
ReceiveMessageWorkerVIAMessenger, ReceiveMessageLeader,
ReceiveMessageLeaderVIAMessenger, ReceiveMessageError,
ProcessingSortingAndStorage, ProcessingGeneration,
ProcessingPrediction, ProcessingDiagnosis, ProcessingRecovery,
ProcessingRemediation}

For the other views, each time there is a transition, part of the CSP, X-Machine, and Unity Logic specifications would represent how, and the conditions under which, the communications would be performed.

3.4.2.2 *Transition Graph* A transition graph derived from these transitions for the ANTS leader spacecraft is shown in Figure 3.2. (Nodes represent the agents, and the edges between represent the weights and actions.)

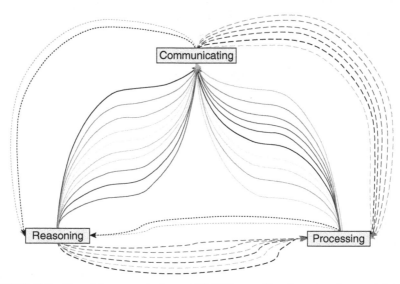

FIGURE 3.2 Transition graph from WSCCS specification showing weights and actions.

3.4.3 X-Machines

X-Machines are defined as the following tuple:

$$L = (Input, Memory, Output, Q, \Phi, F, start, m_0)$$

where the components of the tuple are defined as follows:

- *Input, Memory*, and *Output* are sets of data.
- Q is a finite set of states.
- Φ is a set of (partial) transition functions where each transition function maps *Memory* $\times$ *Input* $\rightarrow$ *Output* $\times$ *Memory*.
- F is the next-state partial function, $F : Q \times \Phi \rightarrow Q$.
- *start* $\in Q$ is the initial state.
- $m_0 \in$ *Memory* is the initial value of memory.

For the ANTS specification, the components of the X-Machines are defined as follows:

- *Input* = {*worker, messenger, leader, error, Deliberative, Reactive, SortAnd-Store, Generate, Predict, Diagnose, Recover, Remediate*}.
- *Memory* is written as a tuple $m = (Goals, Model)$ where *Goals* describes the goals of the mission and *Model* describes the model of the universe maintained by the leader. The initial memory is denoted by ($Goals_0$, $Model_0$). When the goals and/or model changes, the new tuple will be denoted as $m' = (Goals', Model')$.
- *Output* = {*SentMessageWorker, SentMessageMessenger, SentMessageLeader, SentMessageError, ReceivedMessageWorker, ReceivedMessageMessenger, ReceivedMessageLeader, ReceivedMessageError, ReasonedDeliberatively, ReasonedReactively, ProcessedSortingAndStoring, ProcessedGeneration, ProcessedPrediction, ProcessedDiagnosis, ProcessedRecovery, ProcessedRemediation*}.
- Q = {*Start, Communicating, Reasoning, Processing*}.
- Φ = {*SendMessage, ReceiveMessage, Reason, Process*} where these functions are defined as in Table 3.2.

To see the Leader Spacecraft in these terms, consider Table 3.3, which depicts the states, transition functions, and associated inputs, outputs, and memory. A transition diagram for the ANTS leader spacecraft is shown in Figure 3.3. (Nodes represent the states, and the edges between represent the transition functions.)

TABLE 3.2   Leader States and Transitions

Q State	Φ The Agent State	$Q' = F(Q, \Phi)$
Start	SendMessage	Communicating
	ReceiveMessage	Communicating
	Reason	Reasoning
	Process	Processing
Communicating	SendMessage	Communicating
	ReceiveMessage	Communicating
	Reason	Reasoning

TABLE 3.3   ANTS Role: Leader Spacecraft

State	Transition Functions $F(Q, \Phi)$	Function Definition $\Phi(m, \sigma) =$
Start Communicating	Send Msg	$\Phi(m, Worker) = (m', SentMessageWorker)$ $\Phi(m, Messenger) = (m', SentMessageMessenger)$ $\Phi(m, Leader) = (m', SentMessageLeader)$ $\Phi(m, Error) = (m', SentMessageError)$
	RecvMsg	$\Phi(m, Worker) = (m', SentMessageWorker)$ $\Phi(m, Messenger) = (m', SentMessageMessenger)$ $\Phi(m, Leader) = (m', SentMessageLeader)$ $\Phi(m, Error) = (m', SentMessageError)$
Reasoning	Reasoning	$\Phi(m, Deliberative) = (m', ReasonedDeliberatively)$ $\Phi(m, Reactive) = (m', ReasonedDeactively)$
Processing	Processing	$\Phi(m, SortAndStore) = (m',$ $ProcessedSortingAndStoring)$ $\Phi(m, Generate) = (m', ProcessedGeneration)$ $\Phi(m, Predict) = (m', ProcessedPrediction)$ $\Phi(m, Diagnose) = (m', ProcessedDiagnosis)$ $\Phi(m, Recover) = (m', ProcessedRecovery)$ $\Phi(m, Remediate) = (m', ProcessedRemediation)$

For viewpoint specification interactions, all of the above would affect either the CSP specification, the WSCCS specification, or the Unity Logic specification. Since the states are the same (with the exception of the start state), any time there is a state change in the X-Machine specification, the priorities and probabilities in the WSCCS specification, as well as the Unity Logic state machine and predicates, would need to be checked. Due to their similarities, the specifications could be combined with the goals and model data added. For the CSP view, any time there is a change to a communicating state, the communication specifications in CSP would take over, particularly the passing

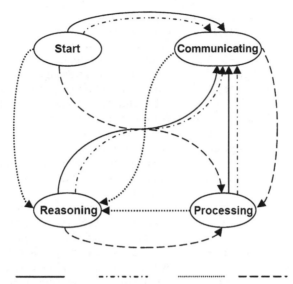

SendMessage ReceiveMessage Reasoning Processing

FIGURE 3.3 Transition diagram for the leader spacecraft as an X-Machine.

of data over the channels. Similarly for Unity Logic, any time there is a communication, the predicates for the logic would affect whether the transition would be taken.

3.4.4 Unity Logic

To model the ANTS leader spacecraft with Unity Logic, we consider states of the leader just as in WSCCS and X-Machines and other state machine-based specification languages. In Unity Logic, we will consider the states of the leader and the actions taken to put the leader in those states, but the notation will appear much closer to classical logic.

Predicates are defined to represent the actions that would put the leader into its various states (Table 3.4). Those predicates then become statements, which, if true, would mean that the leader had performed an action that put it into the corresponding state (see Table 3.5).

The communicating part of the leader program would then be specified using the following assertions (the reasoning and processing would be similar):

$[Communicating]ReasoningDeliberative(Leader)[Reasoning]$
$[Communicating]ReasoningReactive(Leader)[Reasoning]$
$[Communicating]ProcessingSortingAndStorage(Leader)[Processing]$
$[Communicating]ProcessingGeneration(Leader)[Processing]$
$[Communicating]ProcessingPrediction(Leader)[Processing]$

TABLE 3.4   Predicates and Meanings in X-Machine Transition Diagram

Predicate	Meaning
SendMessage(Leader, Worker)	A Leader sent a message to a Worker
SendMessageVIAMessenger (Leader, Worker)	A Leader sent a message to a Worker by relaying it through a Messenger
SendMessage(Leader, Leader)	A Leader sent a message to another Leader
SendMessageVIAMessenger (Leader, Leader)	A Leader sent a message to another Leader by relaying through a Messenger
SendMessageError(Leader)	A Leader sent a message in Error
ReceiveMessage(Leader, Worker)	A Leader received a message from a Worker
ReceiveMessageVIAMessenger (Leader, Worker)	A Leader received a message from a Worker who relayed through a Messenger
ReceiveMessage(Leader, Leader)	A Leader received a message from another Leader
ReceiveMessageVIAMessenger (Leader, Leader)	The Leader received a message from another Leader who relayed it through a Messenger
ReceiveMessageError(Leader)	A Leader received a message in Error
ReasoningDeliberative(Leader)	A Leader is reasoning deliberatively
ReasoningReactive(Leader)	A Leader is reasoning reactively
ProcessingSortingAndStorage (Leader)	The Leader is processing by Sorting, Classifying and/or Storing Data
ProcessingGeneration(Leader)	A Leader is processing by Model Generation
ProcessingPrediction(Leader)	A Leader is processing by prediction of asteroid properties, or by prediction of resource (worker and communication) availability
ProcessingDiagnosis(Leader)	A Leader is processing for Diagnosis
ProcessingRecovery(Leader)	A Leader is processing for Recovery
ProcessingRemediation(Leader)	A Leader is processing for Remediation

TABLE 3.5   Predicates and Meanings in X-Machine Transition Diagram

Program state	Statements which, if true, lead to that program state
	SendMessage (Leader, Worker)
	SendMessageVIAMessenger(Leader, Worker)
	SendMessage(Leader, Leader)
	SendMessageVIAMessenger(Leader, Leader)
	SendMessageError(Leader)
Communicating	ReceiveMessage(Leader, Worker)
	ReceiveMessageVIAMessenger(Leader, Worker)
	ReceiveMessage(Leader, Leader)
	ReceiveMessageVIAMessenger(Leader, Leader)
	ReceiveMessageError(Leader)
Reasoning	ReasoningDeliberative(Leader)
	ReasoningReactive(Leader)
	ProcessingSortingAndStorage(Leader)
	ProcessingGeneration(Leader)
Processing	ProcessingPrediction(Leader)
	ProcessingDiagnosis(Leader)
	ProcessingRecovery(Leader)
	ProcessingRemediation(Leader)

[*Communicating*]*ProcessingDiagnosis*(*Leader*)[*Processing*]
[*Communicating*]*ProcessingRecovery*(*Leader*)[*Processing*]
[*Communicating*]*ProcessingRemediation*(*Leader*)[*Processing*]

Unity Logic then provides a logical syntax equivalent to propositional logic for reasoning about these predicates and the states they imply, as well as for defining specific mathematical, statistical, and other simple calculations to be performed. For the view specification, the predicates would define the conditions when transitions would take place. The state machine specified above is similar to the WSCCS and X-Machine state machines and could be combined with them.

3.5 CONCLUSION

This project has shown how an integration of the formal methods CSP, WSCCS, X-Machines, and Unity Logic can specify and even predict emergent behavior of a swarm-based mission such as the ANTS concept mission. With CSP providing the interprocess communication view, X-Machines providing the state machine and memory views, WSCCS providing the probability and priority views, and Unity Logic providing the logic views, these formal methods could provide what is needed for verifying swarms of spacecraft or other swarm-based systems using a viewpoint integration.

There is overlap between the four formal methods, particularly the state machine aspects of WSCCS, X-Machines, and Unity Logic. Thus, *conserving integration* or a *monolithic integration* could provide a more integrated specification. The monolithic integration starts by going back to the base formalisms (often the first-order logic definition of the language) and then merging the base formalisms and redefining the semantics of the formalisms. With a conserving integration, the base formalisms are integrated more loosely by preserving the base formalisms [44]. Budget and time resources were not sufficient for completion of the work in this direction, but this type of integration would reduce the overlap in the viewpoint specifications and provide a tighter integration of the formal methods, with the complementary types of formal methods each providing only their strengths, as described above.

ACKNOWLEDGMENTS

This work was supported by the NASA Office of Safety and Mission Assurance (OSMA) Software Assurance Research Program (SARP) and managed by the NASA Independent Verification and Validation (IV&V) Facility. This work was also supported in part by the Science Foundation Ireland grant 03/CE2/I303_1 to Lero—the Irish Software Engineering Research Centre. This chapter is substantially based on Reference 34.

REFERENCES

1. I. Bakam, F. Kordon, C. L. Page, and F. Bousquet. Formalization of a spatialized multiagent model using coloured Petri nets for the study of a hunting management system. In *Proceedings of the First International Workshop on Formal Approaches to Agent-Based Systems (FAABS I)*, number 1871 in LNAI, Springer, Greenbelt, MD, April 2000.

2. J. Barnard, J. Whitworth, and M. Woodward. Communicating X-machines. *Information and Software Technology*, 38(6):401–407, 1996.

3. G. Beni. The concept of cellular robotics. In *Proceedings of the 1988 IEEE International Symposium on Intelligent Control*, pp. 57–62. IEEE Computer Society Press, Los Alamitos, CA, 1988.

4. G. Beni and J. Want. Swarm intelligence. In *Proceedings of the Seventh Annual Meeting of the Robotics Society of Japan*, pp. 425–428. RSJ Press, Tokyo, Japan, 1989.

5. M. Blackburn, R. Busser, A. Nauman, R. Knickerbocker, and R. Kasuda. Mars Polar Lander fault identification using model-based testing. In *Proceedings of the 26th Annual IEEE/NASA Software Engineering Workshop (SEW)*, Greenbelt, MD, December 2001.

6. E. Bonabeau, M. Dorigo, and G. Théraulaz. *Swarm Intelligence: From Natural to Artificial Systems*. Oxford University Press, New York, 1999.

7. E. Bonabeau and G. Théraulaz. Swarm smarts. *Scientific American*, 282:72–79, 2000.

8. E. Bonabeau, G. Théraulaz, J.-L. Deneubourg, S. Aron, and S. Camazine. Self-organization in social insects. *Trends in Ecology and Evolution*, 12:188–193, 1997.

9. L. Bonnet, G. Florin, L. Duchien, and L. Seinturier. A method for specifying and proving distributed cooperative algorithms. In *Proceedings of the DIMAS-95*, November 1995.

10. R. Büssow, R. Geisler, and M. Klar. Specifying safety-critical embedded systems with Statecharts and Z: A case study. In Astesiano, ed., *Proceedings of the International Conference on Fundamental Approaches to Software Engineering*, pp. 71–87, number 1382 in LNCS, Springer-Verlag, Berlin, Germany, 1998.

11. S. Carlson. Artificial life: Boids of a feather flock together. *Scientific American*, 283: 112–114, 2000.

12. J. Casani, C. Whetsler, A. Albee, S. Battel, R. Brace, G. Burdick, P. Burr, D. Dippoey, J. Lavell, C. Leising, D. MacPherson, W. Menard, R. Rose, R. Sackheim, and A. Schallenmuller. Report on the loss of the Mars Polar Lander and Deep Space 2 missions. Technical Report JPL D-18709, Jet Propulsion Laboratory, California Institute of Technology, 2000.

13. K. M. Chandy and J. Misra. *Parallel Program Design: A Foundation*. Addison-Wesley Publishing Company, Boston, 1988.

14. E. M. Clare and J. M. Wing. Formal methods: State of the art and future directions. *ACM Computing Surveys*, 28(4):626–643, 1996.

15. P. E. Clark, S. A. Curtis, and M. L. Rilee. ANTS: Applying a new paradigm to Lunar and planetary exploration. In *Proceedings of the Solar System Remote Sensing Symposium*, Pittsburgh, PA, September 20–21, 2002.

16. S. A. Curtis, J. Mica, J. Nuth, G. Marr, M. L. Rilee, and M. K. Bhat. ANTS (Autonomous Nano-Technology Swarm): An artificial intelligence approach to asteroid belt

resource exploration. In *Proceedings of the International Astronautical Federation, 51st Congress*, October 2000.

17. S. A. Curtis, W. F. Truszkowski, M. L. Rilee, and P. E. Clark. ANTS for the human exploration and development of space. In *Proceedings of the IEEE Aerospace Conference*, Big Sky, MT, March 9–16, 2003.

18. J. Derrick, E. Boiten, H. Bowman, and M. Steen. Supporting ODP—Translating LOTOS to Z. In *First IFIP International Workshop on Formal Methods for Open Object-Based Distributed Systems*, pp. 399–406. Chapman & Hall, 1996.

19. C. Fischer. Combination and implementation of processes and data: From CSP-OZ to Java. PhD thesis, Universität Oldenburg, Germany, 2000.

20. A. K. Gala and A. D. Baker. Multi-agent communication in JAFMAS. In *Proceedings of the Workshop on Specifying and Implementing Conversation Policies, Third International Conference on Autonomous Agents (Agents '99)*, Seattle, WA, 1999.

21. A. J. Galloway and W. J. Stoddart. An operational semantics for ZCCS. In M. Hinchey and S. Liu, eds., *Proceedings of the IEEE International Conference on Formal Engineering Methods (ICFEM-97)*, pp. 272–282, Hiroshima, Japan, November 1997. IEEE Computer Society Press, Los Alamitos, CA.

22. D. E. Hiebeler. The swarm simulation system and individual-based modeling. In *Proceedings of the Decision Support 2001: Advanced Technology for Natural Resource Management*, Toronto, Canada, September 1994.

23. M. Hinchey, J. Rash, and C. Rouff. Verification and validation of autonomous systems. In *Proceedings of the SEW-26, 26th Annual NASA/IEEE Software Engineering Workshop*, pp. 136–144, Greenbelt, MD, November 2001. NASA Goddard Space Flight Center, Greenbelt, MD, IEEE Computer Society Press, Los Alamitos, CA.

24. M. G. Hinchey and S. A. Jarvis. *Concurrent Systems: Formal Development in CSP*. International Series in Software Engineering. McGraw-Hill International, London, UK, 1995.

25. M. G. Hinchey, J. L. Rash, and C. A. Rouff. Towards an automated development methodology for dependable systems with application to sensor networks. In *Proceedings of the IEEE Workshop on Information Assurance in Wireless Sensor Networks (WSNIA 2005), Proceedings of the International Performance Computing and Communications Conference (IPCCC-05) (Reprinted in Proceedings of Real Time in Sweden 2005 (RTiS2005), the 8th Biennial SNART Conference on Real-time Systems, 2005)*, Phoenix, AZ, April 7–9, 2005. IEEE Computer Society Press, Los Alamitos, CA.

26. C. A. R. Hoare. Communicating sequential processes. *Communications of the ACM*, 21(8):666–677, 1978.

27. C. A. R. Hoare. *Communicating Sequential Processes*. Prentice Hall International Series in Computer Science. Prentice Hall International, Englewood Cliffs, NJ, 1985.

28. F. Luna and B. Stefansson. *Economic Simulations in Swarm: Agent-Based Modelling and Object Oriented Programming*. Kluwer Academic Publishers, Dordrecht, 2000.

29. W. Michael and L. Holcombe. Mathematical models of cell biochemistry. Technical Report CS-86-4, Sheffield University, UK, 1986.

30. W. Michael and L. Holcombe. Towards a formal description of intracellular biochemical organization. Technical Report CS-86-1, Sheffield University, UK, 1986.

31. W. Michael and L. Holcombe. X-Machines as a basis for system specification. *Software Engineering*, 3(2):69–76, 1988.

32. C. W. Reynolds. Flocks, herds, and schools: A distributed behavioral model. *Computer Graphics*, 21(4):25–34, 1987.

33. C. Rouff, M. Hinchey, J. Pena, and A. Ruiz-Cortes. Using formal methods and agent-oriented software engineering for modeling NASA swarm-based systems. In *IEEE Proceedings of the Swarm Intelligence Symposium*, pp. 348–355, April 2007.

34. C. Rouff, A. Vanderbilt, M. Hinchey, W. Truszkowski, and J. Rash. Formal methods for swarm and autonomic systems. In *Proceedings of the 1st International Symposium on Leveraging Applications of Formal Methods (ISoLA)*, Cyprus, October 30–November 2, 2004.

35. C. Rouff, A. Vanderbilt, M. Hinchey, W. Truszkowski, and J. Rash. Properties of a formal method for prediction of emergent behaviors in swarm-based systems. In *Proceedings of the 2nd IEEE International Conference on Software Engineering and Formal Methods*, Beijing, China, September 2004.

36. C. A. Rouff, M. G. Hinchey, W. F. Truszkowski, and J. L. Rash. Verifying large numbers of cooperating adaptive agents. In *Proceedings of the 11th International Conference on Parallel and Distributed Systems (ICPADS-2005)*, Fukuoka, Japan, July 20–22, 2005.

37. C. A. Rouff, M. G. Hinchey, W. F. Truszkowski, and J. L. Rash. Experiences applying formal approaches in the development of swarm-based space exploration systems. *International Journal of on Software Tools for Technology Transfer. Special Issue on Formal Methods in Industry*, 8(6):587–603, 2006.

38. C. A. Rouff, J. L. Rash, and M. G. Hinchey. Experience using formal methods for specifying a multi-agent system. In *Proceedings of the Sixth IEEE International Conference on Engineering of Complex Computer Systems (ICECCS 2000)*, Tokyo, Japan, 2000. IEEE Computer Society Press, Los Alamitos, CA.

39. C. A. Rouff, W. F. Truszkowski, M. G. Hinchey, and J. L. Rash. Verification of emergent behaviors in swarm based systems. In *Proceedings of the 11th IEEE International Conference on Engineering Computer-Based Systems (ECBS), Workshop on Engineering Autonomic Systems (EASe)*, pp. 443–448, Brno, Czech Republic, May 2004. IEEE Computer Society Press, Los Alamitos, CA.

40. C. A. Rouff, W. F. Truszkowski, M. G. Hinchey, and J. L. Rash. Verification of NASA emergent systems. In *Proceedings of the 9th IEEE International Conference on Engineering of Complex Computer Systems*, Florence, Italy, April 2004. IEEE Computer Society Press, Los Alamitos, CA.

41. C. A. Rouff, W. F. Truszkowski, J. L. Rash, and M. G. Hinchey. A survey of formal methods for intelligent swarms. Technical Report TM-2005-212779, NASA Goddard Space Flight Center, Greenbelt, MD, 2005.

42. M. Savage and M. Askenazi. Arborscapes: A swarm-based multi-agent ecological disturbance model. Working paper 98-06-056, Santa Fe Institute, Santa Fe, NM, 1998.

43. S. Schneider, J. Davies, D. M. Jackson, G. M. Reed, J. Reed, and A. W. Roscoe. Timed CSP: Theory and practice. In *Proceedings of the REX, Real-Time: Theory in Practice Workshop*, pp. 640–675, volume 600 of LNCS, Springer-Verlag, June 3–7, 1991.

44. C. Suhl. RT-Z: An integration of Z and timed CSP. In *Proceedings of the 1st International Conference on Integrated Formal Methods (IFM99)*, York, UK, June 1999.

45. D. J. T. Sumpter, G. B. Blanchard, and D. S. Broomhead. Ants and agents: A process algebra approach to modelling ant colony behaviour. *Bulletin of Mathematical Biology*, 63(5):951–980, 2001.

46. W. Truszkowski, M. Hinchey, J. Rash, and C. Rouff. NASA's swarm missions: The challenge of building autonomous software. *IEEE IT Professional*, 6(5):47–52, 2004.

47. W. F. Truszkowski, L. Hallock, C. A. Rouff, J. Kerlin, J. L. Rash, M. G. Hinchey, and R. Sterritt. *Autonomous and Autonomic Systems with Applications to NASA Intelligent Spacecraft Operations and Exploration Systems*. NASA Monographs in Systems and Software Engineering. Springer-Verlag, London, UK, 2009.

48. W. F. Truszkowski, M. G. Hinchey, J. L. Rash, and C. A. Rouff. Autonomous and autonomic systems: A paradigm for future space exploration missions. *IEEE Transactions on Systems Man and Cybernetics—Part C: Applications and Reviews*, 36(3):279–291, 2006.

49. H. Van Dyke Parunak and R. S. Vanderbok. Managing emergent behaviour in distributed control systems. In *Proceedings of ISA-Tech'97*, Anaheim, CA, 1997.

50. G. Weiss, ed., *Multiagent Systems: A Modern Approach to Distributed Artificial Intelligence*. MIT Press, Cambridge, MA, 1999.

PART III

TRANSPORTATION SYSTEMS

FRAGMENTATION SYSTEMS

CHAPTER 4

SOME TRENDS IN FORMAL METHODS APPLICATIONS TO RAILWAY SIGNALING

ALESSANDRO FANTECHI
Dipartimento di Sistemi e Informatica, Università degli Studi di Firenze, Florence, Italy; and ISTI-CNR, Pisa, Italy

WAN FOKKINK
Sectie Theoretische Informatica, Vrije Universiteit Amsterdam, Amsterdam, The Netherlands; and Specificatie en Verificatie van Embedded Systemen, CWI, Amsterdam, The Netherlands

ANGELO MORZENTI
Dipartimento di Elettronica e Informazione, Politecnico di Milano, Milan, Italy

4.1 INTRODUCTION

National railway systems are managed by transportation service providers that do not develop computer-based systems themselves. Rather, they act as integrators of systems purchased from external suppliers. Service providers therefore have the problem of managing acquisition and integration of purchased subsystems. Hence, such organizations need clear, unambiguous, possibly formal requirement specifications. Both the purchaser and their suppliers must agree on rigorous acceptance procedures, based on verification and validation, functional and safety assessment, and safety approval. Furthermore, uniform, possibly standardized documentation is essential to permit monitoring of system development and to facilitate operation and maintenance. The procurement task is made more difficult by the requirement, under applicable national and international laws, that safety-critical railway systems must satisfy international standards, dictating procedures for design, deployment, and maintenance.

Formal Methods for Industrial Critical Systems: A Survey of Applications, First Edition.
Edited by Stefania Gnesi and Tiziana Margaria.
© 2013 IEEE. Published 2013 by John Wiley & Sons, Inc.

Railway signaling is often considered as one of the most fruitful areas of intervention by formal methods. Many success stories have been told about the application of formal specification and verification techniques in this area. The width of the proposed usage of formal methods in this field is witnessed by the number of references to relevant articles in a (still far from complete) review by Dines Bjørner [7]: 182 references and many others have followed in the last 2 years. Moreover, work performed at railway companies is often not published for confidentiality reasons.

There are two main reasons for the success of formal methods applications to railway signaling. On the one hand, railway signaling has always generated the interest of formal methods researchers, due to its safety criticality, and the absence of complex computations and hard real-time constraints, making it a promising application field. On the other hand, railways have always had a very strong safety culture, based on simple fail-safe principles. In electromechanical equipment, used in most signaling systems before the introduction of computers, gravity was used to bring a system to the fail-safe state (e.g., all signals to red) in any occurrence of a critical event. The fact that computers have no gravity, that is, the impossibility of predicting in general the effects of the occurrence of faults, has long delayed the acceptance of computer-controlled signaling equipment by railway companies. The employment of very stable technology and the quest for the highest possible guarantees have been key aspects for the adoption of computer-controlled equipment in railway applications. Formal proof, or verification, of safety is therefore seen as a necessity.

In this chapter, we offer some insight into the actual industrial usage of formal methods in this field, which does not yet meet the promises of the aforementioned success stories, but is steadily increasing. The external conditions that are driving industrial choices are also discussed, as well as the classification of railway signaling devices into categories more or less amenable to formal methods application. Here we give only some personal and partial views and experiences in the field, and do not intend to exhaustively cover the field of railway signaling applications of formal methods. In particular, we only address the European railway signaling market, where actually the most important applications of formal methods to railways can be found, and which has undergone several dramatic changes in the last decade.

The structure of this chapter is as follows. In Section 4.2, the EN50128 guidelines by the European Committee for Electrotechnical Standardization (CENELEC) regarding the development of software for railway signaling are discussed. Section 4.3 reports on a comparative case study of the applicability of different formal methods to railway signaling. Section 4.4 is devoted to applications in the railway domain of one such formal method, namely B. In Section 4.5, we focus on formal methods applications to railway signaling equipment, which is divided into train control systems and interlocking systems. Finally, Section 4.6 contains some conclusions.

4.2 CENELEC GUIDELINES

The EN50128 guidelines [28], issued by CENELEC, address the development of "Software for Railway Control and Protection Systems," and constitute the main reference for railway signaling equipment manufacturers in Europe, with their use spreading to the other continents and to other sectors of the railway (and other safety related) industry.

The EN50128 document is part of a series of documents regarding the safety of railway control and protection systems, in which the key concept of Software Safety Integrity Level (SSIL) is defined. One of the first steps indicated by these guidelines in the development of a system is to define a Safety Integrity Level (SIL) for each of its components, on the basis of the level of risk associated, by means of a risk assessment process. Assigning different SILs to different components helps to concentrate the efforts (and therefore the production costs) on the critical components. The SILs are 4 (very high), 3 (high), 2 (medium), 1 (low), and 0 (not safety related).

The EN50128 guidelines dictate neither a precise development methodology for software nor any particular programming technique, but they classify a wide range of commonly adopted techniques in terms of a rating (from "forbidden" to "highly recommended" and "mandatory") with respect to the established SIL of the component. Formal methods (in particular, CCS, CSP, HOL, LOTOS, OBJ, Temporal Logic, VDM, Z, and B are cited as examples) are rated as highly recommended for the specification of systems/components with the higher levels of SIL. Formal proof is also highly recommended as a verification activity. Anyway, both are not classified as mandatory, since alternative, more traditional techniques are also accepted. We should notice, however, that this is the first time (the first edition of EN50128 dates back to 1994) that a strong indication about the usage of formal methods appears in standard guidelines.

Indeed, despite CENELEC directives and success stories, formal methods have not permeated the whole railway signaling industries, where much software is still written with traditional means. This is due to the investments needed to build up a formal method culture, and to the high costs of commercial support tools. Moreover, equipment can conform to CENELEC without applying formal methods. Verification by thorough testing can be claimed compliant to EN50128. But the guidelines require, for the highest SILs, that design and verification is carried independently by two separate teams. Relying only on testing shifts an enormous effort (usually more than 50% of the total development effort) on the shoulders of the testing department, which is often considered less important (and hence less funded) than the design department. This becomes a risk for a company that is more and more required by the market to be CENELEC compliant, and the only solution is to shift back the effort to the design team, by introducing formal methods in the specification and design phases. This is a necessity that companies begin to realize, and success stories and CENELEC guidelines have had an important part in the raising of this consciousness.

4.3 SOFTWARE PROCUREMENT IN RAILWAY SIGNALING

This section reports on experiences in a joint project between Politecnico di Milano and Italian State Railway FS, Infrastructure Department (which then became RFI—Rete Ferroviaria Italiana S.p.A.). The purpose of the project was to define procedures and rules for managing software procurement for safety-critical signaling equipment [32]. The latter includes a broad range of devices, governing signals and tracks, railway/road crossings, and train movements. Goals of the project, which were imposed as additional constraints, were

- to cover all phases of system development, from requirements elicitation to implementation, final validation, approval, and acceptance;
- to provide requirements on methods, languages, and tools to be used during software development, without any bias toward any particular technology or tool provider. The only general requirement is technical soundness and being up-to-date with respect to the current advances in computer science;
- to provide results consistent with, and acceptable against, international standards (mainly the EN50128 standard, see Section 4.2);
- to choose methods that are sufficiently mature for industrial usage, are supported by automated tools, and are likely to gain acceptance by average engineers, both in the railway and computer technology domains.

The main working group in the project was composed of two researchers from Politecnico di Milano, expert of formal methods, and two engineers from RFI, skilled in the modeling and analysis of railway signaling equipment. No formal procedure or metric was adopted for the evaluation of the various formal methods; these were analyzed through a detailed, careful investigation of the available technical documentation and scientific literature and on the basis of previous experiences in using the notations and tools. To validate the obtained results and provide some empirical support, a small-scale experiment was conducted, consisting of the formal specification of a simple signaling apparatus. The descriptions obtained in the various notations were compared with respect to compactness and readability of the produced artifacts, as these qualities were considered the most important to favor the practical application of the method.

As a result of the project, requirements and recommendations were issued, tailored to various kinds of systems. The main contribution of the project concerns requirements on specification, verification, and validation. In particular, adoption of formal methods in the specification phase is recommended, when supported by suitable tools and validation and verification techniques. Here we report on the results concerning a comparative evaluation of methods, tools, and notations for formal requirements specification.

4.3.1 System Classification

The recommendations were based on a system classification according to three categories: complexity (low, medium, high), criticality, and presence of temporal requirements. Complexity was assumed to be conventionally determined by the purchaser, while the degree of criticality was determined according to the SIL (see Section 4.2) of the application. The temporal requirements were classified in three categories: time independent, qualitative time, and quantitative time. The time-independent category refers to systems without any particular temporal constraints, for example, performing pure data or signal elaborations. The qualitative time category refers to systems that can restrict to time-ordered values and actions without quantitative information about time instants and time distances. Some improper real-time systems are in this category: systems with strict and binding requirements, but designed to adequately manage every possible delay or anticipation, or the absence of expected events. The quantitative time category comprises hard real-time systems. These systems interact with processes that are not completely manageable or controlled, and that cannot avoid a quantitative expression of their temporal constraints (instead of just an order relation among events) without severe consequences. It is worth pointing out that the category of qualitative time is quite different from the so-called soft real-time systems; that is, systems missing some (quantitatively of qualitatively stated) time constraint are undesirable or annoying but do not cause unacceptable damage; also, they do not correspond to high-throughput systems, which must have the capability of processing high quantities of data, but with time requirements that are expressed in statistical terms. This is because the systems under consideration were in any case critical for safety and economic reasons, so that missing time requirements (even when these are qualitative) is not admitted.

4.3.2 Requirements Analysis and Specification

Table 4.1 shows the prescription on specification and validation techniques and generation of functional test cases, depending on the SIL of the system, its complexity, and its temporal features.

The table is divided into four parts: analysis, syntax checks, degree of specification coverage, and validation accuracy degree. *Analysis* is itself divided into two kinds of activities for the validation of specifications: simulation or trace generation and proof of properties. (1) *Simulation* of the behavior of a system means generating (possibly in an interactive or semiautomatic way) events and actions in a chronological order, while *trace generation* means

TABLE 4.1 Validation Prescriptions

		SIL		Complexity			Ind	Time	
		1,2	3,4	Low	Med	High		Qual	Quant
Analysis	Simulation/trace generation	Yes	Yes	*	*	Yes	*	Yes	Yes
	Property proof — No abstraction	Yes	*	Yes (3)	*	*	*	*	*
	Abstraction	*	*	Yes	*	*	*	*	*
	Generality	Yes	*	Yes (3)	*	*	*	*	*
	Automation	*	*	S	*	*	*	*	*
Syntax checks		Yes	Yes	*	Yes	Yes	*	Yes	Yes
Degree of specification coverage		T	T	*	*	*	*	T(1)	T(1)
Validation accuracy degree		β	$\gamma(2)$	0	α	β	0	$\beta(1)$	$\gamma(1)$

There is no recommendation, neither in favor nor against adoption of the technique.

(1) The indicated coverage or accuracy is a minimum requirement for the temporal parts alone.

(2) It is recommended, but not mandatory at the current state of the art, to use a method with degree of accuracy δ.

(3) Recommended but not mandatory at the current state of the art.

generating (again possibly in a semiautomatic way) execution traces of the system and verifying automatically whether these traces are compatible with the specification. Unlike simulation, in trace generation, events and actions are not necessarily generated in chronological order. (2) *Proof of properties* indicates how far it is possible to prove mathematically (by means of logical demonstrations or exhaustive analysis) that a system possesses properties like safety and absence of deadlock. Such proofs are classified according to four categories: without abstraction, with abstraction, generality, and automation degree. (2.1) *Without abstraction* means that proofs can be executed on the complete specification of the system. They, therefore, have a total degree of certainty: The specified system without doubt possesses the proved property. (2.2) *With abstraction* means that proofs can be executed by introducing suitable approximations (abstractions) of the original specification, for example, by ignoring the actual data in the system. Abstractions make proofs simpler but may reduce the degree of certainty of the result. (2.3) *Generality* means that properties to be proved can be chosen by the user in a general and flexible way, using a suitable, sufficiently expressive mathematical notation. (2.4) *Automation degree* evaluates the support offered by the proof tools: S indicates that at least a semiautomatic support is required (the tools support the verification that the proof is correct, for instance, by preparing a structure for the proof obligations or by automating the trivial parts and subproofs, but must be guided by expert users); otherwise, proofs can be carried out manually.

Syntax checks expresses whether there is tool support for checking that a specification is syntactically correct. For *specification coverage*, the requirement T stands for *total*: All requirements have the same relevance and must therefore be specified; otherwise, it can be the case that some requirements, identified in an unambiguous way and totally isolated from the others, do not have any influences on safety and need not be formally specified. Finally, *validation accuracy* measures the accuracy of the validation of the requirements specification. Values are, in order of increasing accuracy and hence of preference, 0 (informal inspections, walkthrough), α (syntactic control of types, coherence between definition, and use of the entities that compose the specification, i.e., the typical static controls carried out by the compilers of modern programming languages), β (at least one of the following: simulation, animation, generation of traces, symbolic analysis, reachability analysis, proofs of certain properties like absence of deadlock, proof of properties with abstraction), γ (same as β but with a combination of at least two techniques of a different nature, and adoption of suitable metrics in order to measure the coverage degree of a system analysis), and δ (statement and proof of general properties).

Notice that the columns of Table 4.1 deal separately with the various system features, but their prescriptions are intended to be applied in conjunction (in other terms, the more severe requirement applies): For instance, for a system of medium complexity and qualitative temporal features, the required

TABLE 4.2   Prescription on Specification Methods

	SIL		Complexity			Time		
	1,2	3,4	Low	Med	High	Ind	Qual	Quant
Z	Yes	No[a]	Yes	Yes	No[a]	Yes	Yes	No
TRIO	No[a]	No[a]	Yes	No[a]	No[a]	Yes	Yes	Yes
Statecharts	Yes	Yes	Yes	Yes	Yes	Yes	Yes	Yes[b]
SDL	Yes	Yes	Yes	Yes	Yes	Yes	Yes	Yes[b]
UML	No[c]	No	No[c]	No	No	Yes	Yes	No
PN	Yes	No	Yes	No	No	Yes	Yes	Yes[b]
LOTOS	Yes	No	Yes	Yes	No	Yes	Yes	Yes[b]
SCADE	Yes	No[a]	Yes	Yes	Yes	Yes	Yes	Yes[b]
B	Yes	Yes	Yes	Yes	Yes	Yes	Yes	No

[a]The "no" answer derives from the unavailability of tools of a sufficiently consolidated level, which possess all the features required for the "yes" value.
[b]The method is recommended for systems with SIL 1 or 2, while for systems with SIL 3 or 4, the method is acceptable at the current state of the art but not strongly recommended.
[c]The method is recommended only for systems with SIL 1.

validation accuracy degree is β; for a system of low complexity but highly critical (SIL 3 or 4), the required validation accuracy degree is γ.

Finally, Table 4.2 shows the application of the prescriptions of Table 4.1 to an agreed set of formalisms, widely used at the time of the project, considering both language features and available tool support. The analyzed notations and formal methods are Z [46], TRIO [34], Statecharts [36], SDL [23], UML [14], LOTOS [48], Petri nets [45], SCADE [15], and B [1]. Table 4.2 is obtained by comparing, for each notation and corresponding method and tool environment, the characteristic features and the tool support with the requirements expressed in Table 4.1. Not surprisingly, the state of the art appears still unsatisfactory, even for methods and tools that received the best score, in the case of systems with quantitative timing and a high level of complexity. In this case, there is no "strongly recommended" method and tool, the existing ones being only "recommended." This is due to the fact that the available tools for analysis and verification of formal models lack a rigorous formal basis, or are neither certified nor validated by repeated and long-lasting application in an industrial setting. However, as already mentioned in the introduction, in railway signaling, there are in general no complex computations or hard real-time constraints.

4.4   A SUCCESS STORY: THE B METHOD

In the comparative case study from Section 4.3, the B method [1] was shown to be one of the strongest verification approaches. B has rigorous mathematical foundations and a well-developed underlying methodology, and is supported by a reasonably advanced toolset. A series of railway signaling products have benefited from the application of the B method in the design process. The success of B has had a major impact in the sector of railway signaling by influencing the definition of the EN50128 guidelines (see Section 4.2).

The B method targets software development from specification through refinement, down to implementation and automatic code generation, with verification at each stage. It includes a notation—abstract machines—for specifying a system: An abstract machine is defined as a set of states and a set of operations that modify the values of state variables; an invariant predicate is defined on states; for each operation, a precondition and a postcondition are defined, describing the effects of operations on state variables. It must be proved that when executing an operation in a state that satisfies both the precondition and the invariant, the state after the execution of this operation satisfies both the postcondition and the invariant. Moreover, at each refinement step, it must be proved that the required safety properties of the system are preserved. So writing a specification produces a series of proof obligations that need to be discharged by formal proofs. The B method is accompanied by support tools, which include tools for the derivation of proof obligations, theorem provers, and Ada code generation tools.

The B method has been successfully applied to railway signaling systems, especially by Matra Transport and Alstom, mainly in France. The first application has been at the end of the 1980s, concerning the SACEM system for the control of a line of Paris RER [20]. B was introduced while the project was already in progress, in order to ensure the two railway companies exploiting the line (SNCF and RATP) about the correctness of the design. B has been adopted for many later designs of similar systems by the same companies (especially Matra, which is now absorbed by Siemens). One of the most striking application has been for the Paris Météor metro line, which is in operation since October 1998. This line was designed to reach traffic of 40,000 passengers per hour with an interval between trains down to 85 seconds during peak hours. It is being managed by the automatic train operation system developed by Matra, consisting of 86,000 lines of Ada (see Reference 3).

Of the 27,800 proven lemmas during the B development, around 90% were proven automatically by support tools, leaving around 2000 lemmas to be interactively proven. Many errors were found during proof activities. By contrast, no further bugs were detected by the various testing activities that followed the B development. Moreover, no bugs have been reported since the line is in operation.

4.5 CLASSES OF RAILWAY SIGNALING EQUIPMENT

Railway signaling equipment can be roughly divided in two main categories. Train control systems guarantee safe speed and braking control for trains, while interlocking systems establish safe routes through the intricate layout of tracks and points. Several other minor signaling systems can be considered, which are often used to provide input for main signaling systems. Some of them may share the criticality level of main systems. Moreover, some signaling systems actually merge features of both categories above. For the purpose of our discussion, it will, however, be useful to concentrate on the nature of the two major classes identified.

4.5.1 Train Control Systems

A variety of train control systems exist, which may depend on the degree of authority over the driver (ranging from giving a mere support to the driver, to the completely automatic, driverless systems), on different means to convey information to the train (either to the driver or to on-board equipment) and on the nature of this information. However, the basic general principle on which train speed control is based is common: the *braking curve* concept (Fig. 4.1). The preceding train, or a fixed obstacle, defines a curve for the maximal safe speed of the train in any point of the line at a given time. The train has to maintain its own speed below the curve. Since the preceding train moves, the curve follows it, giving free headway to the train. The main challenge is to make sure that knowledge on board of the train regarding the curve is sufficiently accurate.

When information is continuously exchanged between on-board and wayside computers, a guaranteed bandwidth is required, and safe communication protocols need to be used. Hence, in modern train control systems, complexity is shifting from basic safety rules to communication protocols.

The examples of SACEM and Météor systems show that formal methods can be applied to the entire system development. However, when dealing with main lines, matters get complicated by heterogeneity, compatibility, and

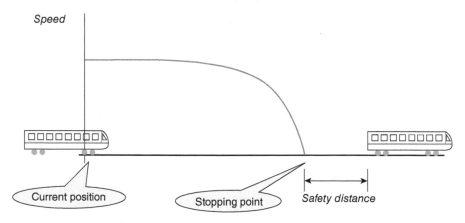

FIGURE 4.1 The braking curve principle.

interoperability issues. The rolling stock is in general intended to be capable of running on differently equipped lines, with mixed freight/passenger traffic. Every national railway has its own tradition, especially for what concerns signaling rules and procedures. Before the advent of the open European market, every national company maintained contacts with (mostly national) signaling equipment providers, and the strict relation, typical of a protected market, between the first and the latter favored a nationwide specific approach to signaling. This has had the effect that different countries in Europe have different train control systems, which require different on-board equipment. The new rules of the open railway market require instead that a train of a company is given equal access to all tracks in Europe. This means that a train should be interoperable. The only way to achieve this goal is currently to equip the cab with several versions of on-board equipment, one for each traversed nation, or to change the locomotive at each border.

For this reason the European Rail Traffic Management Systems/European Train Control System (ERTMS/ETCS) project was launched, aiming at a single train control system for the future Trans-European railway network [25]. The project, after the current initial test phase, plans to gradually install the ERTMS/ETCS equipment side by side to the traditional national equipment, also exploiting the three successive ERTMS/ETCS levels, referring to the increasing degree of information flowing from wayside to on-board equipment. In levels 2 and 3, GSM-R (GSM radio communication specific to the railway industry) is adopted to continuously transfer information to the train on the status of the line ahead.

ERTMS/ETCS makes use of standardized components (European Vital Computer on board, Radio Block Center, Eurobalise, etc.) and protocols (Euroradio), produced by a consortium of the main European signaling manufacturers, based on consolidated techniques. Specifications issued by ERTMS/ETCS [27] are structured as a natural language requirement document, including tables, state diagrams, and sequence charts to add some formality.

Several formal modeling and verification studies have been conducted regarding ETCS protocols and components, starting from a model of ETCS given by colored Petri nets [43], to the use of Statecharts with the aim of proving safety properties by model checking an early version of the radio-based train control system [19], to the studies of real-time properties using stochastic Petri nets [49] or CSP-OZ-DC [29]. The most systematic approach to the formalization of ETCS natural language requirements has been the recent EuRailCheck project by the European Railway Agency [16] where UML diagrams augmented with constraints in a controlled natural language have been exploited to produce formalized requirement fragments. Automated validation analysis of such fragments has then been possible by means of a customization of the NuSMV model checker.

Formal methods have also been used by consortium companies in their development cycle. For example, Ansaldo, after having addressed with SDL and Message Sequence Charts the modeling and verification of the Radio

Block Center [17], has given a formal specification of the Euroradio protocol by means of UML State Diagrams, performing a verification by simulation following given scenarios expressed as UML Sequence Diagrams [26].

In the case of ETCS, the attention of the formal methods community has shifted from the consolidated train control logic (the braking curve principle), to the safety and real-time performance of radio-based control, which is going to be the sole mean by which the conditions of the track ahead are communicated to the train, since even signals will no more be present on the line.

4.5.2   Interlocking Systems

The control and management of a railway area consists of two separate tasks. First, control instructions for the track and points are devised in the logistic layer, which is usually managed by human experts. Second, it has to be guaranteed that the execution of control instructions does not jeopardize safety; that is, collisions and derailments have to be avoided. This is done by means of a so-called interlocking, which is a medium between the infrastructure on the one side, and the logistic layer and its interfaces on the other side.

An interlocking is an embedded system that controls pieces of equipment (like signals, points, track circuits, automatic blocks) so interconnected that their functions should be performed in proper sequence and for which interlocking rules are defined in order to guarantee safe operations. A simple example of an interlocking system is shown in Figure 4.2, taken from a real Italian interlocking system [21]. Line segments represent track segments in the infrastructure; some of them have track circuits, that is, sensors of the presence of a train, which are numbered inside circles; joints between segments represent points. Lollipop-like drawings represent signals of various types. Numbered labels are attached to each important part of a route. This example (a station consisting of a single track line) constitutes of eight allowed routes, two points, eight signals, six track circuits, and two automatic blocks.

A route can be set free only if all points on the route have been correctly placed, and no train is present. The signals can be set to green only if the route in front is set to free. These sentences express two examples of generic principles that hold for every interlocking systems. Such rules aim at allowing only

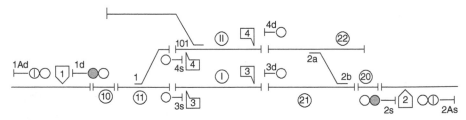

FIGURE 4.2   The simplest track layout.

safe combinations of point positions, signals, and so on, in order to avoid collisions. The signal indications, handled by the interlocking system, govern the correct use of the routes, authorizing the movement of trains. The rules usually enforce a predefined sequence of actions. For instance, issuing a route request command first triggers a check that all the track elements involved in the route are free. In that case, commands are issued for the positioning of points for that route and for locking the track elements. This phase may be followed by a global centralized control over the correct state of the commanded elements, after which the route is locked and signal indications for the route are set.

Note however that the generic rules expressed above need to be conjugated on every specific layout; for instance, the rules should be set for routes 1–3 in Figure 4.2, taking into account point 1, track circuit 10, 11, I, and so on.

Actually, the precise and complete set of such rules depends on the layout of the tracks and points (see, e.g., Reference 30), and also on national policies traditionally established by railway companies or regulatory boards. Since an interlocking system is safety critical, the formalization of such rules is a top requirement.

In the traditional process adopted by many railway companies to develop relay-based interlocking systems, the generic principles were encoded into relay circuit templates. (A relay is an electrically operated switch; electric current through a copper wire that is wound around a core creates a magnetic field that attracts a lever and changes the switch contacts.) When a new interlocking plant was installed, these general principles had to be adapted to the particular layout of the tracks. The adaptation process was also guided by some more or less formalized rules. At the end of the process, there was a diagram containing the command and control circuits for each logical or physical object in the station.

An example of this kind of diagram is shown in Figure 4.3; this diagram, taken from the same Italian interlocking, represents a circuit for the establishment of routes 1–3 in Figure 4.2, taking into account point 1, track circuits 10, 11, I, and so on. The ladder diagram in Figure 4.3 expresses the fact that the energizing of relay CD_1_3 is dependent on many other relay contacts.

Such a circuit is generated based on templates supplied to help the engineers in the design of new stations. The templates are then associated to layout objects and replicated for each object. In a circuit template, there are all the contacts needed to manage that kind of object; the only action to perform on it is the substitution of these generic contacts with the ones dictated by the layout. The structure of all diagrams related to routes is always the same, but the numbers and names of some contacts (serial or parallel) are different from one route to another.

The safety of old times, relay-based, interlocking systems was based on single fail-safe concepts, exploiting the intrinsic characteristics of relay technology. The introduction of computers in the control and command chain has subverted this approach to safety, since failure modes of computer-controlled equipment may be much more diverse and difficult to predict.

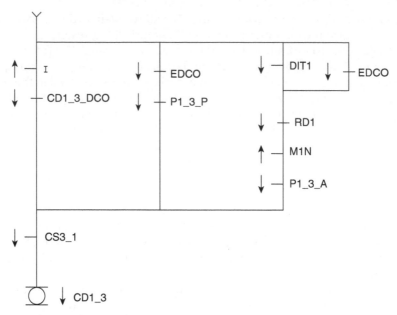

FIGURE 4.3   An instantiated relay schema referred to routes 1–3.

The first approach followed by some railway companies was to maintain the traditional and well-established relay-based principle diagram as the trusted source of information for computer-based interlocking developers, looking for conformance of the new interlocking systems to such sources, by means of costly and tedious, but possibly not exhaustive, testing. This approach has put on manufacturers' shoulders the burden of conceiving a family of interlocking products, together with means to instantiate the generic product by taking into account some proprietary, formalized version of principle diagrams suitable to be (more or less automatically) interpreted or compiled into running code, that has to be shown compliant to the trusted source. Actual approaches have varied from manufacturer to manufacturer as witnessed in References 6, 24, 33, and 42. The development of computer-controlled interlocking systems has seen an increasing interest in the use of formal methods, due to their ability to precisely specify the logical rules that guarantee the safe establishment of routes. B notations (see Section 4.4) are not really suitable to express the interlocking logical rules, since these require the system states (logical variables, corresponding to the old relay states) to be accessed globally by many logical rules, while abstract machines encapsulate their state variables, which are accessible only via operations.

Rather than being adherent to old relay technology, what is needed is an innovative approach that encompasses a complete formalization of the whole system. Domain-specific languages have been proposed for the formalization of interlockings [37, 44], the most prominent one being the European Railway Interlocking Specification (EURIS) [4, 47], which will be discussed in Section 4.5.3. More recently, the possibility of using commercial support tools has pushed forward the use of general-purpose languages, as shown in Section 4.3, and a recent trend has indicated Statecharts (in their Statemate, Stateflow, or UML state diagrams dialects) as a means for defining a standard formalization; see, for example, Reference 2.

The latter trend has to do with the transition from the traditional protected market to the European open market, but on different grounds than for train control systems (see Section 4.5.1). With the previous national protected market, interlocking systems were developed by national manufacturers for the national railway company. Still, railway signaling is the responsibility of the national societies that are in charge of the railway infrastructure (e.g., RFF, RFI, ProRail) and not of the open market railway operators. On the other hand, traditionally national industries have been merged and reorganized in a few multinational companies. They, therefore, have to merge different know-hows about railway signaling production, in order to unify their product lines. In this scenario, the strict collaboration between national railway companies and national railway industries, in which there was no need for a precise specification (every misunderstanding was resolved by phone) vanishes; there is greater reliance on precise contractual specifications to define the responsibility of each involved party.

The European railway community has come to realize that a drastic overhaul of current interlocking design is needed, for four main reasons. First, current methods to design interlockings, like SSI and VPI from Alstom and WESTRACE from Westinghouse Signals, are based on the earlier designs of interlockings using relays, and as a result, do not fully exploit the additional capabilities of computer hardware and software. Second, due to their lack of modularity, current methods are not suitable to build interlocking systems for very large railway stations; dividing such stations into separate parts, which is the most common solution, causes undesirable communication overhead in current methods. Third, different European nations so far use different interlocking technologies, with raising costs due to the lack of standardization. Fourth, formal methods cannot easily be integrated into current methods; see, for example, References 18, 22, and 35, for some work in this direction, mostly based on the adoption of model checking techniques for formal verification of interlocking systems. It is in this light that the Italian railway infrastructure agency has issued the document for software procurement discussed in Section 4.3.

The Euro-Interlocking project has involved the main European railway companies and suppliers to develop both European functional requirements and standardized interfaces for interlocking systems. In this case, interoperability is not an issue, as interlocking systems do not (directly) communicate with trains. Standardization has the sole purpose to reduce costs, by means of standardized components and standardized interlocking rules. Inside Euro-

Interlocking, the EIFFRA working group [40] has focused on textual requirements and requirement management tools such as Telelogic DOORS, together with model-based requirements. This is done by means of UML state diagrams and Statecharts to describe the behavior, and OCL to describe the properties of the interlocking systems. In this context, SNCF-RFF modeled their (relay based) principle schemata using Statemate, producing 90 generic Statecharts for interlocking elements [41]. These have been instantiated on an example medium-sized station, to obtain 115 instances of 25 Statecharts (out of the 90). Simulation by Statemate and visualization of scenarios by Waveforms were used to verify the correctness of the definition and instantiations.

A recent follow-up of Euro-Interlocking is the FP7 INESS project [38], aimed at defining the specifications for a new generation of interlocking systems, with particular attention to properly interface ERTMS systems. UML State Diagrams have been chosen as the modeling language within INESS.

4.5.3 EURIS

The restrictions that the interlocking logics imposes on the states of the system are reasonably consistent, depending mostly on the parameters of the autonomous elements, such as signals and points. Based on this observation, Peter Middelraad from the Dutch company ProRail evolved a modular specification method/language EURIS [4], to describe fully automated interlocking logics. EURIS assumes an object-oriented architecture, which consists of a collection of generic building blocks, representing the elements in the infrastructure such as signals and points, and of two clearly separated entities in the outside world, representing the logistic layer and the infrastructure. The building blocks, which together make up the interlocking logic, communicate with each other by means of messages called telegrams. The building blocks can also exchange telegrams with the two entities that model the logistic layer and the infrastructure. This model can be depicted as in Figure 4.4.

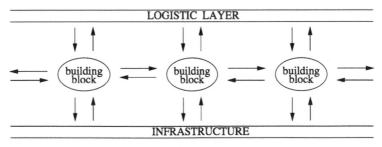

FIGURE 4.4 EURIS architecture.

To give an example, suppose that the logistic layer decides that a train should be moved via route R. This request is passed on to the interlocking layer, which attempts to claim route R; this mission is divided into smaller tasks, which are performed by exchanging telegrams between building blocks. If all building blocks concerned agree that route R can be established without jeopardizing safety, then the interlocking reserves this route, after which it passes on the necessary instructions to the infrastructure.

EURIS not only denotes a specification method, it is also the name for a graphically oriented imperative specification language that is based on this method. A so-called Logic and Sequence Chart (LSC) specifies a building block. Each LSC consists of the graphical representation of procedures, which can adapt and test the values of variables, and which can ultimately trigger the transmission of a telegram. Such telegrams can be received by neighboring building blocks, by the overlying logistic layer, and by the underlying infrastructure. Conversely, each building block can also receive telegrams from neighboring building blocks, from the logistic layer and from the infrastructure. The communication channels between the building blocks, the logistic layer, the infrastructure, and the initial values of variables are recorded outside the LSCs.

In EURIS, the heart of a specification defines the way that different kinds of building blocks handle incoming telegrams. Intuitively, these building blocks represent the separate elements in the infrastructure, such as signals and points. As soon as all types of building blocks have been specified in full detail, the specification of a particular railway area layout is constructed by simply connecting its separate building blocks in the appropriate manner. The object-oriented approach of EURIS allows the design of interlockings for large railway stations without extra effort, and makes it possible to have different interlocking design patterns for different countries.

UniSpec [4] is a particular instance of the EURIS method, which has been developed by ProRail as a complete set of generic elements to compose interlocking. A simulator enables the animation of the behavior of a UniSpec specification. After designing a set of LSCs, the user can join instantiations of these LSCs according to the topology of a railway area. The result is checked for design rule errors and compiled, after which situations at the controlled railway area can be simulated via a graphical interface.

In a project funded by the Dutch company Holland Railconsult, researchers from Utrecht University formulated a formal operational semantics for EURIS [5], which, following the EURIS simulator, is based on a discrete time model. This semantics was presented in the setting of discrete-time process algebra. In a follow-up project, funded by ProRail, researchers from CWI in Amsterdam devised a textual variant of EURIS called LARIS [31], with the aim of improving the clarity of the graphical LSCs. Verification efforts of EURIS specifications were undertaken at CWI in Amsterdam. A prototype compiler from EURIS to μCRL [8] was implemented, and the EURIS specification of the

Dutch station Woerden-Harmelen was tackled with the help of the μCRL toolset. Thus, a symbolic version of the state space of this interlocking system has become available for analysis. The correctness of a EURIS specification of an (smaller) imaginary railway station was established using the μCRL toolset.

The verification effort concerning Woerden-Harmelen resulted in several advances in the realm of formal verification. Namely, the state space belonging to the interlocking system at this station is so large that new verification techniques had to be implemented for the μCRL toolset, to cope with such large state spaces. They are based on partial order reduction [12], distributed state space generation [13], and minimization of such a distributed state space [9–11].

The ownership of EURIS has shifted from ProRail to Siemens, aimed at guaranteeing stronger commercial support and tool development. Currently, EURIS is at the heart of the GRACE toolset of Siemens [39].

4.6 CONCLUSIONS

We have seen that the history of application of formal methods to railway signaling is not disjoint from the history of the organization of railways, which has undergone dramatic changes in the last decades, due to the advent of the European Community enforced open market. A shift toward behavioral, state machine-based formalisms has been witnessed, with more attention toward formalisms supported by commercial tools. Tools that give the ability of simulating and model-checking specifications, and of generating code from them will have an added value. But these tools may be very expensive, prohibitive for small companies that produce software for major ones or produce minor equipment, which should anyway satisfy directives. Still some more time will pass before a clear satisfactory indication will emerge.

Formal methods for specification and verification are—slowly but steadily—reaching some appreciation and use in the industrial environment: There are many notations, methods, and (prototypal) tools originating from the academia, which, however, lack industrial strength in terms of tool stability, documentation, and user support; on the other hand, there are a few technically sound methods and tools coming from the industry. Thorough verification of complex, hard real-time systems is still infeasible in practice using the (industrial strength) tools. The verification technology is, however, rapidly evolving.

International standards like EN50128 can have a positive role in promoting the adoption of systematic and technically sound development methods, but can also be technically outdated, obscure, ambiguous, or too accommodating. The need for a revision of CENELEC norms has brought to a current revision proposal by the TC9X/SC9XA Technical Committee, which has been published recently, and which includes many more references to formal modeling and formal verification techniques.

REFERENCES

1. J. R. Abrial. *The B-Book*. Cambridge University Press, 1996.

2. M. Banci and A. Fantechi. Geographical vs. functional modelling by statecharts of interlocking systems. In *Proceedings 9th Workshop on Formal Methods for Industrial Critical Systems (FMICS'04), Linz, Volume 133 of Electronic Notes in Computer Science*, pp. 3–19. Elsevier, 2005.

3. P. Behm, P. Benoit, A. Faivre, and J. M. Meynadier. Météor: A successful application of B in a large project. In *Proceedings World Congress on Formal Methods in the Development of Computing Systems (FM'99)*, pp. 369–387, Volume 1708 of Lecture Notes in Computer Science, Springer, Toulouse, 1999.

4. J. Berger, P. Middelraad, and A. J. Smith. EURIS, European railway interlocking specification. In *Proceedings IRSE'93*, pp. 70–82, Institution of Railway Signal Engineers, 1993.

5. J. A. Bergstra, W. J. Fokkink, W. M. T. Mennen, and S. F. M. van Vlijmen. Railway Logic via EURIS. Quaestiones Infinitae XXII, Zeno Institute of Philosophy, Utrecht, 1997 (in Dutch).

6. C. Bernardeschi, A. Fantechi, S. Gnesi, S. Larosa, G. Mongardi, and D. Romano. A formal verification environment for railway signaling system design. *Formal Methods in System Design*, 12(2):139–161, 1998.

7. D. Bjørner. New results and trends in formal techniques and tools for the development of software for transportation systems—A review. In *Proceedings 4th Symposium on Formal Methods for Railway Operation and Control Systems (FORMS'03)*, L'Harmattan Hongrie, Budapest, 2003.

8. S. C. C. Blom, W. J. Fokkink, J. F. Groote, I. A. van Langevelde, B. Lisser, and J. C. van de Pol. μCRL: A toolset for analysing algebraic specifications. In *Proceedings 13th Conference on Computer Aided Verification (CAV'01)*, pp. 250–254, Volume 2102 of Lecture Notes in Computer Science, Springer, Paris, 2001.

9. S. C. C. Blom and S. Orzan. A distributed algorithm for strong bisimulation reduction of state spaces. In *Proceedings 1st Workshop on Parallel and Distributed Model Checking (PDMC'02), Brno, Volume 68(4) of Electronic Notes in Theoretical Computer Science*, Elsevier, 2002.

10. S. C. C. Blom and S. Orzan. Distributed state space minimization. In *Proceedings 8th Workshop on Formal Methods for Industrial Critical Systems (FMICS'03), Trondheim, Volume 80 of Electronic Notes in Theoretical Computer Science*, Elsevier, 2003.

11. S. C. C. Blom and S. Orzan. Distributed branching bisimulation reduction of state spaces. In *Proceedings 2nd Workshop on Parallel and Distributed Model Checking (PDMC'03), Boulder, Volume 89 of Electronic Notes in Theoretical Computer Science*, Elsevier, 2003.

12. S. C. C. Blom and J. C. van de Pol. State space reduction by proving confluence. In *Proceedings 14th Conference on Computer Aided Verification (CAV'02)*, pp. 596–609, Volume 2404 of Lecture Notes in Computer Science, Springer, Copenhagen, 2002.

13. S. C. C. Blom, I. A. van Langevelde, and B. Lisser. Compressed and distributed file formats for labeled transition systems. In *Proceedings 2nd Workshop on Parallel*

and Distributed Model Checking (PDMC'03), Boulder, Volume 89 of Electronic Notes in Theoretical Computer Science, Elsevier, 2003.

14. G. Booch, J. Rumbaugh, and I. Jacobson. *The Unified Modeling Language User Guide.* Addison-Wesley, 1999.

15. F. Boussinot and R. de Simone. The Esterel language. Another look at real time programming. *Proceedings of the IEEE,* 79(9):1293–1304, 1991.

16. R. Cavada, A. Cimatti, A. Mariotti, C. Mattarei, A. Micheli, S. Mover, M. Pensallorto, M. Roveri, A. Susi, and S. Tonetta. EuRailCheck: Tool support for requirements validation. In *ASE 2009,* Auckland, New Zealand, November 16–20, 2009.

17. A. Chiappini, A. Cimatti, C. Porzia, G. Rotondo, R. Sebastiani, P. Traverso, and A. Villafiorita. Formal specification and development of a safety-critical train management system. In *Proceedings 18th Conference on Computer Safety, Reliability and Security (SAFECOMP'99),* pp. 410–419, Volume 1698 of Lecture Notes in Computer Science 1698, Springer, Toulouse, 1999.

18. A. Cimatti, F. Giunchiglia, G. Mongardi, D. Romano, F. Torielli, and P. Traverso. Formal verification of a railway interlocking system using model checking. *Formal Aspects of Computing,* 10(4):361–380, 1998.

19. W. Damm and J. Klose. Verification of a radio-based signaling system using the STATEMATE verification environment. *Formal Methods in System Design,* 19(2):121–141, 2001.

20. C. DaSilva, B. Dehbonei, and F. Mejia. Formal specification in the development of industrial applications: Subway speed control system. In *Proceedings 5th IFIP Conference on Formal Description Techniques for Distributed Systems and Communication Protocols (FORTE'92),* pp. 199–213, Perros-Guirec, North-Holland, 1993.

21. P. E. Debarbieri, F. Valdambrini, and E. Antonelli. A.C.E.I. Telecomandati per linee a semplice binario, schemi I0/19. CIFI Collana di testi per la preparazione agli esami di abilitazione, Quaderno 12, 1987.

22. C. Eisner. Using symbolic CTL model checking to verify the railway stations of Hoorn-Kersenboogerd and Heerhugowaard. *Software Tools for Technology Transfer,* 4(1):107–124, 2002.

23. J. Ellsberger, D. Hogrefe, and A. Sarma. *SDL—Formal Object-oriented Language for Communicating Systems.* Prentice Hall, 1997.

24. L. H. Eriksson. Specifying railway interlocking requirements for practical use. In *SAFECOMP'96—Proceedings of the 15th International Conference on Computer Safety, Reliability and Security,* Springer-Verlag, 1996.

25. UNIFE, ERTMS, 2012, Available at: http://www.ertms-online.com.

26. R. Esposito, A. Lazzaro, P. Marmo, and A. Sanseviero. Formal verification of ERTMS Euroradio safety critical protocol. In *Proceedings 4th Symposium on Formal Methods for Railway Operation and Control Systems (FORMS'03),* L'Harmattan Hongrie, Budapest, 2003.

27. European Railway Agency, ERTMS, List of Mandatory Specifications and Standards, 2012. Available at: http://www.era.europa.eu/Core-Activities/ERTMS/Pages/List-Of-Mandatory-Specifications-and-Standards.aspx.

28. European Committee for Electrotechnical Standardization. EN 50128, Railway Applications Communications, Signaling and Processing Systems Software for Railway Control and Protection Systems, 2001.

29. J. Faber. Verifying real-time aspects of the European train control system. In *Proceedings 17th Nordic Workshop on Programming Theory (NWPT'05)*, Copenhagen, 2005.

30. W. J. Fokkink. Safety criteria for the vital processor interlocking at Hoorn-Kersenboogerd. In *Proceedings 5th Conference on Computers in Railways (COMPRAIL'96)*, pp. 101–110, Computational Mechanics Publications, Berlin, 1996.

31. W. J. Fokkink, J. F. Groote, M. J. Hollenberg, and S. F. M. van Vlijmen. LARIS 1.0: Language for Railway Interlocking Specifications. CWI Publications Miscellaneous, Stichting Mathematisch Centrum, 2000.

32. U. Foschi, M. Giuliani, A. Morzenti, M. Pradella, and P. San Pietro. The role of formal methods in software procurement for the railway transportation industry. In *Proceedings 4th Symposium on Formal Methods for Railway Operation and Control Systems (FORMS'03)*, L'Harmattan Hongrie, Budapest, 2003.

33. B. Fringuelli, E. Lamma, P. Mello, and G. Santocchia. Knowledge-based technology for controlling railway stations. *IEEE Intelligent Systems*, 7(6):45–52, 1992.

34. C. Ghezzi, D. Mandrioli, and A. Morzenti. TRIO: A logic language for executable specifications of real-time systems. *Journal of Systems and Software*, 12(2):107–123, 1990.

35. J. F. Groote, J. W. C. Koorn, and S. F. M. van Vlijmen. The safety guaranteeing system at station Hoorn-Kersenboogerd. In *Proceedings 10th IEEE Conference on Computer Assurance (COMPASS'95)*, pp. 131–150, IEEE Computer Society Press, Gaithersburg, 1995.

36. D. Harel. Statecharts: A visual formalism for complex systems. *Science of Computer Programming*, 8(3):231–274, 1987.

37. A. E. Haxthausen and J. Peleska. Generation of executable railway control components from domain-specific descriptions. In *Proceedings 4th Symposium on Formal Methods for Railway Operation and Control Systems (FORMS'03)*, pp. 83–90, L'Harmattan Hongrie, Budapest, 2003.

38. INESS project, 2009. Available at: http://projects.uic.asso.fr/

39. B. Jung. Die methode und werkzeuge GRACE. In *Formale Techniken für die Eisenbahn-sicherung (FORMS'00)*, Fortschritt-Berichte VDI, Reihe 12, Nr. 441, VDI Verlag, 2000.

40. N. H. König and S. Einer. The Euro-Interlocking formalized functional requirements approach (EIFFRA). In *Proceedings 4th Symposium on Formal Methods for Railway Operation and Control Systems (FORMS'03)*, L'Harmattan Hongrie, Budapest, 2003.

41. P. Le Bouar. Interlocking SNCF functional requirements description. Euro-Interlocking Project, Paris, May 2003.

42. G. LeGoff. Using synchronous languages for interlocking. In *First International Conference on Computer Application in Transportation Systems*, 1996.

43. M. Meyer zu Hörste and E. Schnieder. Formal modelling and simulation of train control systems using Petri nets. In *Proceedings World Congress on Formal Methods*

in the Development of Computing Systems (FM'99), p. 1867, Volume 1709 of Lecture Notes in Computer Science, Springer, Toulouse, 1999.

44. M. J. Morley. Safety in railway signalling data: A behavioural analysis. In *Proceedings 6th Workshop on Higher Order Logic Theorem Proving and its Applications (HUG'93), Vancouver, Volume 740 of Lecture Notes in Computer Science*, pp. 464–474. Springer, 1993.

45. T. Murata. Petri nets: Properties, analysis and applications. *Proceedings of the IEEE*, 77(4):541–580, 1989.

46. J. M. Spivey. *Introducing Z: A Specification Language and Its Formal Semantics*. Cambridge University Press, 1998.

47. F. J. van Dijk, W. J. Fokkink, G. P. Kolk, P. H. J. van de Ven, and S. F. M. van Vlijmen. EURIS, a specification method for distributed interlockings. In *Proceedings 17th Conference on Computer Safety, Reliability and Security (SAFECOMP'98)*, pp. 296–305, Volume 1516 of Lecture Notes in Computer Science, Springer, Heidelberg, 1998.

48. P. van Eijk, C. A. Vissers, and M. Diaz. *The Formal Description Technique LOTOS*. Elsevier, 1989.

49. A. Zimmermann and G. Hommel. Towards modeling and evaluation of ETCS real-time communication and operation. *Journal of Systems and Software*, 77(1):47–54, 2005.

CHAPTER 5

SYMBOLIC MODEL CHECKING FOR AVIONICS

RADU I. SIMINICEANU
National Institute of Aerospace, Hampton, VA

GIANFRANCO CIARDO
Department of Computer Science and Engineering, University of California, Riverside, CA

5.1 INTRODUCTION

Since the 1970s, both on-board flight management systems and air traffic management operations on the ground have become significantly more automated. The cockpits of commercial and military airplanes are now heavily computerized. The general term for this class of equipment is *avionics*. This includes digital electronic devices, components, and entire subsystems used for

- navigation, such as the global positioning system (GPS);
- control, for example, autopilot systems;
- communications, for example, Automatic Dependent Surveillance-Broadcast (ADS-B), which in turn is based on GPS;
- conflict detection and resolution (CD&R) protocols, for example, the Traffic Collision Avoidance System (TCAS) and the Runway Incursion Prevention System (RIPS);
- flight data recorders;
- integrated display systems;
- entire aircraft management systems, for example, the Integrated Modular Avionics (IMA); and
- unmanned vehicle systems (UASs).

Formal Methods for Industrial Critical Systems: A Survey of Applications, First Edition.
Edited by Stefania Gnesi and Tiziana Margaria.
© 2013 IEEE. Published 2013 by John Wiley & Sons, Inc.

For safety-critical avionics, regulatory authorities (the Federal Aviation Administration [FAA], the Civil Aeronautics Authority [CAA] or the Department of Defense [DoD]) require software development standards, such as MIL-STD-2167 for military systems and RTCA DO-178B for civil aircraft. This is both a challenge and an opportunity for the formal methods community, whose technology has not been initially included in the regulations, but has since made tremendous progress and is now strongly recommended in the process of building dependable systems [39].

The challenges in verifying avionics systems can be attributed to two main factors:

- The *hybrid* nature of the embedded systems: Both discrete and continuous variables are needed to faithfully model concepts such as (continuous) aircraft trajectories, the physics behind the operating environment (e.g., temperature, pressure, speed, and acceleration), and most notably "real time."
- The degree of *complexity* of the systems: The number of subcomponents, their size, and the interactions between these components can be quite large.

Hybrid systems analysis has been around for almost two decades. But, as pointed out in Reference 43, the research community has from the beginning adopted a methodology based on accepting the foundations of the theory of computation as "transformation of data and not about physical dynamics." Thus, real time has been modeled by retrofitting basic abstract models, such as automata, with temporal properties. This is the way timed automata [2] and other incarnations (timed I/O automata, timeout automata, calendar automata) were conceived. Despite massive research efforts, especially in establishing the formal mathematical foundations, progress in terms of practical applications has virtually stalled and has not moved beyond systems with more than a dozen continuous variables. For avionics systems, a basic 3-D collision avoidance protocol, for example, requires at least six real variables to represent the coordinates of an aircraft and an intruder, and six more to represent the 3-D speed vectors, thus is already beyond the means of today's capabilities.

Satisfiability Modulo Theories (SMT) solvers for linear arithmetic and uninterpreted functions have been used to efficiently verify real-time designs [33]. However, the approach is still limited to models with a relatively small number of discrete states and timing constraints that can be expressed as linear inequalities.

Until the field of hybrid system verification reaches a higher level of maturity, a verification practitioner must resort to more traditional, yet relatively scalable, techniques, such as discrete-state *model checking*. Therefore, the first and foremost task is finding appropriate *abstraction techniques* that allow the analysis of infinite-state spaces in the form of behaviorally equivalent finite models.

Once a suitable abstraction is found, the second challenge is addressing the issue of *state-space explosion*. One possibility is to develop reduction techniques (such as partial order reduction, symmetry reduction, or compositional approaches) that reduce the state space to manageable sizes. Another is to improve the model checking algorithms themselves, as is the case for the saturation algorithm [18] presented in Section 5.2.6. This approach to model checking, initially proposed as a very efficient iteration strategy for generating the state spaces of globally asynchronous, locally synchronous systems, has been gradually improved so that it is now able to tackle a much larger class of problems. In the most recent version, it supports on-the-fly variable domain computation (when the lower and upper bounds for variable values are not known a priori), and it is now also able to analyze models that do not satisfy "Kronecker consistency," as previously required.

In the following, we present our experience in applying the methodology outlined above (i.e., discrete-state model checking of abstracted models) to an industrial size application: the NASA Runway Safety Monitor (RSM) software [35]. This classical approach seems to have maintained a good track record in the industry, as also illustrated by recent reports from ONERA and Airbus [5, 51].

We do not pretend or intend to do a *comparison* of this approach with other formal verification tools and techniques, since this is not the custom practice in the industry, where the toolsets and skillsets of the personnel determine quite strictly the verification technology used in each project. We do try, however, to carefully justify our modeling and analysis decisions and share our perspectives and lessons learned from what turned out to be a rather successful project.

5.2 APPLICATION: THE RUNWAY SAFETY MONITOR

The RSM is part of the RIPS [40]. Designed and implemented by Lockheed Martin engineers, RSM is intended to be incorporated in the Integrated Display System (IDS) [4], a suite of cockpit applications that NASA has been developing since 1993. IDS also includes other conflict detection and prevention algorithms, such as TCAS II [44]. The IDS design enables RSM to exploit existing data communications facilities, displays, GPS, ground surveillance system information, and data links.

Collision avoidance protocols are already in operation. TCAS [44] has been in use since 1994 and is now required by the FAA on all commercial U.S. aircraft. TCAS has a full formal specification, but it has been verified only partially, due to its complexity [11, 37]. Other protocols, such as Small Aircraft Transportation System (SATS) [1], developed at NASA Langley to help ensure safe landings of general aviation craft at towerless regional airports, and Airborne Information for Lateral Spacing (AILS) [10], an alerting algorithm for parallel landing scenarios, have been instead formally verified [32].

5.2.1 Purpose of RSM

The goal of the RSM is to detect runway incursions, defined by the FAA as "any occurrence at an airport involving an aircraft, vehicle, person, or object on the ground, that creates a collision hazard or results in the loss of separation with an aircraft taking off, intending to take off, landing, or intending to land."

Since most air safety incidents occur on or near runways, the RSM plays a key role in accident avoidance. RSM is not intended to *prevent* incursions, but to *detect* them and *alert* the pilots. Prevention is provided by other components of RIPS in the form of a number of IDS capabilities such as heads-up display, electronic moving map, cockpit display of traffic information, and taxi routing. Experimental studies conducted by Lockheed Martin [35, 53] show that incursion situations are less likely to occur when IDS technology is employed on aircraft. RSM should greatly improve this positive effect.

5.2.2 RSM Design

Figure 5.1 shows the high-level architecture of the RSM algorithm. RSM runs on a cockpit-installed device and is activated prior to takeoff and landing procedures at airports. An independent copy of RSM runs on each aircraft and refers to the aircraft on which it is operating as *ownship* and to other aircraft, ground vehicles using the same runway, or even physical obstacles such as equipment, as *targets*.

RSM monitors traffic in a zone surrounding the runway where the takeoff or landing can occur. This is a 3-D volume running up to 220 ft laterally from each edge of the runway, up to 400 ft of altitude above the runway, and 1.1 nautical miles from each runway end (this corresponds to a 3° glide slope for takeoff and landing trajectories).

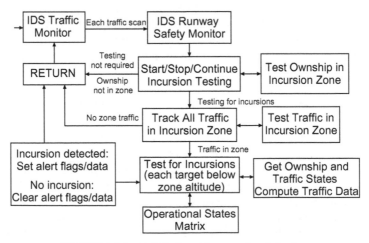

FIGURE 5.1 RSM algorithm top-level design.

The protocol, implemented as a C-language program, consists of a repeat loop over three major phases. In the first phase, RSM gathers traffic information from radar updates received through a data link. It identifies each target present in the monitored zone and stores its 3-D physical coordinates. The frequency of the updates may not be constant, updates can be lost, and data might even be faulty. The implications of data link errors or omissions are not addressed in this study, but present a challenging task for future studies. These errors have already been the subject of some experimental measurements [53], and their analysis calls for a *stochastic* flavor not captured in our model, which is instead concerned only with *logical* errors.

In the second phase, the algorithm determines the *status* of each target, from a predetermined set of values: taxi, pre-takeoff, takeoff, climb out, landing, roll out, and fly-through modes. We discuss in detail the meaning of these states in Section 5.3.

The third phase is responsible for detecting incursions and is performed for each target based on the spatial attributes (position, heading, and acceleration) of ownship and target, plus some logical conditions. Table 5.1 in Section 5.3.2, shows the *operational state matrix* of this phase. The safety analysis focused on verifying that the decision criteria listed in the table are able to detect all possible incursion scenarios.

5.2.3 Formal Verification of RSM

We adopted a model-based approach to verification, rather than attempting to verify the actual C code itself, for two reasons. First, expressing the main safety property ("no missed alarms") requires representing the environment (e.g., the movement of targets, which is only tracked by the software, while the laws governing the dynamics of the targets are not represented in the code). Second, temporal logic model checking is not known to be able to handle code of this size (in contrast to other static analysis techniques that have been applied to avionics software [28]).

We argue that a discrete-state model is adequate for this application (and, for similar air traffic monitoring applications, be they en route or airportal) because, in any behavior observable by the software, the state of the system is already discretized, as aircraft positions are taken at regular time intervals and not continuously.

Before proceeding with the description of our extracted model of RSM, we review the main features of the symbolic verification technique we have developed in the course of the last years.

5.2.4 Structural Symbolic Model Checking

When applying symbolic model checking to large and complex systems, the memory and time requirements can quickly become a formidable obstacle. To mitigate this problem, one can try to exploit the special characteristics of the system under study. Our technique, which we call *structural symbolic model checking* [14, 23], is particularly successful in this regard when applied to globally asynchronous, locally synchronous systems [12]. Its main idea is to recognize *locality* (i.e., the fact that most events affect only a few of the many state variables) and use it to perform a *saturation-style* fixed-point iteration instead of a more traditional breadth-first-style iteration (i.e., events are explored in a particular locality-guided order that can greatly reduce the peak size of the decision diagrams).

We represent discrete-state models as a triple $(\mathcal{S}_{pot}, \mathcal{S}_{init}, \mathcal{N})$, where $\mathcal{S}_{pot}$ is the set of *potential states* of the model, $\mathcal{S}_{init} \subseteq \mathcal{S}_{pot}$ is the set of *initial states*, and $\mathcal{N} : \mathcal{S}_{pot} \rightarrow 2^{\mathcal{S}_{pot}}$ is the *next-state function* specifying the states reachable from each state in a single step. In practice, the model is described compactly in some high-level formalism (e.g., Petri nets or process algebras), but the size of $\mathcal{S}_{pot}$ is usually very large. A fundamental question is then to determine the set of states that are actually reachable from the initial states through repeated applications of the next-state function. Formally, the *(reachable) state space* $\mathcal{S}_{rch} \subseteq \mathcal{S}_{pot}$ is the smallest superset of $\mathcal{S}_{init}$ closed with respect to $\mathcal{N}$:

$$\mathcal{S}_{rch} = \mathcal{S}_{init} \cup \mathcal{N}(\mathcal{S}_{init}) \cup \mathcal{N}(\mathcal{N}(\mathcal{S}_{init})) \cup \cdots = \mathcal{N}^*(\mathcal{S}_{init}),$$

where "*" denotes reflexive and transitive closure and $\mathcal{N}(\mathcal{X}) = \bigcup_{i \in \mathcal{X}} \mathcal{N}(i)$.

The first step in structuring the model is to decompose the model into K *submodels*, or, in other words, write a *(global)* state $\mathbf{i}$ as a K-tuple $(\mathbf{i}_K, \ldots, \mathbf{i}_1)$, where $\mathbf{i}_k$ is the *local* state of submodel k, for $K \geq k \geq 1$. Thus, the potential state space is given by the cross-product of K *local state spaces*, $\mathcal{S}_{pot} = \mathcal{S}_K \times \cdots \times \mathcal{S}_1$.

Assuming for now that each $\mathcal{S}_k$ is known a priori, we can map each of its local states $\mathbf{i}_k$ to an index i_k in the range $\{0, 1, \ldots, n_k - 1\}$, where $n_k = |\mathcal{S}_k|$. Then, we can identify $\mathcal{S}_k$ with $\{0, 1, \ldots, n_k - 1\}$ and encode any set $\mathcal{X} \subseteq \mathcal{S}_{pot}$ in a *quasi-reduced ordered multiway decision diagram* [41, 42, 48] (MDD) over $\mathcal{S}_{pot}$. Formally, an MDD is a directed acyclic edge-labeled multigraph where

- each node p belongs to a *level* in $\{K, \ldots, 1, 0\}$. If the level is $k > 0$, we also say that the node refers to *variable* x_k;
- level 0 can only contain the two *terminal* nodes *Zero* and *One*;
- there is a unique *root* node r with no incoming arcs, and it is either at level K or it is the terminal node *Zero*;
- a node p at level $k > 0$ has n_k outgoing edges, labeled from 0 to $n_k - 1$. The edge labeled by i_k points to a node q, which is either the terminal *Zero* or a node at level $k - 1$; we write $p[i_k] = q$;
- there are no *duplicate* nodes: If p and q are at level k and $p[i_k] = q[i_k]$ for all $i_k \in \mathcal{S}_k$, then $p = q$.

Note that MDDs are a generalization of the very successful BDDs [6], which are restricted to binary choices at each node, thus require multiple Boolean variables to encode a single index i_k whenever $n_k > 1$.

The MDD encodes a set of states $\mathcal{B}(r)$, defined by the recursive formula

$$\mathcal{B}(p) = \begin{cases} \emptyset & \text{if } p = Zero \\ \{i_1 : p[i_1] = One\} & \text{if } p \text{ is at level 1} \\ \bigcup_{i_k \in S_k} \{i_k\} \times \mathcal{B}(p[i_k]) & \text{if } p \text{ is at level } k > 1 \end{cases}.$$

In symbolic algorithms, several sets of states $\mathcal{X}^{(1)}, \ldots, \mathcal{X}^{(m)}$, all subsets of $\mathcal{S}_{pot}$, may need to be stored at the same time. This is achieved through an *MDD forest* that stores the roots $r^{(1)}, \ldots, r^{(m)}$ of these MDDs and forces them to *share* nodes, so that duplicates are avoided even across different MDDs. A fundamental property of the MDDs just defined is that they are *canonical*: For a given variable order $x_K, \ldots, x_1$, two nodes representing the same set are isomorphic and, when using an MDD forest, this situation is easily recognized in $O(1)$ time using hash table techniques.

In addition to the compact representation of sets of states provided by MDDs, symbolic methods also require a compact representation of the next-state function. Since $\mathcal{N}$ can be seen as the set of pairs (i, j) such that $j \in \mathcal{N}(i)$, we can store this set using a $2K$-level MDD over the "from" variables $x_K, \ldots,$ x_1 and the "to" variables $y_K, \ldots, y_1$. However, this monolithic MDD encoding often requires excessive memory. The second structuring step is then to decompose $\mathcal{N}$ into a *disjunction* of next-state functions [9]: $\mathcal{N}(i) = \cup_{a \in \mathcal{E}} \mathcal{N}_a(i)$, where $\mathcal{E}$ is a finite set of *events* and $\mathcal{N}_\alpha$ is the next-state function associated with event α. Then, we say that $\mathcal{N}_\alpha(i)$ is the set of states the system can enter when α occurs, or *fires*, in state i, and that α is *disabled* in i if $\mathcal{N}_a(i) = \emptyset$, and *enabled* otherwise. Usually, storing $|\mathcal{E}|$ MDDs in an MDD forest with the *interleaved* variable ordering $(x_K, y_K, \ldots, x_1, y_1)$ greatly improves the memory requirements for storing $\mathcal{N}$ [20].

The structural approach goes a step further and partitions each $\mathcal{N}_\alpha$ according to the K state variables. An efficient approach [17, 48] adopts a Kronecker representation [31] inspired by the work on Markov chains [7], assuming that the model is *Kronecker consistent*, that is, that $\mathcal{N}_\alpha$ can be *conjunctively* decomposed into K local next-state functions $\mathcal{N}_{k,\alpha}: \mathcal{S}_k \to 2^{\mathcal{S}_k}$, for $K \geq k \geq 1$, satisfying

$$\forall (i_K, \ldots, i_1) \in \mathcal{S}_{pot}, \mathcal{N}_\alpha(i_K, \ldots, i_1) = \mathcal{N}_{K,\alpha}(i_K) \times \cdots \times \mathcal{N}_{1,\alpha}(i_1).$$

Defining $K \cdot |\mathcal{E}|$ matrices $\mathbf{N}_{k,\alpha} \in \{0, 1\}^{n_k \times n_k}$, with $\mathbf{N}_{k,\alpha}[i_k, j_k] = 1 \Leftrightarrow j_k \in \mathcal{N}_{k,\alpha}(i_k)$, we encode $\mathcal{N}_\alpha$ as a Kronecker product: $j \in \mathcal{N}_\alpha(i) \Leftrightarrow \otimes_{K \geq k \geq 1} \mathbf{N}_{k,\alpha}[i_k, j_k] = 1$, where a state i is interpreted as a *mixed-base* index in $\mathcal{S}_{pot}$ and $\otimes$ indicates the (Boolean) Kronecker product of matrices.

The Kronecker encoding of $\mathcal{N}$ is quite memory efficient also because it can be used to recognize and exploit *event locality*. We say that event α is *independent* of level k if $\mathbf{N}_{k,\alpha} = \mathbf{I}$, the identity matrix. For globally asynchronous, locally synchronous models, most events affect only a few state variables and are independent of all others. Only the matrices $\mathbf{N}_{k,\alpha} \neq \mathbf{I}$ require actual storage, and their number in practice is often $O(|\mathcal{E}|)$ instead of $O(K \cdot |\mathcal{E}|)$. Furthermore, these matrices are extremely sparse in practice and often require just $O(n_k)$ memory instead of $O(n_k^2)$.

5.2.5 The Saturation Algorithm for Symbolic State-Space Generation

Recognizing event locality is essential not only for a Kronecker representation of $\mathcal{N}$, but also for the *saturation* algorithm [18]. Let $Top(\alpha)$ and $Bot(\alpha)$ denote the highest and lowest levels for which $\mathbf{N}_{k,\alpha} \neq \mathbf{I}$. We say that a node p at level k is *saturated* if it is a fixed point with respect to all events α such that $Top(\alpha) \leq k$; that is,

$$\forall i_K, \ldots, i_{k+1} \in \mathcal{S}_K \times \cdots \times \mathcal{S}_{k+1}, Top(\alpha) \leq k \Rightarrow,$$

$$\{(i_K, \ldots, i_{k+1})\} \times \mathcal{B}(p) \supseteq \mathcal{N}_\alpha(\{(i_K, \ldots, i_{k+1})\} \times \mathcal{B}(p)).$$

This is succinctly written as $\mathcal{B}(p) \supseteq \mathcal{N}_{\leq k}(\mathcal{B}(p))$ by defining $\mathcal{N}_{\leq k} = \cup_{\alpha:Top(a)\leq k}\mathcal{N}_a$ and allowing the application of $\mathcal{N}_\alpha$ to a set $\mathcal{X} \subseteq \mathcal{S}_l \times \cdots \times \mathcal{S}_1$ with $l \geq Top(\alpha)$, since $\mathcal{N}_\alpha$ leaves all local states above $Top(\alpha)$ unchanged.

The saturation algorithm starts with the MDD encoding the initial states $\mathcal{S}_{init}$ and saturates its nodes bottom-up. A simplified high-level pseudocode for the algorithm is shown in Figure 5.2, where $\mathcal{E}_k = \{\alpha: Top(\alpha) = k\}$.

Saturation employs multiple nested lightweight, fixed-point iterations, unlike the traditional breadth-first approach, which applies every $\mathcal{N}_\alpha$ to the entire set of known states, or to the entire set of newly discovered states, at every iteration. Whenever *saturate* operates on a node p at level k, its descendants have been already saturated. To saturate p, the algorithm repeatedly fires on p all events α with $Top(\alpha) = k$ until reaching a fixed point, with the proviso that, if a firing creates new nodes at levels below k, they are saturated immediately, prior to completing the saturation of p.

Results in Reference 18 show that saturation greatly outperforms breadth-first symbolic exploration by several orders of magnitude in both memory and time, making it arguably the most efficient symbolic fixed-point iteration strategy for state-space generation of globally asynchronous, locally synchronous discrete event systems.

While the algorithm we presented assumes that the local state space $\mathcal{S}_k$ is known prior to calling *StateSpaceGeneration*, this is not a requirement. The saturation algorithm has been extended so that new local states can be discovered *on-the-fly* using explicit local state-space explorations interleaved with the global symbolic state-space generation just presented [19]. While the algorithmic implementation becomes substantially more difficult in this case, the

---

$StateSpaceGeneration(r)$ • *r is the root of the MDD encoding S_{init}*
1. for $k = 1$ to K do   • *saturate the initial nodes bottom up*
2. for each node p at level k in the MDD rooted at r do $Saturate(p)$

$Saturate(p)$ • *let k be the level of node p*
1. repeat   • *update p so that it satisfies the fixed point*
   $\mathcal{B}(p) = \mathcal{B}(p) \cup \mathcal{N}_{\leq k}(\mathcal{B}(p))$
2. pick a $i_k \in \mathcal{S}_k$ s.t. $p[i_k] \neq Zero$ and an $\alpha \in \mathcal{E}_k$ s.t. $\mathcal{N}_\alpha(i_k) \neq \emptyset$
   • *a state in $\{i_k\} \times \mathcal{B}(p[i_k])$ may enable α*
3. for each $j_k \in \mathcal{N}_\alpha(i_k)$ do set $p[j_k]$ to $Union(p[j_k], FireSat(\alpha, p[i_k]))$
   • *update p in place*
4. until p does not change
5. return $MakeUnique(p)$ • *if p duplicates a node d, remove p and return d*

$FireSat(\alpha, p)$ • *let k be the level of node p, note that $Top(\alpha) > k$*
1. if $Bot(\alpha) > k$ then return p • *end condition for the firing recursion*
2. if $f = FireSat(\alpha, p)$ has been previously computed then return f
   • *look up the $FiringCache$*
3. create a new node f at level k with all edges pointing to $Zero$
   • *cannot modify p in place, . . .*
4. for each $i_k \in \mathcal{S}_k$ s.t. $p[i_k] \neq Zero$ and each $j_k \in \mathcal{N}_\alpha(i_k)$ do
5. set $f[j_k]$ to $Union(f[j_k], FireSat(\alpha, p[i_k]))$
   • *. . . but can modify f in place*
6. return $Saturate(f)$

$Union(p, q)$ • *let k be the level of nodes p and q*
1. if $p = Zero$ or $q = One$ or $p = q$ then return q
2. if $q = Zero$ or $p = One$ then return p
3. if $u = Union(p, q)$ has been previously computed then return u
   • *look up the $UnionCache$*
4. create a new node u at level k with all edges pointing to $Zero$
5. for each $i_k \in \mathcal{S}_k$ do set $u[i_k]$ to $Union(p[i_k], q[i_k])$
6. return $MakeUnique(u)$ • *if u duplicates a node d, remove u and return d*

FIGURE 5.2 State-space generation using MDDs, Kronecker, and a saturation-style iteration.

theoretical complexity remains the same, and the ease of modeling is substantially enhanced in practice, as the modeler need not worry about the bounds of the local state variables.

5.2.6 Saturation-Based Model Checking

The advantages of using a Kronecker representation for the next-state function apply also to a breadth-first iteration for state-space generation, and to the more general iterations required for symbolic Computation Tree Logic (CTL) model checking [25, 46], even though the latter is much more challenging.

It is well known that a CTL formula can be expressed using the three operators EX, EU, and EG, plus the Boolean operators $\neg$, $\wedge$, and $\vee$. Clearly, saturation is not applicable to the computation of the EX operator, since this involves the application of exactly one step of the next-state function $\mathcal{N}$, while any fixed-point algorithm, including saturation, is concerned with arbitrarily long sequences of steps in the evolution of the model. Analogously, the EG operator starts with a set of states $\mathcal{P}$ satisfying a particular condition p, and iteratively *removes* from $\mathcal{P}$ any state i that does not have a transition to a state $j \in \mathcal{P}$. In other words, unlike state-space generation, where a state j can be *added* to the set of states $\mathcal{S}_{rch}$ if there is *any* event α such that $j \in \mathcal{N}_{\alpha}(i)$ for some state $i \in \mathcal{S}_{rch}$, the condition for removing a state in the EG iterations requires to examine *all* events. Consequently, saturation does not appear to be directly applicable to EG either.

For the EU operator, however, the situation is much better [23]. First, consider the EF operator, which can be seen as a special case of EU, since EFq is equivalent to E[*true*Uq]. To symbolically compute the set of states satisfying EFq, we can start from the set $\mathcal{Q}$ of states satisfying condition q, and "walk the model backwards," adding to $\mathcal{Q}$ all the states that can transition to a state in $\mathcal{Q}$. This is exactly the state-space generation problem, where the initial set of states is $\mathcal{Q}$ and the next-state function is the inverse of the original next-state function of the model, that is, $i \in \mathcal{N}^{-1}(j)$ iff $j \in \mathcal{N}(i)$; thus, saturation naturally applies, with all its benefits. It is worth observing that, with our Kronecker encoding of $\mathcal{N}$, it is sufficient to use the *transpose* matrices $\mathbf{N}_{k,\alpha}^{T}$ to describe the backward evolution of the model.

When tackling the general problem of computing the state satisfying condition E[$p \cup q$], however, the original saturation algorithm cannot be directly applied, since we must ensure that, as we walk backward from the states in $\mathcal{Q}$, we do not stray from the states in $\mathcal{P}$ (satisfying p). The solution proposed in Reference 23 partitions the events $\mathcal{E}$ into *safe* events $\mathcal{E}_S$ and *unsafe* events $\mathcal{E}_U$. The distinguishing characteristic of the former set is that, for any safe event α and any state $j \in \mathcal{P} \cup \mathcal{Q}$, $i \in \mathcal{N}_{\alpha}^{-1}(j)$ implies that $i \in \mathcal{P} \cup \mathcal{Q}$ as well; that is, it is not possible to move from a state not satisfying p or q to a state satisfying p or q by firing α. The cost to classify all events is essentially just that of one breadth-first iteration (each event must be fired backward once). Then, we can compute the set of states satisfying E[pUq] by alternating a backward saturation step on the safe events (i.e., EF with the set of events $\mathcal{E}_S$) with a backward breadth-first step (i.e., EX with the set of events $\mathcal{E}_U$), until no more states can be added. The efficiency of this saturation-based EU algorithm depends on the model, and, in particular, on how many events can be classified as safe. In the best case, all events are safe (e.g., in the EF case), while, in the worst case, no event is safe (the complexity is then that of the traditional symbolic breadth-first algorithm, although still with the advantages of a Kronecker representation for $\mathcal{N}$).

An alternative approach to employ saturation for the EU computation was recently proposed [55], where each next-state function $\mathcal{N}_{\alpha}$ is modified by being *constrained* to stay in $\mathcal{P}$ when going backward, through an intersection with $\mathcal{P} \times S_{pot}$, performed either before beginning the computation, or on-the-fly during the fixed-point iteration. This new approach is even more efficient than the one in Reference 23, but it had not been discovered at the time we conducted the study described in this chapter.

5.2.7 The Stochastic and Model-Checking Analyzer for Reliability and Timing (SMART) Tool

The symbolic techniques we discussed are implemented in the tool SMART [16]. Given a description of a system as an extended Petri net [49], SMART can generate the state space, verify temporal logic properties, and compute numerical solutions for timing and stochastic analysis. SMART implements a wide range of explicit as well as symbolic methods. In addition to using MDDs to encode sets of states and either Kronecker operators, matrix diagrams [21, 47], or MDDs to encode the next-state function, SMART also employs a special form of edge-valued MDDs (EV$^+$MDDs) [22] for the generation of minimal-length counterexamples and witnesses in CTL model checking.

The SMART input is an extended Petri net with Turing-equivalent extensions (immediate transitions, marking dependent arc cardinalities, and transition guards) [49], which must have a finite-state space. Each SMART input file defines one or more structured (i.e., partitioned into submodels) models. A model can be parameterized and defines a set of *measures*, which, in our case, can be thought of as logical queries to be evaluated by systematic state exploration.

The SMART User Manual is available online [15].

5.3 A DISCRETE MODEL OF RSM

5.3.1 Abstraction on Integer and Real Variables

Automated abstraction techniques are desirable and have been successfully used in many applications. The best known techniques include abstract interpretation [29], domain abstraction [30], data abstraction [26, 27, 38], predicate abstraction [34, 45], automated abstraction refinement (CEGAR) [8, 24], approximation [3, 50, 52], data equivalence [13], slicing [36], and verification of regular infinite-state spaces [54].

Manual abstraction has been seen as more problematic, as it usually requires a good understanding of the system and how this evolves. In many cases, however, a manually built model can be tailored to the strengths of the tool that is used. Therefore, manual abstraction can often yield better results, because the modeler has more *control* over the process. While automation is highly desirable, the very generality of the automated approaches can lead to their demise. For example, generated abstractions can be inefficient, inaccurate, or suffer from the Zeno effect in the case of CEGAR.

Moreover, in our particular case, we exploit the fact that saturation targets the analysis of globally asynchronous, locally synchronous systems. By modeling the continuous environment and the discrete system events such that there is a high degree of event locality in the model, saturation-based model checking succeeds in building the state space of the abstract model. No further reduction techniques (partial order reduction, symmetry, predicate abstraction) are needed, but some of them could be completely orthogonal to the discretization method, and thus could be applied on top of the reduced model. Also, the discretization not being so drastic (as it could be in the case of applying predicate abstraction), the system behaviors still closely resemble actual aircraft trajectories.

5.3.2   The SMART Model of RSM

Unlike using a predicate abstraction technique that would ultimately divide the entire 3-D space into (possibly irregular, but logically equivalent) regions, we decided to establish a fixed number of variables (the coordinates on the three axes), then divide their domain into segments. In taking this decision, we took into account two facts. First, there was no actual formal specification of the desired set of properties of the protocol that would drive the predicate abstraction. Second, our type of discretization leads to modeled executions that are closer to the geometry of airplane motion in space, which is thus better understood by the design engineers, who have no training in, and possibly no clear understanding of, abstraction techniques.

In the end, we chose the system variables by partitioning the model into $n + 1$ submodels where n is the number of targets moving inside the zone. The variables of submodel 0 describe the state of ownship, while those of the other n submodels describe the state of each target. For submodel i, $0 \leq i \leq n$, the relevant attributes are the following:

Location. A 3-D vector (x_i, y_i, z_i), where the X-axis is across the width of the runway, the Y-axis is along the length, and the Z-axis is on the vertical.

Speed and Heading. A second 3-D vector (vx_i, vy_i, vz_i).

Acceleration along the Runway. ay_i.

Status. An enumerated-type variable, $status_i$.

Alarm Flag. A Boolean variable, $alarm_i$.

Phase. An enumerated-type variable, $phase_i$.

The variable domains are the following (the subscript i is omitted for readability):

- The coordinates x, y, z could be as simple as $x, y, z \in \{0, 1, 2\}$, where 0 means out of the monitored zone, 1 means in the vicinity, and 2 means on the runway. However, we chose a finer representation: $x \in \{0, \ldots, max_x\}$, $y \in \{0, \ldots, max_y\}$, and $z \in \{0, \ldots, max_z\}$, where 0 means outside the zone, and the constants max_x, max_y, and max_z can be adjusted to the modeler's preference. In other words, location (0, 0, 0) represents all positions outside the zone. A target that exits the zone, or has not yet entered it, has this location.

- The speed values vx, vy, vz could be assigned the domain $\{0, \pm1, \pm2\}$, where 0 means not moving, ±1 means moving slowly (below the predetermined *taxi speed threshold TS* of 45 knots), and ±2 means moving fast (above *TS*). Again, a better representation is $vx, vy, vz \in \{-max_{speed}, \ldots 0, \ldots, max_{speed}\}$ using another parameter max_{speed}.
- The acceleration a_y has only two relevant values: nonnegative or strictly negative.
- The *status* is one of $\{out, taxi, takeoff, climb, land, rollout, flythru\}$.
- The *phase* is one of $\{radar\_update, set\_status, detect\}$.

The variable *phase* works like a program counter for the execution of the algorithm by each participant, which loops through three steps:

phase = *radar_update*: Update location of targets.

phase = *set_status*: Update status of targets.

phase = *detect*: Set or reset alarm.

We next discuss the modeling decisions taken for each of these three steps.

5.3.2.1 3-D Motion of Targets

Our discretization method divides the monitored space into a 3-D grid. The possible positions of the aircraft are a finite number of grid cells, from the discrete domain $\{(0, 0, 0)\} \cup \{1, \ldots, max_x\} \times \{1, \ldots, max_y\} \times \{1, \ldots, max_z\}$. Similarly, continuous trajectories have to be represented by discretized trajectories through the cells of the 3-D grid. Three alternatives were considered.

First is the projection method, which assigns to every possible continuous trajectory its corresponding discrete path in the grid. An example of such a projection is given in Figure 5.3 (in 2-D space, for the sake of readability). The grid cells in the figure have the size of 100 units (feet), and the snapshots are taken after each 0.5 time units (seconds). The speed units are measured in axis divisions traversed after each update. The problem with this method is the difficulty in discerning between physical possibilities and impossibilities. There is no efficient way of ruling out all anomalies. For example, a target could change its real location, while its discretized location is not. The dependency between the speed and the number of time units a target may remain in one grid cell is also very difficult to establish: It could be one move (at high speed), or more (at low speed), but no upper bound on the number of time units allowed within one grid cell can be computed in the discretized model.

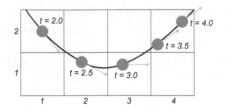

Real trajectory: (51.5, 161.3), (128.5, 93.6), (220.1, 80.3), (318.5, 111.2), ...
Discretized trajectory: (1,2),   (2,1),   (3,1),   (4,2),   ...
Discretized speed: (+1,-1),   (+1,-1),   (+1,0),   (+1,+1), ...

FIGURE 5.3   Example projection of continuous trajectory in 2-D.

Therefore, we have considered a different approach to modeling the motion of targets, that proved to be more practical. One alternative allows nearly free movement of a target, in the sense that a move to an adjacent cell is always allowed. In principle, a target is free to remain in the current cell or to move to any of the neighboring 26 cells, corresponding to a nondeterministic decrease, no change, or increase in the coordinates x, y, and z. However, the changes must be consistent with the heading. On the one hand, the restriction to allow transitions *only* between adjacent cells excludes a large number of trajectories, most of which are truly physically impossible. On the other hand, we have to argue that no realistic trajectory is excluded by the model. This is indeed true when the cell size is sufficiently large. In our simplest model, which captured all the interesting properties, the size of a grid cell is 900 ft. Given that the location updates arrive on the data link every 0.5 seconds, a target can skip a grid cell and move to a cell two discrete positions away only if it travels at speeds exceeding 1800 ft/s $\approx$ 1227 mph (or $\approx$ 1975 km/h). This is over 1.6 times the speed of sound. Although it is not entirely safe to assume that these speeds are not encountered on civil airport runways, their exclusion from our model is reasonable and helps simplify the analysis. Moreover, a rough discretization also mitigates state-space explosion, as the number of possible states becomes manageable. Figure 5.4 shows the possible moves of a target in this second model (also in 2-D space, for clarity).

This second model might still include unrealistic trajectories, such as oscillating back and forth between two adjacent cells (when the corresponding speed components alternate from positive to negative and back) or staying forever in one cell, even with a positive speed.

If a more thorough elimination of unwanted trajectories is desired, a third alternative that forbids abrupt variations in speed can be considered. In other words, both the coordinates x, y, z and the speed components vx, vy, vz can change by at most one in absolute value. This further restriction can be achieved by allowing only the increase, decrease, and no change of speed at each timestep, together with a consistent update of the coordinates: For

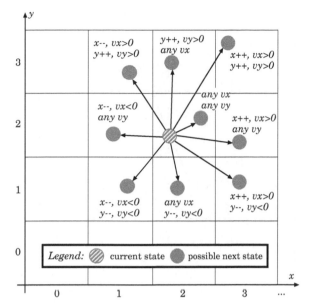

FIGURE 5.4 Possible 2-D movements of a target ("free motion" model).

example, the variable x cannot be decreasing when the speed component vx is nonnegative.

In comparison to the free motion model, Figure 5.5 shows the possible next states (in 2-D space) for a target whose speed components are $vx = 3$ and $vy = 3$ in the current state. In this case, only four new locations are possible, corresponding to the no change or increase in x and, independently, y. The reduced number of choices is due to the strictly positive value of the speed, which does not allow any move in the negative axis direction. Only when one speed component is 0 in the current state, the target can move in both directions of the corresponding axis. The speed is derived from two subsequent position observations, thus a target needs to be able to move from one cell to an adjacent one (e.g., from $x = 3$ to $x = 4$) even when the corresponding speed in that direction is 0 ($vx = 0$); at the next step, the speed will reflect this change ($vx = 1$), as seen in Figure 5.6. In this model, at least two steps are required to go from positive to negative speed (and vice versa). This implies that "zigzagging" is not possible, a fact that could have a significant importance in the analysis, as seen in Section 5.3.3.

5.3.2.2 Status Definitions In the second phase of the execution loop, the status variable of each aircraft is deterministically updated using the other state information. In our model, the status values are as follows:

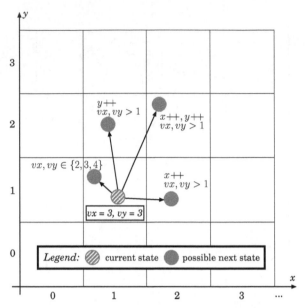

FIGURE 5.5 Possible movements from a state satisfying $vx = 3$, $vy = 3$ ("restricted" model).

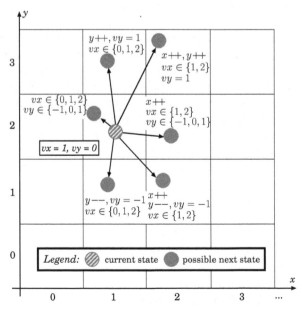

FIGURE 5.6 Possible movements from a state satisfying $vx = 1$, $vy = 0$ ("restricted" model).

out: not in the monitored zone

$$\equiv (x = 0) \wedge (y = 0) \wedge (z = 0)$$

taxi: on the ground, either at low speed or not with a runway heading

$$\equiv (z = 1) \wedge ((|vx| \le TS \wedge |vy| \le TS) \vee (vx \ne 0))$$

takeoff: on the ground, with a runway heading, accelerating

$$\equiv (z = 1) \wedge (|vy| > TS) \wedge (vx = 0) \wedge (a_y \ge 0)$$

rollout: on the ground, with a runway heading, decelerating

$$\equiv (z = 1) \wedge (|vy| > TS) \wedge (vx = 0) \wedge (a_y < 0)$$

climbout: airborne, with a runway heading, strictly positive vertical speed

$$\equiv (z > 1) \wedge (vx = 0) \wedge (vz > 0)$$

land: airborne, with a runway heading, negative vertical speed

$$\equiv (z > 1) \wedge (vx = 0) \wedge (vz \le 0)$$

flythru: airborne, not in *climbout* or *land* mode

$$\equiv (z > 1) \wedge (vx \ne 0)$$

5.3.2.3 Setting the Alarm The third and most important phase of the RSM algorithm is setting the alarm flag for every target. In pseudocode, this corresponds to a single variable assignment statement: Set the (Boolean) value of each *alarm$_i$* based on different combinations of the current values of the other variables, as listed in the operational state matrix of Table 5.1.

TABLE 5.1 Operational State Matrix for Setting the RSM Alarm

Target → Taxi		*takeoff*	*climbout*	*land*	*rollout*	*flythru*
Ownship ↓						
taxi	–	a ∧ f	a ∧ f	a ∧ f	a ∧ c ∧ f	–
takeoff	a ∧ f	d ∨ e	d ∨ e	d ∨ e	a ∨ d	b ∧ c
climbout	a ∧ f	d ∨ e	d ∨ e	d ∨ e	d ∨ e	b ∧ c
land	a ∧ f	d ∨ e	d ∨ e	d ∨ e	a ∨ d	b ∧ c
rollout	a ∧ c ∧ f	a ∨ d	a ∨ d	a ∨ d	d ∨ e	b ∧ c
flythru	–	b ∧ c	b ∧ c	b ∧ c	b ∧ c	–

a, distance closing; b, in takeoff or landing path; c, distance less than minimum separation; d, takeoff or landing in the same direction, less than minimum separation; e, takeoff or landing in the opposite direction, closing; f, taxi or stationary on or near runway.

Modeling this rather complex assignment statement in a Petri net is difficult because of two factors. First, predicates such as "distance is closing" or "in the takeoff path" potentially involve geometry and linear equations and are difficult to express in a discretized model. However, certain factors help make our task easier: The designers kept the concepts simple and analytic geometry can be avoided on a case-by-case basis. For example, "distance to target i is closing" should normally be evaluated by comparing the value of the expression $\sqrt{(x_0 - x_i)^2 + (y_0 - y_i)^2 + (z_0 - z_i)^2}$ in the current and previous states. This could further imply that the previous location of each target should be stored in a set of auxiliary variables, say $oldx_i$, $oldy_i$, $oldz_i$, further increasing the state space. However, this can be avoided by exploiting the information derived from each aircraft's status. For example, if ownship is taxiing and target i is taking off, we know that $z_0 = 1, vx_0, vy_0 \leq TS, z_i = 1, vx_i = 0, |vy_i| > TS$, and $vz_0 = vz_i = 0$; that is, the target is on the ground, lined up with the runway, and moving faster than the taxi speed limit. For the distance to be closing, it is enough that ownship is in front of the target, depending on which direction this is moving. Hence, in this situation, the predicate can be expressed as

$$a \equiv (vy_i > 0 \wedge y_0 > y_i) \vee (vy_i < 0 \wedge y_0 < y_i).$$

We can similarly express the other predicates as follows:

$$b \wedge c \equiv (vy_0 > 0 \wedge y_0 \leq y_i \leq y_0 + 1 \wedge |x_0 - x_i| \leq 1 \wedge z_i \leq 2)$$

$$(vy_0 < 0 \wedge y_0 - 1 \leq y_i \leq y_0 \wedge |x_0 - x_i| \leq 1 \wedge z_i \leq 2),$$

$$d \equiv vy_0 \cdot vy_i > 0 \wedge |x_0 - x_i| \leq 1 \wedge |y_0 - y_i| \leq 1,$$

$$e \equiv (vy_0 > 0 \wedge vy_i < 0 \wedge y_i \geq y_0) \vee (vy_0 < 0 \wedge vy_i > 0 \wedge y_i \leq y_0),$$

$$f \equiv 1 < x_i < max_x,$$

where the above example formulae are derived for the following pairs of states, respectively: $b \wedge c$ for takeoff–flythru, d and e for takeoff–takeoff.

Table 5.2 shows the state-space measurements on the SMART model with one target. Missing entries in the table correspond to parameter choices that required excessive runtime or memory.

Our attempts to use other tools have failed: The symbolic model checker NuSMV runs out of memory even before starting the generation, as the binary decision diagram (BDD) encoding of the transition relation is too large, while the explicit model checker SPIN explores a very small fraction of the state space (less than $1/10^6$ even when using partial order reduction) to be able to expose any problem.

TABLE 5.2   State-Space Generation Measurements on the RSM Model

$max_{speed} \rightarrow$	2	3	4	5
↓ Grid size	State-space generation time (seconds)			
$3 \times 5 \times 4$	75.92	105.17	179.28	252.25
$3 \times 7 \times 4$	195.54	324.65	604.23	805.95
$3 \times 10 \times 5$	995.18	2212.24	4668.55	7348.27
$5 \times 10 \times 7$	48257.30	–	–	–
	Memory consumption (MB)			
$3 \times 5 \times 4$	11.19	21.20	32.58	49.39
$3 \times 7 \times 4$	18.27	36.02	56.91	87.25
$3 \times 10 \times 5$	42.59	83.53	138.56	218.85
$5 \times 10 \times 7$	246.22	–	–	–

5.3.3 Model Checking RSM

The verification effort was concentrated on determining whether the operational matrix in Table 5.1 ensures the absence of missed alarm scenarios. Since a formal description of this requirement was not included in the protocol specification, we had to explore different ways to express this property.

The following predicates are used to define the notions of interest (subscripts o and t refer to ownship and target, respectively):

$$detect \equiv phase_o = detect \land phase_t = detect$$
$$sep \equiv distance(o, t) > \text{minimum separation}$$
$$alarm \equiv alarm_t = \text{true}$$
$$track \equiv status_o \notin \{taxi, flythru\} \lor status_t \notin \{taxi, flythru\}$$

5.3.3.1 Safety Property

Is there a tracked state where minimum separation is not satisfied and the alarm is off?

- In CTL syntax: $EF(detect \land track \land \neg alarm)$

The model checker returns a witness to this condition where the predicate "distance is closing" is not satisfied in the current state. This is the case of the third snapshot of Figure 5.7. However, this might not correspond to an unwanted behavior, since the alarm might have been set in a previous state, when the minimum separation was first lost. The value of the alarm variable also depends on whether the alarm is "aged" or not for a few more cycles.

We observe that the "memoryless" nature of the query influences the result, as we look at the property in a particular snapshot of time, without considering

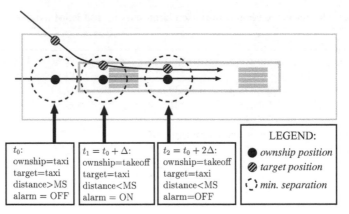

FIGURE 5.7   Scenario for violation of the first safety property (at ground level).

the sequence of events leading to the current state. To get a better understanding of the system, we next investigate the states of the system immediately after the minimum separation distance between two aircraft is violated.

5.3.3.2   The Transition That Causes Loss of Separation

Is there a state where minimum separation is lost by transitioning to the current state while the alarm is off?

- $EF(detect \wedge track \wedge sep \wedge E[(\neg detect)\ U\ (detect \wedge track \wedge \neg sep \wedge \neg alarm)])$

A witness for this query (see Fig. 5.8) has ownship in a landing or climbout state, the target flying across the runway faster than ownship, moving within separation distance from the side, at an angle. The condition for setting an alarm in this circumstance is "distance less than minimum separation **and** target in takeoff or landing path." The second term is not satisfied; hence, no alarm is raised. Aircraft can actually collide (trajectories intersect in Fig. 5.8), while none of the participants gets a warning.

This case was corrected by the RSM developers by adding "distance less than minimum separation" as part of the criterion for this combination of states.

Note that we include the predicate *track* in both states (before and after the transition), as incursions are defined for at least one aircraft taking off or landing. However, this additional constraint could mask some other undesired behaviors. Therefore, we next investigate a more general property.

5.3.3.3   A Stronger Safety Property

Is there a tracked state where minimum separation is lost, reachable without ever previously setting the alarm?

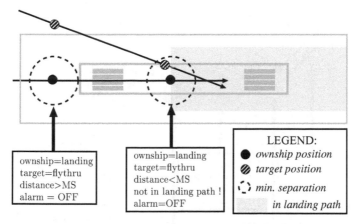

FIGURE 5.8   Scenario 2, airborne: flythru target in conflict with landing aircraft.

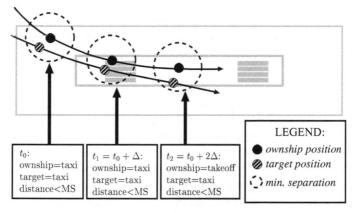

FIGURE 5.9   Scenario 3 (at ground level): taxiing target interferes with ownship taking off.

- $E[(\neg alarm) \cup (detect \wedge track \wedge \neg sep \wedge \neg alarm)]$

The model checker finds several scenarios that satisfy this query. As shown in Figure 5.9, the aircraft may enter the monitored area taxiing (not aligned to the runway) and already at close distance to each other. Note that this combination of states is explicitly ignored by the algorithm, since it does not fit the definition of an incursion. However, once on the runway, ownship can change direction and align itself to the runway. Thereafter, it is categorized as a takeoff (or climbout, if it becomes airborne). The other aircraft can stay within minimum separation, but not closing in: It can be either behind ownship or, more dangerously, in front of it. No alarm is raised because the criterion "distance is closing" is, again, not satisfied. If the distance between two aircraft

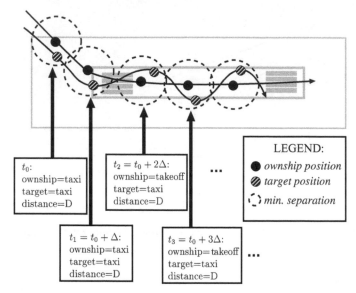

FIGURE 5.10 Scenario 4: (at ground level): target zigzags around ownship taking off.

at entry is very small, there might not be enough time for an escape maneuver, even if, later on, the alarm is indeed triggered by closing in.

Figure 5.9 shows a counterexample to this last safety property. An identical scenario exists for the airborne pair of states that is not tracked (the *flythru* status).

In order to determine whether this situation is of real concern or not, we have to look at possible continuations of the scenario after the potentially bad state is reached. If the distance is closing in the next state, a warning will be issued and the "missed alarm" situation will cease to exist. One way for a malicious agent to perpetuate the problem is shown in Figure 5.10. The target can stay within minimum separation radius for a longer period of time if it "zigzags" and at each radar update has the same discretized distance to ownship. The target *must* zigzag to maintain the distance, since following a parallel path to ownship will cause RSM to consider it as taking off. The alarm criteria for the new combination of operational states is "taking off in the same direction and distance less than minimum separation." Therefore, an alarm will be issued as soon as the target stops zigzagging.

The case when the target is not an aircraft but a vehicle, such as a service truck, adds a degree of freedom for malicious behavior by the target (see scenario 5, Fig. 5.11). Initially, ground vehicles were always considered in taxi mode by the protocol, regardless of their speed, heading, and physical coordinates. Therefore, as in scenario 4, the target may follow ownship at close distance, and even continue chasing ownship after it is lined up for takeoff and

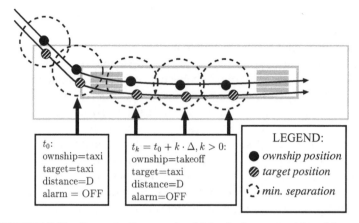

FIGURE 5.11   Scenario 5: ground vehicle shadows ownship taking off.

accelerating. No flag will be raised for the same reasons as in scenario 4. The RSM developers took into account our findings and eliminated the special treatment given to ground vehicles. This fully addresses the situation in scenario 5.

The situation in scenario 4 was not addressed. It was deemed of far less concern, as it is extremely difficult to realize in practice, even intentionally by a very skillful saboteur. At the same time, there is some benefit in exposing it: The designer is aware of this low-probability event. Also, by the fact that is the only remaining unwanted behavior in the system, it serves as a validation for phase 3 of the RSM algorithm.

5.4 DISCUSSION

5.4.1 Lessons Learned

With all its inevitable shortcomings, the verification of RSM has had an undeniable value. The designers of the RSM algorithm were presented with a list of findings, which were not exposed during the testing activities, involving aircraft and ground vehicles, already under way at Dallas/Fort Worth International Airport.

Testing is still essential to certification, regardless of the costs, because it is performed on the product itself, not on abstract models. In some instances, however, the costs of testing can be considerable. Each of the two testing sessions (prior to our formal analysis team joining the effort) required the cooperation of several parties (airport officials, air traffic managers, airlines) to secure the resources: two airport runways reserved for an entire day, volunteer pilots, test evaluation engineers. Additionally, a custom-built van was needed to simulate an aircraft on the ground [53]. In light of these facts, it is arguably more productive to include the formal verification task as early as possible in the design process.

The merit of the model-based technique is that, besides being considerably less expensive, it is more comprehensive. We were able to analyze all possible scenarios in our model and found scenarios of potential concern that occur with extremely low probability or under very peculiar conditions. These are almost impossible to expose during either testing procedures, which usually afford no more than a dozen test flights a day, or simulation sessions. When compared with the actual state-space sizes (of the order of 10^{13}–10^{42} states, depending on the choice of parameters), this shows the need for exhaustive analysis. Another outcome of the formal analysis was that identifying the problems in the abstract models and suggesting modifications to the protocol to eliminate them has significantly increased the level of confidence in the correctness of the design.

The success was facilitated by many factors: There were clear specifications and a good path of communication between design engineers and the formal methods team, while the application itself had the "right" size (amenable for full state-space construction) and the "right" blend of continuous and discrete-state components.

5.4.2 Level of Effort

The verification of RSM was a medium-scale project with a duration of 12 months. A team of three people worked in various stages of the analysis, for a total of 9 man-months of work. Of this, approximately 6 man-months was dedicated to modeling decisions, during which three regular meetings with the design engineers were scheduled. The final 3 man-months was spent with the verification per se: formulating queries, analyzing, and synthesizing the answers. The understanding of RSM was greatly helped by the designers' effort to keep the specification and implementation as clear as possible. Overall, while the human effort was predominant in all stages of the analysis, mostly due to the lack of automation in the modeling process and to the novelty of the problem area for the modelers, the impact of efficient model-checking tools was crucial in completing the study.

5.4.3 Fault Tolerance

An aspect not covered in the above RSM analysis is fault tolerance. While our work verifies the correct operation of RSM under no-fault assumptions, the presence of faults on the data link may significantly impact the correct operation of the algorithm. This type of analysis requires the inclusion of probabilistic aspects in the model. A natural extension of this study is to include faulty behaviors, of either benign nature (missed or late updates) or malicious/Byzantine (inconsistent data between participants).

5.4.4 Challenges

Besides the habitual challenges of making model checking practical (mitigating huge state spaces, arguing for the soundness of the abstraction), the RSM experience also revealed some novel facts. First, a good discretization method and powerful tools could be quintessential in tackling the complexity of this type of applications. Some embedded applications immediately suggest a discretization rule. In this case, the algorithm uses snapshots of aircraft positions taken at regular time intervals, so that in fact the state of the system is already discretized. On the negative side, verifying the actual C code was still out of reach.

In what regard the efficiency of evaluating temporal logic formulae, not all types of properties could be efficiently verified. In general, for safety and reachability properties, good strategies exist, while liveness and fairness properties are more costly to evaluate.

Overall, we can conclude that model checking is a viable alternative for validating the correctness of avionics protocols, given its ability to find nontrivial errors that are usually not exposed during simulation or testing.

REFERENCES

1. C. Adams, M. Consiglio, K. Jones, and D. Williams. SATS HVO Operational Concept: Nominal Operations, 2003.
2. R. Alur and D. L. Dill. Automata for modeling real-time systems. In *Automata, Languages and Programming, 17th International Colloquium, (ICALP)*, pp. 322–335, 1990.
3. T. Ball, R. Majumdar, T. Millstein, and S. K. Rajamani. Automatic predicate abstraction of C programs. *ACM SIGPLAN Notices*, 36(5):203–213, 2001.
4. S. O. Beskenis, D. F. Green, P. V. Hyer, and E. J. Johnson. Integrated Display System for Low Visibility Landing and Surface Operations. NASA Contractor Report 208446, NASA Langley, Hampton, VA, July 1998.
5. T. Bochot, P. Virelizier, H. Waeselynck, and V. Wiels. Model checking flight control systems: The airbus experience. In *ICSE Companion*, pp. 18–27, 2009.
6. R. E. Bryant. Graph-based algorithms for Boolean function manipulation. *IEEE Transactions on Computers*, 35(8):677–691, 1986.
7. P. Buchholz, G. Ciardo, S. Donatelli, and P. Kemper. Complexity of memory-efficient Kronecker operations with applications to the solution of Markov models. *INFORMS Journal on Computing*, 12(3):203–222, 2000.
8. T. Bultan, R. Gerber, and W. Pugh. Model-checking concurrent systems with unbounded integer variables: Symbolic representations, approximations, and experimental results. *ACM Transactions on Programming Languages and Systems*, 21(4):747–789, 1999.
9. J. R. Burch, E. M. Clarke, and D. E. Long. Symbolic model checking with partitioned transition relations. In A. Halaas and P.B. Denyer, eds., *International Conference on*

Very Large Scale Integration, pp. 49–58, Edinburgh, Scotland, August 1991. IFIP Transactions, North-Holland.

10. V. Carreño and C. Muñoz. Formal analysis of parallel landing scenarios. In *Proceedings of the 19th Digital Avionics Systems Conference*, Philadelphia, 2000.

11. W. Chan, R. Anderson, P. Beame, S. Burns, F. Modugno, D. Notkin, and J. Reese. Model checking large software specifications. *IEEE Transactions on Software Engineering*, 24(7):498–520, 1998.

12. D. M. Chapiro. Globally-asynchronous locally-synchronous systems. PhD thesis, Stanford University, October 1984.

13. Y. Choi, S. Rayadurgam, and M. P. E. Heimdahl. Automatic abstraction for model checking software software systems with interrelated numeric constraints. In *Proceedings of the 9th ACM SIGSOFT Symposium on the Foundation of Software Engeneering (FSE)*, pp. 164–174, volume 26, 5, ACM Press, New York, September 10–14, 2001.

14. G. Ciardo. What a structural world. In R. German and B. Haverkort, eds., *Proceedings of the 9th International Workshop on Petri Nets and Performance Models (PNPM'01)*, pp. 3–16, Keynote paper, IEEE Computer Society Press, Aachen, Germany, September 2001.

15. G. Ciardo, et al. SMART: Stochastic Model Checking Analyzer for Reliability and Timing, User Manual. 2004. Available at: http://www.cs.ucr.edu/~ciardo/SMART/.

16. G. Ciardo, R. L. Jones III, A. S. Miner, and R. Siminiceanu. Logic and stochastic modeling with SMART. *Performance Evaluation*, 63(6):578–608, 2006.

17. G. Ciardo, G. Lüttgen, and R. Siminiceanu. Efficient symbolic state-space construction for asynchronous systems. In M. Nielsen and D. Simpson, eds., *Proceedings of the 21st International Conference on Applications and Theory of Petri Nets*, pp. 103–122, LNCS 1825, Springer-Verlag, Aarhus, Denmark, June 2000.

18. G. Ciardo, G. Lüttgen, and R. Siminiceanu. Saturation: An efficient iteration strategy for symbolic state space generation. In T. Margaria and W. Yi, eds., *Proceedings of the Tools and Algorithms for the Construction and Analysis of Systems (TACAS)*, pp. 328–342, LNCS 2031, Springer-Verlag, Genova, Italy, April 2001.

19. G. Ciardo, R. Marmorstein, and R. Siminiceanu. Saturation unbound. In H. Garavel and J. Hatcliff, eds., *Proceedings of the Tools and Algorithms for the Construction and Analysis of Systems (TACAS)*, pp. 379–393, LNCS 2619, Springer-Verlag, Warsaw, Poland, April 2003.

20. G. Ciardo, R. Marmorstein, and R. Siminiceanu. The saturation algorithm for symbolic state space exploration. *Software Tools for Technology Transfer*, 8(1):4–25, 2006.

21. G. Ciardo and A. S. Miner. A data structure for the efficient Kronecker solution of GSPNs. In P. Buchholz, ed., *Proceedings of the 8th International Workshop on Petri Nets and Performance Models (PNPM'99)*, pp. 22–31, IEEE Computer Society Press, Zaragoza, Spain, September 1999.

22. G. Ciardo and R. Siminiceanu. Using edge-valued decision diagrams for symbolic generation of shortest paths. In M. D. Aagaard and J. W. O'Leary, eds., *Proceedings of the Fourth International Conference on Formal Methods in Computer-Aided Design (FMCAD)*, pp. 256–273, LNCS 2517, Springer-Verlag, Portland, OR, November 2002.

23. G. Ciardo and R. Siminiceanu. Structural symbolic CTL model checking of asynchronous systems. In W. Hunt, Jr. and F. Somenzi, eds., *Computer Aided Verification (CAV'03)*, pp. 40–53, LNCS 2725, Springer-Verlag, Boulder, CO, July 2003.

24. E. Clarke, D. Grumberg, and D. Long. Model checking and abstraction. *ACM Transactions on Programming Languages and Systems*, 16(5):1512–1542, 1994.

25. E. M. Clarke and E. A. Emerson. Design and synthesis of synchronization skeletons using branching time temporal logic. In *Proceedings of the IBM Workshop on Logics of Programs*, pp. 52–71, LNCS 131, Springer-Verlag, London, UK, 1981.

26. M. Colón and T. E. Uribe. Generating finite-state abstractions of reactive systems using decision procedures. In *Proceedings of the Computer Aided Verification (CAV)*, 1998.

27. J. C. Corbett, M. B. Dwyer, J. Hatcliff, S. Laubach, C. S. Păsăreanu, Robby, and H. Zheng. Bandera: Extracting finite-state models from Java source code. In *International Conference on Software Engineering*, pp. 439–448, 2000.

28. P. Cousot. Proving the absence of run-time errors in safety-critical avionics code. In *EMSOFT*, pp. 7–9, 2007.

29. P. Cousot and R. Cousot. Abstract interpretation: A unified lattice model for static analysis of programs by construction or approximation of fixpoints. In *POPL*, pp. 238–252, 1977.

30. D. Dams, R. Gerth, G. Dohmen, R. Herrmann, P. Kelb, and H. Pargmann. Model checking using adaptive state and data abstraction. In *Proceedings of the 6th International Computer Aided Verification Conference*, pp. 455–467, 1994.

31. M. Davio. Kronecker products and shuffle algebra. *IEEE Transactions on Computers*, C-30:116–125, 1981.

32. G. Dowek, C. Muñoz, and V. Carreño. Abstract model of the sats concept of operations: Initial results and recommendations. NASA Contractor Report 213006, NASA Langley, Hampton, VA, March 2004.

33. B. Dutertre and M. Sorea. Modeling and verification of a fault-tolerant real-time startup protocol using calendar automata. In *Formal Techniques, Modelling and Analysis of Timed and Fault-Tolerant Systems, Joint International Conferences on Formal Modelling and Analysis of Timed Systems (FORMATS/FTRTFT)*, pp. 199–214, 2004.

34. S. Graf and H. Saïdi. Construction of abstract state graphs with PVS. In *Proceedings of the Computer Aided Verification (CAV)*, 1997.

35. D. F. Green, Jr. Runway Safety Monitor algorithm for runway incursion detection and alerting. NASA Contractor Report 211416, NASA Langley, Hampton, VA, January 2002.

36. J. Hatcliff, M. Dwyer, and S. Laubach. Staging static analyses using abstraction-based program specialization. *Lecture Notes in Computer Science*, 1490:134–151, 1998.

37. M. P. E. Heimdahl. Experiences and lessons from the analysis of TCAS II. In *Proceedings of the 1996 ACM SIGSOFT International Symposium on Software Testing and Analysis*, pp. 79–83. ACM Press, 1996.

38. C. Heitmeyer, J. Kirby, Jr., B. Labaw, M. Archer, and R. Bharadwaj. Using abstraction and model checking to detect safety violations in requirements specifications. *IEEE Transactions on Software Engineering*, 24(11):927–948, 1998.

39. D. Jackson, M. Thomas, and L. I. Millett. *Software for Dependable Systems: Sufficient Evidence?* National Academies Press, 2007.

40. D. Jensen. NASA's solution to runway incursion. *Avionics Magazine*, pp. 34–39, November 2003.

41. T. Kam, T. Villa, R. Brayton, and A. Sangiovanni-Vincentelli. Multi-valued decision diagrams: Theory and applications. *Multiple-Valued Logic*, 4(1–2):9–62, 1998.

42. S. Kimura and E. M. Clarke. A parallel algorithm for constructing binary decision diagrams. In *Proceedings of the International Conference on Computer Design (ICCD)*, pp. 220–223, IEEE Computer Society Press, Cambridge, MA, September 1990.

43. E. A. Lee. Computing needs time. *Communications of the ACM*, 52(5):70–79, 2009.

44. C. Livadas, J. Lygeros, and N. A. Lynch. High-level modeling and analysis of TCAS. In *Proceedings of the IEEE Real-Time Systems Symposium (RTSS)*, 1999.

45. Z. Manna, M. Colón, B. Finkbeiner, H. Sipma, and T. E. Uribe. Abstraction and modular verification of infinite-state reactive systems. In *Proceedings of the Requirements Targeting Software and Systems Engineering (RTSE)*, 1997.

46. K. L. McMillan. *Symbolic Model Checking*. Kluwer, 1993.

47. A. S. Miner. Efficient solution of GSPNs using canonical matrix diagrams. In R. German and B. Haverkort, eds., *Proceedings of the 9th International Workshop on Petri Nets and Performance Models (PNPM'01)*, pp. 101–110, IEEE Computer Society Press, Aachen, Germany, September 2001.

48. A. S. Miner and G. Ciardo. Efficient reachability set generation and storage using decision diagrams. In H. Kleijn and S. Donatelli, eds., *Proceedings of the 20th International Conference on Applications and Theory of Petri Nets*, pp. 6–25, LNCS 1639, Springer-Verlag, Williamsburg, VA, June 1999.

49. T. Murata. Petri nets: Properties, analysis and applications. *Proceedings of the IEEE*, 77(4):541–579, 1989.

50. K. S. Namjoshi and R. P. Kurshan. Syntactic program transformations for automatic abstraction. In *12th Conference on Computer Aided Verification*, number 1855 in LNCS, 2000.

51. J. Souyris, V. Wiels, D. Delmas, and H. Delseny. Formal verification of avionics software products. In *FM*, pp. 532–546, 2009.

52. S. Tasiran, R. Alur, R. P. Kurshan, and R. K. Brayton. Verifying abstractions of timed systems. In *Proceedings of the International Conference on Concurrency Theory (CONCUR)*, 1996.

53. J. Timmerman. Runway Incursion Prevention System, ADS-B and DGPS data link analysis, Dallas—Ft. Worth International Airport. NASA Contractor Report 211242, NASA Langley, Hampton, VA, November 2001.

54. P. Wolper and B. Boigelot. Verifying systems with infinite but regular state spaces. In *Proceedings of the Computer Aided Verification (CAV)*, 1998.

55. Y. Zhao and G. Ciardo. Symbolic CTL model checking of asynchronous systems using constrained saturation. In Z. Liu and A. P. Ravn, eds., *Proceedings of the 7th International Symposium on Automated Technology for Verification and Analysis (ATVA)*, pp. 368–381, LNCS 5799, Springer-Verlag, Macao SAR, China, October 2009.

TELECOMMUNICATIONS

TELECOMMUNICATIONS

CHAPTER 6

APPLYING FORMAL METHODS TO TELECOMMUNICATION SERVICES WITH ACTIVE NETWORKS

MARÍA DEL MAR GALLARDO, JESÚS MARTÍNEZ,
and PEDRO MERINO

Dpto. de Lenguajes y Ciencias de la Computacion, University of Málaga, Málaga, Spain

6.1 OVERVIEW

This chapter examines the application of formal methods to a recent paradigm for developing telecommunication services, the active networks approach [7, 21]. Work dealing with the formalization and verification of protocols already exists within this application domain. However, we have found that more powerful methods can be used for this purpose. In particular, we present the use of one of the most prestigious tools, SPIN, and we explain some of the advantages it offers. The main goal of this chapter is to provide a survey of the use of formal methods in this application domain. An additional goal is to compare our approach with previous ones.

We start by describing proposals dealing with active networks and formal methods: Maude [12, 28], ACTIVESPEC [23], Unity [5], and the Verisim framework [4]. Then, we describe our recent work using the SPIN model checker [17, 19].

In order to be fair, we describe the advantages/disadvantages of every approach focusing on the same three main aspects: *formal modeling of active networks*, *property specification*, and their *analysis capabilities*. Since the SPIN approach is novel, we devote more space to its description.

Formal Methods for Industrial Critical Systems: A Survey of Applications, First Edition.
Edited by Stefania Gnesi and Tiziana Margaria.
© 2013 IEEE. Published 2013 by John Wiley & Sons, Inc.

The chapter is organized as follows: Sections 6.2 and 6.3 contain a brief description of the problem domain. Section 6.4 presents some previous experiences in the literature. Section 6.5 focuses on the use of the explicit model checker SPIN for modeling and verifying active services with examples. Finally, we give some conclusions.

6.2 ACTIVE NETWORKS

Users of current telecommunication networks are constantly demanding new and more powerful services. This is the case of videoconferencing services, real-time applications, group communications, mobility, or peer-to-peer services. The main motivation to develop active networks in the 1990s was the lack of flexibility of computer networks and the Internet to incorporate these new protocols and services. This lack of flexibility has at least two origins. On the one hand, standardization bodies such as ITU-T, IEEE, or IETF require a long process to get a new protocol approved and implemented in most network nodes and terminals. On the other hand, the incorporation of new services may require restarting many critical nodes in the network, with serious effects on millions of users.

The basic idea of active networks is to open some nodes with specific application programming interfaces (APIs) that allow the fast implementation of new experimental services. Since the early 1990s, several communities have concentrated their efforts in defining node architectures, execution platforms, and description languages to be used by developers. In this context, it is worth noting the work done by IEEE toward the IEEE P1520 Standards Initiative for Programmable Network Interfaces, and the series of International Working Conference on Active Networks (IWAN) conferences organized by the Technical Committee 6 (TC6—Communications Systems) of the International Federation for Information Processing (IFIP).

The introduction of this paradigm has produced reusable technologies in aspects such as agents, mobile code, middleware, operating systems, reconfigurable hardware, packet scheduling in routers, routing protocols, network management or secure code injection, and execution. With regard to applications, active networks have a reasonable impact on application domains such as electronic mail [22], video distribution [6, 16], and overlay and virtual networks [25].

Although the initial interest of having an open Internet has now decreased, all these technologies have given rise to new opportunities in the fields of network virtualization, ad hoc networks, autonomic networks, sensor networks, and content-aware distribution, among others.

See References 20 and 21 for a complete picture of this technology and its applications and the future reuse of these advances.

6.3 THE CAPSULE APPROACH

An active network allows the introduction of new services, which can be deployed faster than if they were to follow the usually slow standardization process. One way to introduce the new services is allowing routers and/or switches (nodes) to perform customized computations that can modify the contents of a packet, create new packets, or even store and read information in the node.

Several programming models for active nodes were presented in References 2, 27, 30, and 31, along with other proposals for packet formats and processing. The effort of communicating all existing platforms relied on two standards. The first one was an architecture for active networking, which considers different execution environments (EEs), thus allowing different kinds of nodes [29]. With this approach, the functionality of an active network node is divided between the EE, responsible for providing network abstractions, and the node operating system (NodeOS), which manages access to the network resources. As shown in Figure 6.1, this architecture allows for the presence of multiple EEs in an active node, where the expressive power provided by the environment could be a complete Turing machine. The NodeOS is responsible for implementing the set of abstractions that will provide access to the node resources. This access should be protected by a security enforcement engine that requests the code's credentials before performing critical tasks. The operating system also gives access to the communication channels to send and receive packets, along with some restricted data storage capabilities.

Another important standard in this novel paradigm was the definition of a transport protocol (ANEP) for active packets on top of the nonactive Internet [1]. This protocol is used to support the worldwide active network abone. The

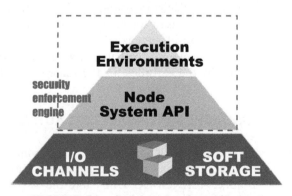

FIGURE 6.1 Active network architecture.

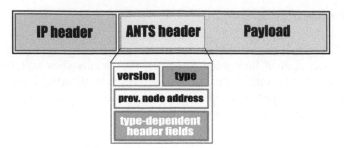

FIGURE 6.2 The capsule format used by ANTS.

Active Network Transport System (ANTS) programming model constitutes one of the most used active architectures. It includes a Java toolkit where protocols can be automatically deployed at both the intermediate nodes and at the end systems by a mobile code technique. Packets, called *capsules*, are processed according to their specific code (payload). This code can use operations available in the node as four kinds of primitives: *capsule manipulation* (accessing the header and the payload), *control operations* (allowing the capsule to create new capsules, copy and discard themselves), *environment access* (reading state information in the node, like routing tables), and *node storage* (manipulating an existing store with application defined objects). Every capsule is identified by its type and its payload (see Fig. 6.2). One active network protocol is supposed to be implemented with a number of instances of different kinds of capsules.

The code for processing a capsule is set at the sender end and cannot change within the network. The processing routine for the capsule has limited capabilities, since it is defined by distrusted users. This capsule is forwarded by nonactive nodes using routing information, but the code is only executed on particular nodes. Therefore, after receiving the capsule, active nodes execute its associated routine. The encapsulated code is used to decide if it will continue being forwarded to its destination, a decision usually included at the end of the processing code. The mechanism used to transport the code depends on the real implementation. The proposal suggested for ANTS is to load code on demand and to cache it to improve performance. By default, the soft storage in the nodes is only shared by the capsules for the same protocol.

6.4 PREVIOUS APPROACHES ON ANALYZING ACTIVE NETWORKS

This section focuses on surveying existing proposals in the literature that use formal methods to describe and analyze active networks. The selected tools and approaches are Maude, ACTIVESPEC, Unity, and the Verisim framework. The next section will be devoted to model-checking active networks with the SPIN model checker.

6.4.1 Maude

Maude is a reflective language supporting rewriting logic specification [24] and programming for a wide range of applications. The support of logical reflection makes Maude remarkably extensible. It supports an extensible algebra of module composition operations, allowing advanced metaprogramming and metalanguage applications. In many applications, Maude is used to create executable environments for different logics, theorem provers, languages, and models of computation. Regarding active network specifications, Maude has been used in the modeling of the reliable broadcast protocol (rbp) [12] along with the operational semantics of the plan language [28] developed within the context of the Switchware project [2]. In Maude, the specification of an active network architecture must be built from scratch; that is, we have to formalize nodes, networks (node instances and their relationships), EEs, and their concurrency model, as well as the execution language semantics for variables, expressions, sentences, node resource manipulation, or routing policies. For instance, in Reference 12, the authors have to build a complete formalization of primitives for message passing, which will act as the main abstraction for network communications.

Figure 6.3 shows one of the modeling approaches used to create a rewriting rule to describe a broadcast send. The left part of the arrow indicates the previous situation, and the right part is the update of the rule.

Maude version 2 now incorporates a model checker [13], which allows the specification of propositional temporal logic formulas. It was used in Reference 28 to find a bug in a reduced version of their proposed active configuration. Unfortunately, there were no details regarding this reduction of the original Maude model carried out prior to being analyzed using the model checker. A thorough study of Reference 13 shows that this module needed further testing in more realistic environments.

```
crl [Send] :
 < A : Node | nbs : OIDSET,
             states : states(state(A,passive),IDSTATUSPFUN),
             parents : IDIDPFUN,
             seqNos : seqNos(seqNo(A,N),IDINTPFUN),
             nbsStates : IDIDSTATUSPFUN >
 =>
 < A : Node | states : assignIdStatusPFun(IDSTATUSPFUN, A, active),
             parents : assignIdIdPFun(IDIDPFUN, A, A),
             seqNos : assignIdIntPFun(IDINTPFUN, A, N + 1),
             nbsStates : assignAllIdIdStatusPFun(
                         IDIDSTATUSPFUN, A, OIDSET, active) >
 (multimsg N + 1 To OIDSET From A Src A)
 if OIDSET =/= mtnbs .
```

FIGURE 6.3 Rewriting rule to model broadcasting ad hoc in Maude (extracted from Reference 12).

```
Packets [
  Address : TYPE,      % Addresses
  PacketType : TYPE, % Packet type identifiers
  Payload : TYPE       % Payload data type
] : THEORY BEGIN

PacketID : TYPE+ Packet : TYPE = [#
  ptype : PacketType,
  src : Address,
  dest : Address,
  pid : PacketID,
  payload : Payload
#] packet_exists : AXIOM (EXISTS (pkt : Packet) : TRUE) IMPORTING
Queue[Packet]

END Packets
```

FIGURE 6.4   ActiveSPEC capsule definition (extracted from Reference 23).

6.4.2   ActiveSPEC

ActiveSPEC [23] constitutes a framework to formally specify active services and resources using advanced features of the pvs [9] theorem prover. The methodology provided includes definitions for packets (see Fig. 6.4), nodes, and a predefined set of services, security policies, and resources. Developers may use the theorem prover to verify that a packet processed by an EE satisfies some authorization requirements. Security policies will include the definition of preconditions and postconditions to be fulfilled before and after the execution of the packet, respectively. Currently, these specifications are entered manually by following the recommendations of the framework. Figure 6.4 shows the definition of capsules (packets) in ActiveSPEC along with a precondition indicating the existence of a packet in a queue before it is consumed.

A similar proposal, called ActiveNodeSPEC, analyzes the concurrent use of resources in a node. None of these frameworks are concerned with protocol safety, because they do not implement mechanisms to execute any active packet content. Because they focus on different aspects, ActiveSPEC and ActiveNodeSPEC must be used independently of each other.

The framework supports the definition of properties and security policies as pvs theorems. Therefore, ActiveSPEC uses theorem proving as its analysis technique, which usually requests interactive verification.

6.4.3   Unity

Unity [8] is a small parallel language that allows process composition. The execution of sentences is done in a nondeterministic manner from available ones. It does not support types, control flow, or an implicit execution sequence order. This formalism was used to model an active protocol in Reference 5. The authors designed an abstract interface representing those programmable capabilities exported by an active node, independently of the active platform

```
Program {Node} Program at each active node v initially
   NO v.state, discCnt, errCnt = idle, 0, 0
assign
   N1 < < []x : v.inC[x] E v.inC :
   v.state, v.inC[x], v.Msg, v.LH := newPkt, tail(v.inC[x]), head(v.inC[x]), x >
   || < || i :: v.rt.i.usage := 0 )
   > if v.idle ^ (v.inC[x] != null)
   ...
```

FIGURE 6.5   Part of a node definition in Unity (extracted from Reference 5).

```
alarm LoopInv[at][nxt][dst] = sendroute[at][dst] when
   ((at!=nxt) && (at!=dst) && (nxt!=dst) &&
   (obs_nexthop[at][dst] == nxt) &&
   ((obs_seqno[at][dst] > obs_seqno[nxt][dst]) ||
   (obs_seqno[at][dst] == obs_seqno[nxt][dst]) &&
   (obs_seqno[at][dst] <= obs_seqno[at][dst])))
```

FIGURE 6.6   Example of a property described in MEDL (see Reference 4).

and type of injected code. The interface established a relationship between the EE and the code to be executed, and communications were modeled using shared memory (see Fig. 6.5). In spite of the differences with typical transition-based languages, Unity is claimed to be flexible enough to represent programs in a compact way, constituting a basic support for testing the global state of an active node when the injected code fulfills some restrictions.

Regarding properties, Unity includes features to define progress and safety temporal properties, using some temporal logic operators. It also allows the definition of pre- and postconditions over states. The approach in Reference 5 uses manual proofs of Unity properties, and as far as we know, there is no automated verification support to be used with the proposed active behavior.

6.4.4   Verisim

The Verisim project has developed a toolkit to perform correctness analysis of properties over network simulation traces [4]. This approach uses the outputs of the multiprotocol *ns2* simulator, a well-known academic tool that performs network simulations by programming OTcl scripts to configure nodes, links, protocol stacks, and end applications. A suitable extension for the deployment of active services as an extension of the *ns2* simulator can be found in Reference 26.

Verisim incorporates the Meta-Event Definition Language (MEDL), an LTL extension to define patterns over *ns2* execution traces. MEDL is oriented to perform the so-called monitoring and checking, by defining requirements with events and conditions over traces (see Fig. 6.6 for an example). Safety is described in terms of conditions that must always be true and alarms that must never be raised. MEDL makes use of auxiliary variables to record execution history.

The Verisim technique can be considered a kind of automated runtime analysis. Therefore, it does not perform exhaustive analysis on the model.

6.5 MODEL CHECKING ACTIVE NETWORKS WITH SPIN

In the last few years, SPIN has become one of the most used model checkers in both academic and industrial areas [19]. It supports the verification of the usual safety properties (like deadlock absence) in systems written in the modeling language PROMELA, as well as the analysis of complex requirements expressed with linear temporal logic. It is also used as the platform to try new powerful algorithms to attack the state-explosion problem.

PROMELA is a language designed to describe systems composed of concurrent asynchronous communicating processes. A PROMELA model consists of a finite set of processes $M = Proc_1\|...\|Proc_n$, global and local channels, and global and local variables. Processes communicate via message passing through channels. Communication may be asynchronous using channels as bounded buffers, and synchronous using channels with size zero. Global channels and variables determine the environment in which processes run, while local channels and variables establish the internal local state of processes. A PROMELA process is defined as a sequence of possibly labeled sentences preceded by the declarative part. It also provides mechanisms to express nondeterministic executions.

The SPIN model checker verifies LTL formulas against PROMELA models. Well-formed LTL formulas are inductively constructed from a set of atomic propositions (in PROMELA, propositions are tests on data, channels, or labels), the standard Boolean operators, and the *temporal operators*: *always* "□,"*eventually* "◊,"and *until* "U." Formulas are interpreted with respect to model state sequences (traces) $t_i = s_i \rightarrowtail s_{i+1} \rightarrowtail \cdots$. Each sequence represents a possible model execution from state s_i. The use of *temporal operators* permits the construction of formulas that depend on the current and future states of a configuration trace.

By default, given an LTL formula, SPIN translates it into a Büchi automaton that represents an undesirable behavior (which is claimed to be impossible). Then, verification consists of an exhaustive exploration of the state space searching for executions that satisfy the automaton. If such an execution exists, then the tool reports it as a counterexample for the property. If the model is explored and a counterexample is not found, then the model satisfies the LTL property as a *universal property*. The same verification scheme can be used to check whether a formula cannot be satisfied by any path (*refutation of existential properties*). These two ways of using LTL are presented in a graphical user interface called XSPIN.

Although there are many examples where verification can be done with standard exhaustive verification, SPIN also implements optimization techniques to deal with complex systems. *Partial order reduction* replaces several interleaved sequences of events (sentences) with only one that represents the whole set. *State compression* reduces the use of memory by compressing the representation of the states without losing information. *Bit-state hashing* represents states as bits in a hash table, so in many cases, the analysis is only partial.

6.5.1   Modeling Active Networks in PROMELA

We will consider an example of how to construct a model for an ANTS-like active protocol in PROMELA, remembering that a verification model should be as small as possible, making sure that it represents the exact details needed for the properties to be analyzed. The basic elements to be abstracted in this example are (1) network links and the topology, (2) the active NodeOS, and (3) the active applications to be executed within active nodes, along with the end-to-end applications. These elements are depicted in Figure 6.7. Therefore, the resulting model will have a part representing the active nodes (operating system facilities + EE) and a specific part for both the new active applications and the topology considered. The former will be common for every active configuration, and the latter will change depending on the active service being proposed.

6.5.1.1 Building Capsules   In active ANTS terminology, a capsule is an active packet, which can be modeled as a new data type in PROMELA, as shown in Figure 6.8. Regarding fields in the packet of Figure 6.2, the PROMELA version contains only four mandatory fields: the origin and destination addresses, the previous node that executed the capsule, and a reference for its associated code, which will be executed when arriving at a new node. The basic *capsule*

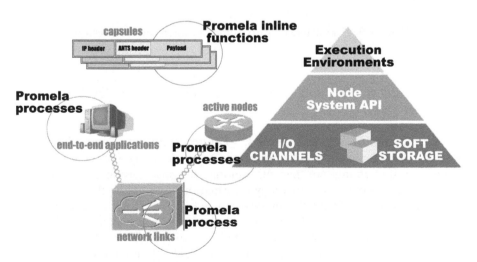

FIGURE 6.7   Overview of the PROMELA model for an active network.

```
typedef Capsule{
    address src;   /*source address of the IP datagram*/
    address dst;   /*destination address of the IP datagram*/
    address prev;  /*previous active node. Reserved to Active Nodes*/
    codeRef ref;   /*type of capsule (it makes reference to an active application code)*/
    /*Specific data fields must be inserted from here*/
};
```

FIGURE 6.8 PROMELA definition of an ANTS-like capsule.

```
active proctype AbstractNetworkService(){

    Capsule capsule;
    address from;
endService:
    do
    :: atomic{ to_network ? from,capsule->
        if
        /*packet destined to the same network*/
        :: (getNetworkFromAddress(from))==(getNetworkFromAddress(capsule.dst))->
            if
            ::(getHostFromAddress(capsule.dst)==0)-> /*router*/
                    from_network[getNetworkFromAddress(capsule.dst)]!capsule;
            ::else-> /*host*/
                    from_network[getHostFromAddress(capsule.dst)]!capsule;
            fi
        /*packet destined to another network from a Host*/
        ::((getNetworkFromAddress(from))!=(getNetworkFromAddress(capsule.dst)))
          && (getHostFromAddress(from)!=0) ->
                    from_network[getNetworkFromAddress(from)]!capsule;

        /*packet destined to another network from a Router*/
        ::((getNetworkFromAddress(from))!=(getNetworkFromAddress(capsule.dst)))
          && (getHostFromAddress(from)==0)->
                    from_network[NODE[getNetworkFromAddress(from)].route]!capsule;
#if WITH_LOSSES
        ::skip
#endif
        fi;
      }
    od
}
```

FIGURE 6.9 Unreliable network communication service in PROMELA.

type may be extended with specific fields if needed when developing new active protocols.

6.5.1.2 Common Parts: Nodes, Communication, and Environments

Communications in PROMELA may be modeled by a process that performs the interchange of packets among networks, using asynchronous channels and following the topology information supplied by the designer at system initialization. Using this process, active routers are not concerned with specific routing processing duties, reducing both the interleaving and the size of the stored states in the verification step. The *AbstractNetworkService* shown in Figure 6.9 is a basic transport facility for unreliable communications, following the connectionless nature of the ANTS toolkit [29]. When a new capsule arrives, its destination field is checked. If the destination network is the same as the one the host/node that sent the capsule belongs to, the network service can deliver the capsule directly. However, if the destination is another network in the model, the service has to detect whether the capsule was received from a router or from a host. If the capsule came from a router, the service has to query its routing information in order to select a router to perform the next hop. If the capsule came from a host, the service forwards it to the local network router.

The active routers have been modeled as processes to allow the execution of active applications. The abstraction for these entities in PROMELA constitutes a mixture of the NodeOS and the EE functionalities. An important design requirement is to assume that active applications have been previously loaded in the active nodes when the system is started, because the way in which that code reaches the node is independent of the active service that is going to be analyzed. For instance, the EE in Figure 6.10 includes the code needed for the reception of capsule packets from the network and the execution of the corresponding active application associated to the reference code. As can be seen, the reception channel *from_network_to_i* has been defined as read-only, one optimization available in SPIN to minimize the effect of the state explosion in verifications. When a capsule arrives, its reference type field is checked and the EE selects the appropriate procedure that will process the capsule. In the example shown in Figure 6.10, three types of capsules exist.

In order to manipulate the capsule, there are several functions to obtain the basic fields in its header (*getSrc*, *getDst*, *getPrev*). The *setDst* and the *newCapsule* functions change the destination of the capsule and create a new one to be forwarded, respectively. Some other functions include ones for explicit forwarding and routing along with the primitives responsible for the

```
proctype EE(address _this_address){

    chan from_network_to_i = from_network[getNetworkFromAddress(_this_address)];
    xr from_network_to_i;
    Capsule capsule;
endEE:
    do
    :: atomic{ from_network_to_i?capsule ->
                if /*time to process capsules*/
                /*Code for processing active applications will be inserted here*/
                ::(capsule.ref==DATA)-> capsuleDATA();
                ::(capsule.ref==NACK)-> capsuleNACK();
                ::(capsule.ref==ACK)-> capsuleACK();
                ::else-> /*references that were not previously registered*/
                    if
                    ::(capsule.dst == _this_address)-> /*silently discarded*/
                    ::else-> to_network!_this_address,capsule;
                    fi
                fi;
        }
    od
}
```

FIGURE 6.10   An execution environment example.

manipulation of a soft-store data cache in the node (*cacheGet, cachePut, cacheRemove*), also employed in the ANTS literature [30].

6.5.1.3 *Creating Network Topologies*   Active network designers deal with a network topology when deploying a new network service. In order to abstract a real topology for the purposes of verification, PROMELA topologies consist of networks, each of which is identified by a natural number. The basic connectivity mechanisms are point-to-point links between networks, each one containing an active node. Thus, the identifiers of these active nodes (their global addresses) are the same as the ones assigned to their corresponding networks, avoiding the need for some other complex routing mechanisms. Active hosts execute end-to-end applications, which are also attached to networks. Their global addresses are composed of two different parts: the network to which they belong and a valid host identifier. The host identifier is selected from the natural number set starting with the next free value not previously used when defining networks. The *hostAddress(idNet,idHost)* function automatically obtains the resulting global address from valid network and hosts identifiers. Figure 6.11 shows a valid scenario for an active network topology composed of two networks, each one with its corresponding active node (identified as 0 and 1).

When starting the system, designers have to provide this topology information. That is, they have to explicitly declare the routes for each active node in the model. Finally, they start the sender and receiver instances along with the active nodes, using the *start_router(idNet)* function.

6.5.2   Example: Verifying an Active Protocol

Figures 6.8–6.11 correspond to parts of an example for verifying an active multicast protocol [14]. The chosen protocol, called RMANP [6], constitutes a complex protocol for multicast applications on active networks. It is worth noting that it is the ANTS-oriented version of the Reliable Multicast Protocol (RMNP) presented in Reference 3. RMANP was designed to take advantage of

```
/* Network topology for verification:              /--receiver(3)
                        sender(2)---n(0)---n(1)-
*/                                                \--receiver(4)
init{
 atomic{
    NODE[0].route = 1;
    NODE[1].route = 0;

    address addrRcv = hostAddress(1,3);
    ...
    start_router(0); /*n0*/
    start_router(1); /*n1*/
 }
}
```

FIGURE 6.11   Creating a network topology in PROMELA.

active networks making active nodes participate in processing acknowledgement (ACK) and retransmission request (NACK) messages. Aggregation of multiple ACKs into a single capsule (MACK) to the source prevents the implosion of confirmations. The storage of nonconfirmed data in active nodes saves traffic when particular data are requested to be retransmitted to the destination applications. The node may also filter NACK messages to the source, only allowing those requesting new data to pass through. Regarding quality of service, RMANP considers three kinds of traffic: reliable, unreliable, and reliable with temporal constraints. The PROMELA model presented in Reference 14 only included the suitable capsules (DATA, ACK, and NACK) to model a reliable service, the most complex one. Therefore, the active code in these capsules only included behavior oriented to verifying properties in the protocol. Using the topology depicted in Figure 6.11 for model checking, the first network included the source of the data: a sender providing data to the active node using a sliding window protocol. The second network consisted of a process modeling a multicast reception group.

As an example of the code for the capsules, Figure 6.12 shows an example of the NACK capsule for this protocol. The active node intercepts a retransmission request to analyze the NACK sequence field, providing the data requested if they are available in its cache memory. The operation of inserting data into the cache corresponds to the execution of a DATA capsule (see more details in Reference 14).

The fixed part and the specific part of the active network architecture in PROMELA for RMANP is deadlock free. Besides, the capsule's code is oriented to verifying some LTL formulas with SPIN. For instance, the LTL property shown in Figure 6.13 shows a universal property that must hold in every possible scenario of the RMANP service proposed. Each proposition in the formula (those marked with #define) corresponds to labeled transitions of the active code in the capsules of the protocol.

```
typedef Capsule{
    address src;
    address dst;
    address prev;
    codeRef ref;
    byte seq;    /*RMANP specific field*/
    mtype data; /*payload*/
};

inline capsuleNACK(){
 short tmp;
 tmp = cacheGet(last_unack);
 if
 ::(tmp==capsule.seq)-> //send data from cache
   capsule.data = cacheGet(storing_key(tmp));
   sendCapsuleTo(getSrc(),DATA)
 ::else -> sendTo(getDst()) //forward to source
 fi
}
```

FIGURE 6.12 A NACK capsule for the RMANP protocol.

```
LTL property (RestrictedScope):  [](retransmission_requested -> <> data_from_EEs)

  #define retransmission_requested   receiver[1]@retransm_req
  #define data_form_EEs     (data_from_EE0 || data_from_EE1)
  #define data_from_EE0     (EE[1]@retransm_EE_from_nack || EE[1]@retransm_EE_from_ack)
  #define data_from_EE1     (EE[2]@retransm_EE_from_nack || EE[2]@retransm_EE_from_ack)
```

FIGURE 6.13 Universal property verified with the SPIN version of the RMANP protocol.

6.5.3 Modeling More Realistic Code in SPIN

One of the main problems of using any of the formalisms described (including PROMELA) is the need to manually abstract the behavior and structure of the applications that are going to be verified. In fact, this method is quite prone to errors. Therefore, methods to guide the automatic extraction of a (verification) model from source code are always demanded [10, 11, 15]. In the active network domain, this should involve not only parsing and converting the Java code for capsules, but also providing the abstract representation of the active node API (interfaces and behavior) and the IP routing algorithms.

In order to facilitate these tasks, SPIN has recently incorporated some extensions to allow the execution of C-embedded code within PROMELA. With this new capability of the model checker, it is now possible to enrich the verification models with more realistic behaviors, therefore increasing confidence in the results obtained.

Figure 6.14 shows a possible modification of the previous PROMELA model for the network (Fig. 6.9). In this new variant, we have used the new *c_decl* primitive to embed new C types in the model. Here, we depict the c_NodeResources type, which can be contrasted with its previous simplified version in PROMELA (now properly renamed to pml_NodeResources). Therefore, we can manage more complex abstract data types, such as a route table (a two-dimensional array with two columns, the destination network and the output interface) or a *least recent used* cache (not shown in the figure, although included in an external .h file). In the example, we can now allow a router to have more than two interfaces, thus allowing more complex topologies than the one depicted in Figure 6.11.

C variables can be declared within the model using the *c_state* primitive, where they are explicitly attached to the state vector or hidden from it. In the example in Figure 6.14, we declare a global array named nodeRes[]. It is also possible to declare C variables within the local scope of a PROMELA proctype.

The execution of pure C code in an atomic way is available inside the *c_expr* and *c_code* primitives. The former requires a non-side-effect Boolean expression over a C code fragment, whereas the latter is a more general primitive that allows manipulation for both PROMELA or C variables. Figure 6.14 shows how c_code can be used within a NetworkService proctype in order to include a more realistic behavior for a route forwarding algorithm. It is worth noting that PROMELA variables are accessible within the C code fragment using the

```
/*Promela version of a the NodeResources type*/
typedef pml_NodeResources{
address route; /* only an output interface is allowed*/
short cache[STORAGE_RESOURCES]=FREE;
/*Beware thinking in Cache as an LRU one. We have modeled it as a Hash Table instead,
  so be careful with the STORAGE_RESOURCES limit and your special needs*/
};

/*C version of a the NodeResources type*/
c_decl{
#include "nodetypes.h"
  typedef struct{
    short myAddress; /*node address of this node*/
    short routeTable[MAX_ROUTES][2];
    /*1st column: destination address, 2nd: output interface (channel id)*/
    struct LRU cache;
    /*now this cache is an array with extra information to get the Least Recently Used index*/
  }c_NodeResources;
}

c_state "c_NodeResources nodeRes[TOTAL_NODES]" "Global" /* goes inside the state vector */

/*C version of NetworkService (not as abstract as before) */
active proctype NetworkService(){

  Capsule capsule;
  address from;
  short output_channel_id ;
endService:
    do
    :: atomic{ to_network ? from,capsule->
        c_code{
            PNetworkService->output_channel_id = getRoute(PNetworkService->from,PNetworkService->capsule.dst);
            printf("Capsule will be forwarded to: %d\n", now.nodeRes[PNetworkService->output_channel_id].myAddress);
        }
        if
        ::(output_channel_id != -1) ->
            if
            ::from_network[output_channel_id]!capsule;
            #if WITH_LOSSES
            ::skip
            #endif
            fi
        ::else /* forwarding error ...*/
        fi;
      }
    od
}
```

FIGURE 6.14 Embedding c code in SPIN.

prefix *now.* for global variables and *Pproctype_name->* for variables in the scope of a proctype (named *proctype_name*). In the example of the figure, we use an external C function (getRoute()) to calculate the appropriate output channel to forward capsules.

In summary, these SPIN extensions help users create PROMELA models that are closer to the final code they are trying to verify. The use of C functions and algorithms within the model are of great interest, because they are executed atomically. However, they usually also entail having to manage more data in the verification, which can lead more easily to the state-explosion problem.

6.6 CONCLUSIONS

Using PROMELA as the modeling formalism for active protocols and LTL to describe their properties has advantages over previous approaches. Regarding *specification formalisms*, none of the languages described in Section 6.4 were designed to describe communication protocols. Therefore, they are not close enough to the ones used by protocol engineers, who usually take transition-based languages into account. PROMELA incorporates features to work with protocols: messages, communication channels, losses, and reordering or concurrency models, which constitutes a direct support to specify active network architectures. Moreover, PROMELA shares many similarities with imperative languages usually used when implementing the final code (Java or C). This makes it less difficult to write PROMELA code as compared with some other formal method-based proposals such as Maude or Unity, and makes it possible to implement efficient (and automatic) model extractors from the final source code.

Regarding properties, LTL is supported by almost all the proposals described, except ACTIVESPEC. It is worth noting that the use of temporal logic without extensions, such as the use of auxiliary variables in MEDL, is more efficient. SPIN can also use the complete range of LTL operators, instead of the reduced ones used in Unity. Moreover, for those users with no expertise in logics, SPIN offers some complementary notations to represent properties using the graphic TimeLine Editor tool [18], or embedded observers (synchronized automata).

Finally, the most realistic analysis tools are those that perform automatic verification, that is, the exhaustive exploration of all possible execution scenarios.

REFERENCES

1. D. S. Alexander, et al. Active Network Encapsulation Protocol (ANEP). 1997. Available at: http://www.cis.upenn.edu/~switchware/ANEP/.
2. D. S. Alexander, et al. The Switchware active network architecture. *IEEE Communications Magazine*, 1998.
3. A. Azcorra, M. Calderon, and M. Sedano. A strategy for comparing reliable multicast protocols applied to RMNP and CTES. In *IEEE Conference on Protocols for Multimedia Systems—Multimedia Networking (MmNet'97)*, 1997.
4. K. Bhargavan, C. A. Gunter, M. Kim, I. Lee, D. Obradovic, O. Sokolsky, and M. Viswanathan. Verisim: Formal analysis of network simulations. *IEEE Transactions on Software Engineering*, 28(2):129–145, 2002.
5. S. Bhattacharjee, K. Calvert, and E. Zegura. Reasoning about active network protocols. In *IEEE ICNP'98*, 1998.
6. M. Calderon, M. Sedano, A. Azcorra, and C. Alonso. Active network support for multicast applications. *IEEE Network*, 12(3):46–52, 1998.
7. K. L. Calvert, S. Bhattacharjee, E. Zegura, and J. Sterbenz. Directions in active network research. *IEEE Communications Magazine*, 36(10):72–78, 1998.
8. K. Chandy and J. Misra. *Parallel Program Design*. Addison-Wesley, 1998.
9. J. Crow, et al. A tutorial introduction to PVS. Presented at *WIFT'95*, 1995.

10. P. de la Camara, M. M. Gallardo, P. Merino, and D. Sanan. Checking the reliability of socket based communication software. *STTT*, 11(5):359–374, 2009.

11. P. de la Camara, R. J. Castro, M. M. Gallardo, and P. Merino. Verification support for ARINC-653 avionics software, software testing, verification and reliability. *Software Testing, Verification and Reliability*, 21(4):267–298, 2011.

12. G. Denker, et al. Specifying a Reliable Broadcasting Protocol in Maude. Internal Report, Computer Science Laboratory, SRI International, Menlo Park, CA, 1999.

13. S. Eker, J. Meseguer, and A. Sridharanarayanan. The Maude LTL model checker. *Electronic Notes in Theoretical Computer Science*, 71, 2002.

14. M. M. Gallardo, J. Martinez, and P. Merino. Model checking active networks with SPIN. *Computer Communications*, 28:609–622, 2005.

15. K. Havelund and T. Pressburger. Model checking Java programs using Java pathfinder. *STTT*, 2(4):366–381, 2000.

16. D. He, G. Muller, and J. L. Lawall. Distributing MPEG movies over the internet using programmable networks. In *Proceedings of the 22nd International Conference on Distributed Computing Systems (ICDCS'02)*, 2002.

17. G. J. Holzmann. The model checker SPIN. *IEEE Transactions on Software Engineering*, 23(5):279–295, 1997.

18. G. J. Holzmann. *The SPIN MODEL CHECKER. Primer and Reference Manual*. Addison-Wesley, 2003.

19. G. J. Holzmann. On-the-fly LTL Model Checking with SPIN. Available at: http://spinroot.com/spin/whatispin.html

20. S. A. Hussain. *Active and Programmable Networks for Adaptive Architectures and Services*. Auerbach Publications, 2006.

21. D. Hutchison, S. Denazis, L. Lefevre, G. Minden, and J. Gary. Active and programmable networks. In *IFIP TC6 7th International Working Conference*, IWAN 2005, Sophia Antipolis, France, Springer-Verlag, November 21–23, 2005. Revised Papers, 2009.

22. S. Kamouskos and A. Vasilakos. Active electronic mail, in SAC. 2002.

23. C. Kong, D. Dieckman, and P. Alexander. Formal Modeling of Active Network Nodes Using PVS. *Workshop on Formal Methods in Software Practice (FMSP-00)*, 2000.

24. J. Meseguer. Conditional rewriting logic as a unified model of concurrency. *Theoretical Computer Science*, 96:73–155, 2002.

25. N. M. Mosharaf Kabir Chowdhury and R. Boutaba. A Survey of Network Virtualization, University of Waterloo, Ontario, Canada. Technical Report CS-2008-25, 2008.

26. G. Rodriguez, P. Merino, and M. M. Gallardo. An extension of the ns simulator for active network research. *Computer Communications*, 25:189–197, 2002.

27. B. Schwartz, et al. Smart packets for active networks. *ACM Transactions on Computer Systems*, 18(1):67–88, 2000.

28. M. Stehr and C. Talcott. PLAN in Maude. Specifying an active network programming language. *Electronic Notes in Theoretical Computer Science*, 71, Elsevier, 2002.

29. D. Tennenhouse and D. Wetherall. Towards an active network architecture. *Computer Communication Review*, 26:2, 1996.

30. D. J. Wetherall, J. V. Guttag, and D. L. Tennenhouse. ANTS: Network services without the red tape. *IEEE Computer*, 1999.

31. Y. Yemini and S. da Silva. Towards programmable networks. In *IFIP/IEEE International Workshop on Distributed Systems: Operations and Management*. L'Aquila, Italy, October, 1996.

CHAPTER 7

PRACTICAL APPLICATIONS OF PROBABILISTIC MODEL CHECKING TO COMMUNICATION PROTOCOLS

MARIE DUFLOT
LORIA, Equipe MOSEL/VERIDIS, Vandoeuvre-lès-Nancy, France

MARTA KWIATKOWSKA
Department of Computer Science, University of Oxford, Oxford, UK

GETHIN NORMAN
Department of Computing Science, University of Glasgow, Glasgow, UK

DAVID PARKER
School of Computer Science, University of Birmingham, Birmingham, UK

SYLVAIN PEYRONNET
LRI, INRIA Université Paris-Sud XI, Orsay, France

CLAUDINE PICARONNY
LSV, CNRS & ENS de Cachan, Cachan, France

JEREMY SPROSTON
Dipartimento di Informatica, Università degli Studi di Torino, Torino, Italy

7.1 INTRODUCTION

Computer-controlled devices are today ubiquitous in many areas of industry, including business- and safety-critical domains. For this reason, the use of communication protocols, devised to govern the interactions between such devices, is extremely widespread. Recent years have also seen considerable growth in the development and deployment of formal verification methods, used to establish the correctness of and identify faults in a wide array of real-life systems, a fact evidenced by the breadth of topics covered in this volume.

Formal Methods for Industrial Critical Systems: A Survey of Applications, First Edition.
Edited by Stefania Gnesi and Tiziana Margaria.
© 2013 IEEE. Published 2013 by John Wiley & Sons, Inc.

In this chapter, we describe work that has been carried out to apply formal verification techniques to communication protocols. Such systems represent a particularly challenging case in this respect because, in order to successfully model and analyze them, several key aspects must be incorporated: *concurrency* between multiple components, potentially operating in different locations and at unknown speeds; precise, *real-time* constraints, imposed by the protocols and the mediums under which they are designed to operate; and *randomization*, which is often used to break symmetry between devices communicating using the same protocol.

Probabilistic model checking is a formal verification technique for the analysis of systems that exhibit stochastic behavior. It involves the construction of a probabilistic model of some real-life system followed by a mathematical analysis of this model in order to determine useful properties of the original system. Unlike conventional verification techniques, probabilistic model checking can be used to ascertain not only correctness, but also quantitative measures such as performance and reliability. These techniques can be applied to a range of probabilistic models, typically variants of Markov chains, but of particular relevance here are their application to *probabilistic timed automata* (PTAs), a model that can ably express nondeterministic, real-time, and probabilistic behavior. In this chapter, we give an overview of PTAs, probabilistic model checking, and the corresponding implementation techniques and tools. Furthermore, we illustrate their usefulness in the domain of communication protocols through a case study: the IEEE 802.3 (Carrier Sense Multiple Access/ Collision Detection [CSMA/CD]) protocol, as used for example in networking over Ethernet.

7.2 PTAs

PTAs are a formalism for modeling systems whose behavior exhibits nondeterministic, real-time, and probabilistic characteristics [25]. PTAs are an extension of timed automata [1], one of the most prominent formalisms for the formal verification of real-time systems.

In this section, we illustrate a number of basic concepts of (probabilistic) timed automata using the example in Figure 7.1. The figure shows an automaton modeling a simple communication protocol, in which a station attempts

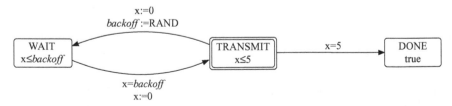

FIGURE 7.1 An example of a probabilistic timed automaton.

to transmit onto a bus. If the station's transmission is interrupted by a transmission from another station (a collision), then the station suspends its activity, waiting a randomly chosen amount of time, before starting to send its message again. The *control states* of the model, TRANSMIT, WAIT, and DONE, are shown by the nodes of the graph, and the possible transitions between the control states are indicated by the graph's edges. In the initial state, TRANSMIT, denoted by the double border, a transmission is being made by the system. When 5 time units have elapsed from the start of transmission, the message has been sent successfully, and the model moves to state DONE. Dependency on time can be represented by *clocks*, *guards*, and *resets* on edges, and *invariants* in states. A clock is a real-valued variable that has the value 0 at the start of execution of the system, which increases at the same rate as real time while the model remains within the same control state. The illustrated model has a single clock, x. The guard of the edge from TRANSMIT to DONE is $x = 5$ and specifies that the edge can be traversed when the value of the clock x equals 5. The invariant of the state TRANSMIT is $x \leq 5$ and specifies that control must pass from TRANSMIT before the value of the clock x exceeds 5.

The edge from TRANSMIT to WAIT is not labeled with a guard, which is interpreted as denoting that the edge can always be traversed from TRANSMIT, regardless of the value of the clock x. Whether this edge is taken or not, at any point in time in which the automaton is in the state TRANSMIT, is a *nondeterministic* choice. The traversal of this edge corresponds to interruption of the transmission caused by the simultaneous transmission on the bus by another station in the network. The edge features a clock reset denoted by $x:=0$, which indicates that, on entry to state WAIT, the clock x is reset to the value 0. In addition to clocks, we also allow finite-domain variables to be referred to in resets, guards, and invariants; furthermore, we also allow *probabilistic resets* of such variables, in contrast to the case of clock resets, which assign 0 deterministically to clocks. On traversal of the edge from TRANSMIT to WAIT, the finite-domain variable backoff is set to a random value according to the assignment *backoff*:=**RAND** (where **RAND** is a probability distribution over a number of possible values of *backoff*, e.g., the uniform distribution over the natural numbers between 3 and 10). Furthermore, the value of *backoff* is subsequently used within the invariant of the state WAIT, and the guard of the edge from WAIT to TRANSMIT, in order to ensure that, when the value of the clock x reaches the value of *backoff*, control returns to the state TRANSMIT.

The example of Figure 7.1 is an example of a PTA. We note that replacing the probabilistic assignment *backoff*:=**RAND** by a nonprobabilistic assignment results in a standard timed automaton. Although not illustrated by the example, PTA can also be extended with a set of *events*, which label edges. These events can then be used to define the *parallel composition* of a number of PTAs, where each such automaton is regarded as a subcomponent of the overall system, and where the automata synchronize on shared events. Such events will be used in Section 7.4 to define the parallel composition of PTAs of a bus and two stations operating according to the CSMA/CD protocol. The parallel composition operator was introduced in Reference 27, based on precedents for timed automata [1] and probabilistic transition systems [33].

The semantics of a PTA are formally defined as an infinite-state Markov decision process (MDP), a probabilistic model that supports nondeterministic choice, and in which transitions are made in discrete steps. The MDP will generally comprise infinite states because the clocks of the PTA are real-valued variables. Similarly, the transitions available in a state in which time can elapse will also be infinite in number because these correspond to real-valued durations. Analysis of a PTA, which typically constitutes formal verification of one or more properties specified in temporal logic, is therefore nontrivial because model-checking algorithms usually operate on finite-state models. However, based on analogous work on model checking of (nonprobabilistic) timed automata, we can obtain faithful finite-state representations of PTAs, which can be used in the analysis of a wide range of correctness properties or performance indices. One example of such a representation is based on *digital clocks*, in which the clocks of the PTA are interpreted as taking integer values, rather than real values [23]. This approach requires that the comparisons involving clocks in guards and invariants are nonstrict; however, this is a common property in PTA models of real-life systems, such as the CSMA/CD protocol considered in this chapter. The digital clocks approach has been, to date, the most successful in practice of the finite-state representations proposed for PTAs: It has been used to verify the CSMA/CD protocol [10, 28], part of the IEEE 802.11 standard for wireless local area networks [26, 31], the FireWire root contention protocol [27], and the IPv4 Zeroconf protocol [23].

Alternative approaches for the analysis of PTAs have been developed based on the manipulation of *zones*, that is, convex polyhedra. In Reference 25, such an approach, based on a forward traversal of the state space, is introduced. Subsequent work in Reference 22 extends its applicability through the use of abstraction refinement and stochastic games. On the other hand, the techniques developed in Reference 28 are based on a backward exploration of the state space and have since been applied to the analysis of cost and reward properties [5, 12].

7.3 PROBABILISTIC MODEL CHECKING

Probabilistic model checking is a formal verification technique for the modeling and analysis of systems that exhibit stochastic behavior. It can be applied to several different types of probabilistic model. The three most commonly used are discrete-time Markov chains (DTMCs), in which time is modeled as discrete steps, and randomness as discrete probabilistic choices; MDPs, which extend DTMCs with the ability to represent nondeterministic behavior; and continuous-time Markov chains (CTMCs), which do not permit nondeterminism but allow specification of real (continuous) time behavior, through the use of exponential distributions. In this chapter, we focus principally on MDPs since, as described in the previous section, in many cases, analysis of PTAs reduces to analysis of MDPs. We also refer to DTMCs, which can be seen as a special case of MDPs where nondeterminism is absent.

Properties of DTMCs and MDPs are usually expressed in temporal logics, such as probabilistic computation tree logic (PCTL) [6, 15] and linear temporal logic (LTL) [9]. Using such logics, one can reason about quantities such as

- "the probability the protocol eventually terminates,"
- "the probability that each request is followed by either an acknowledgement or a time-out signal," and
- "the probability that a message is successfully received within $35 \mu s$."

In the case of MDPs, it is in fact not possible to compute exact probability values such as these due to the presence of nondeterminism in the model. In this situation, the values computed are the *minimum* or *maximum* probabilities over all possible resolutions of nondeterminism. This corresponds to a *best-case* or *worst-case* analysis (depending on the meaning of the probabilities). Furthermore, it is also often useful, both for DTMCs and MDPs, to compute the minimum or maximum probability over a range of possible configurations or parameters of a model, producing a different kind of best/worst-case analysis. Finally, we note that it is also possible to augment DTMCs and MDPs with real-valued *costs* or *rewards*, which can represent a wide range of measures, for example, "system power consumption," "number of lost messages," or "message queue size." It is then possible to reason about the (possibly minimum or maximum) *expected* value of these measures, for example,

- "the expected power consumption during the first 20s of system operation,"
- "the expected number of messages lost before protocol termination," and
- "the expected number of messages queued for delivery after $500 \mu s$."

7.3.1 Techniques for Probabilistic Model Checking

7.3.1.1 Numerical Solution The conventional approach to probabilistic model checking is to construct a representation of the entire probabilistic model, and from this derive one or more numerical problems that will yield results for the properties of the model to be analyzed. The first phase of this process often requires only an analysis of the underlying graph of the probabilistic model (e.g., reachability-based techniques). The remainder (which often represents the bottleneck in terms of efficiency) requires numerical computation to be performed. Commonly, solution of either a linear equation system (for DTMCs) or a linear optimization problem (for MDPs) is required. Although such problems can be solved exactly with *direct methods* (e.g., Gaussian elimination or Simplex, respectively) for efficiency reasons, *iterative methods* (e.g., Gauss–Seidel or dynamic programming, respectively) are typically used. These converge toward the correct solution with each iteration and are terminated when convergence indicates that the desired precision has been reached. See, for example, Reference 32 for more details.

7.3.1.2 *Approximate Probabilistic Computation*

An alternative approach is to use a combination of discrete event simulation and Monte Carlo methods to estimate the probability associated with a PCTL formula [17]. This is done by generating random paths of depth k in a DTMC and computing the value of a random variable that estimates $Prob_k[\psi]$, the probability that a formula ψ is satisfied on paths of depth at most k. More specifically, the algorithm that performs this process takes as input a succinct representation of DTMC x, a formula, a positive integer k, and two parameters ε and δ, producing a value $A(x, \varepsilon, \delta)$. This is a *fully polynomial randomized approximation scheme*, meaning that the result satisfies

$$Prob[|A(x, \varepsilon, \delta) - \mu(x)| \le \varepsilon] \ge 1 - \delta,$$

where $\mu(x)$ is the exact value of $Prob_k[\psi]$. We call ε the approximation parameter and δ the *confidence parameter*. The algorithm must generate $O(\varepsilon^{-2}, \log(\delta^{-1}))$ paths through the DTMC. The main advantage of this approach is that, because random paths can be generated from only a succinct representation of the DTMC, it avoids the (potentially very costly) construction of the model and its state space, hence using a very small amount of memory. A related technique based on *acceptance sampling* and *hypothesis testing* [37] also uses random sampling in conjunction with discrete event simulation but is tailored to checking whether the probability of satisfying a formula meets a given bound.

7.3.2 Probabilistic Model Checking Tools

PRISM [18, 29] is an open-source probabilistic model checker developed initially at the University of Birmingham and now at the University of Oxford. It provides support for analysis of DTMCs, MDPs, and CTMCs. Models are described in the PRISM modeling language, a relatively simple, state-based language based on the reactive modules formalism [2], and properties are specified in a logic that incorporates LTL, PCTL, continuous stochastic logic (CSL) (a variant of PCTL for CTMCs), and a number of custom extensions. PRISM also supports the modeling and analysis of costs and rewards. One of the key features of PRISM is its symbolic implementation techniques using data structures based on binary decision diagrams (BDDs). These allow compact representation and efficient manipulation of extremely large probabilistic models, by exploiting structure and regularity derived from their high-level description. Such techniques have been successfully applied to the probabilistic verification of models with as many as 10^{10} states (see, e.g., References 11 and 24).

APMC (Approximate Probabilistic Model Checker) [3, 17] is a distributed model checker developed in a joint collaboration between the universities of Paris VII and Paris-Sud XI. It uses an efficient Monte Carlo method to approximate satisfaction probabilities of PCTL properties of DTMCs, as described in the previous section. A recent version is also capable of verifying CTMCs, but it was not used in this work. The tool comprises two parts. The first is a compiler that produces an ad hoc verifier (including a path generator and a checker) for a DTMC, described in the PRISM language, and a property. APMC implements different strategies to generate the code of this program with respect to the synchronizations of the reactive modules: The most efficient is called "sync at compile time," which precomputes all the combinations of rules, thus building the synchronized succinct model representation.

The second component is a deployer that takes the ad hoc verifier and a set of available computing resources, deploys the verifier on these computers and collects the resulting approximate satisfaction probability for the formula on the model. APMC implements a massively (but natural) distributed method of model checking. The deployment is performed following a tree topology in order to make the deployment efficient and scalable. For instance, this provides a logarithmic latency to aggregate the results from all nodes to the root. A drawback of this topology is that the system may over generate and verify some samples, but it ensures that there is no point of contention in the system. More information about the implementation of APMC can be found in Reference 14.

7.3.2.1 *Other Tools*

Several other implementations of model checking for MDPs exist. LiQuor [8] performs explicit-state model checking of LTL on MDPs modeled in an expressive language called PROBMELA, a probabilistic extension of SPIN's PROMELA language. RAPTURE [19] employs iterative abstraction-refinement techniques for verifying a subset of PCTL properties. ProbDiVinE [4] supports parallel and distributed LTL model checking. There are also many other tools that include support for probabilistic model checking of DTMCs and CTMCs. These include MRMC [21], the PEPA Plug-in Project [34], CASPA [30], the APNN-Toolbox [7], and Ymer [36].

7.4 CASE STUDY: CSMA/CD

In this section, we present an illustrative case study of a randomized communication protocol, analyzed using PTA and probabilistic model checking. We use the CSMA/CD protocol, which is a fundamental part of the IEEE 802.3 international standard (Ethernet Network Communication protocol).

This protocol has been extensively studied with a variety of methods: simulation [35], analytical methods [13, 20], and real-time model checking [38]. The first accurate formal analysis with respect to the probabilistic aspects of the protocol was undertaken in References 10 and 28, where the system was modeled by a PTA and the correctness of the probabilistic behavior of the protocol verified by analyzing minimum and maximum probabilities for reachability and time-bounded reachability properties.

The two papers take differing approaches to tackling the state-space explosion problem commonly encountered in probabilistic (and real time) model checking. In Reference 10, time is discretized (using the digital clocks approach, mentioned in Section 7.2), and the resulting model is analyzed using PRISM [18, 29] and APMC [3, 17]. In Reference 28, the PTA model is analyzed using a probabilistic extension of the model checking approach for classical timed automata [16], implemented in a prototype extension of PRISM.

7.4.1 The Protocol

CSMA/CD is a distributed network arbitration protocol by which multiple network interface cards (NICs), referred to here as *stations*, may communicate over a single channel, known as the *carrier* or *bus*. All stations can send messages onto the network (*multiple access*) and each station can detect whether the bus is idle or is transmitting a message from another station (*carrier sense*). When a station senses that the bus is busy, it will wait before trying to transmit its own message. However, because of the propagation delay of signals across the network, it is possible that stations will try to transmit messages simultaneously. When this happens, a collision occurs, both messages are lost and the stations receive a garbled signal. In this way, the stations are able to observe that messages have been lost (*collision detection*). According to CSMA/CD, after this situation has occurred, stations reschedule their own transmission by independently choosing a random delay (known as *backoff* time), before which retransmission will be attempted. This random backoff time is chosen uniformly over an interval whose length increases exponentially with the number of collisions that have already occurred. We focus here on the half duplex version of the protocol where only one message can be carried at a time.

7.4.2 The PTA Model

The model of the CSMA/CD protocol used here is a combination of the models from References 10, 28, and 38 and considers the case of two stations. The PTA comprises three components operating in parallel, representing the two stations and the bus. The model has two parameters, σ and λ, representing the time taken for data to propagate along the bus and the time required for an entire message to be sent.

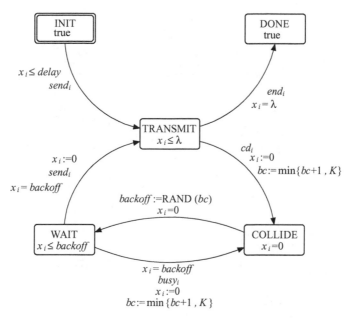

FIGURE 7.2   Probabilistic timed automaton model of a station.

The PTA for station i (where $i = 1, 2$) is shown in Figure 7.2. Each station has a clock x_i. It starts in the INIT state and tries to reach the DONE state where the message has been correctly sent to the other station. When the station wants to send a message (after a certain delay *delay*), it moves to state TRANSMIT. If no collision is detected within time λ, then the message will be delivered correctly and the station moves to DONE. Otherwise, a collision is detected (label cd_i) within σ time units, and the station moves to the COLLIDE state. It then draws a random waiting delay and waits for the corresponding time. When the waiting time is over, there are two options: If the bus is free, the station tries resending the message. If the bus is busy, the station increases the value of the collision counter bc (up to a maximum value K) and selects another random delay.

The PTA for the bus connecting the two stations is shown in Figure 7.3. The bus starts in state INIT and moves to state TRANSMIT when one of the stations begins sending a message. If nothing else happens, the station will finish its transmission (label end_i). In the state TRANSMIT, the second station can only send a message before time σ, which represents the propagation time on the bus. After this time, the station senses that the bus is busy and does not send. The bus uses the clocks y_1 and y_2 to implement this process. If two sending actions occur within time σ, then the bus moves to the COLLIDE state. When receiving the other station's message, both stations will detect the collision, stop sending, and the bus will return to the INIT state.

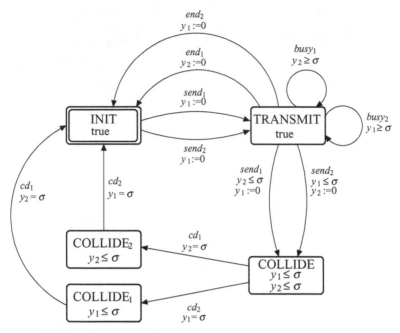

FIGURE 7.3 Probabilistic timed automaton model of the bus.

7.4.3 Analysis of the Model

The PTA model from the previous section has been analyzed using the digital clocks approach, mentioned in Section 7.2. Probabilistic model checking of the resulting MDP was performed with the two tools PRISM and APMC. For the CSMA/CD model parameters σ and λ, we used values of 2 and 65, respectively. The choice of the delay before which stations initially send a message (delay) is assumed to be nondeterministic (either 0, 1, or 2) for the PRISM analysis to ensure that all possibilities are considered. Using APMC, this is not possible so the choice is randomized.

Experiments with PRISM were run on a 2.6-GHz Pentium IV laptop with 1-GB RAM running Red Hat Linux. Iterative numerical computations were terminated when the maximum relative error between elements of solution vectors from successive iterations dropped below 10^{-6}.

APMC experiments were performed on a heterogeneous grid of 500 Athlon 3000+ workstations with 1-GB RAM running NetBSD and twenty 3-GHz Pentium IV workstations with 512-MB RAM mostly running Debian Linux, connected via 100-MB Ethernet. APMC was executed as a "cycle stealer," that is, running in the background of the workstations, while they were used by students and staff at École pour l'Informatique et les Techniques Avancées (EPITA). Hence, timing statistics for the cost of verification are imprecise. However, all experiments were completed in 2 days during a period of low

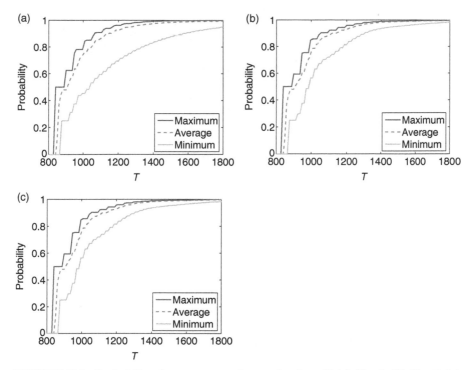

FIGURE 7.4   Probability that a message is sent by time T. (a) $K = 1$; (b) $K = 5$; (c) $K = 10$.

average load on the network. In all cases, the most efficient APMC strategy "sync at compile time" was used and, unless specified otherwise, the approximation parameter ε and confidence parameter δ were fixed at $\varepsilon = 10^{-2}$ and $\delta = 10^{-10}$, respectively.

7.4.3.1   *Probability of Message Transmission*   The first property we consider is the probability that a message has been successfully sent by a certain time point T. In Figure 7.4, we show results computed for three values of the maximum backoff limit K (1, 5, and 10; the value specified in the standard is 10) and a range of values of T. We give the *maximum* and *minimum* transmission probability over all nondeterministic choices, as computed by PRISM, and the *average* values, assuming a uniform choice over initial delays, as computed by APMC.

The results show that using larger values of K increases both the minimum, maximum, and average probabilities of sending a message by time T. Since we have constructed our model in such a way that the stations initially collide, the probability is 0 for any time bound T, which does not allow the stations to enter backoff and send a message. Notice that the exact plots in the graphs (minimum and maximum) contain discrete jumps. These correspond to the fact

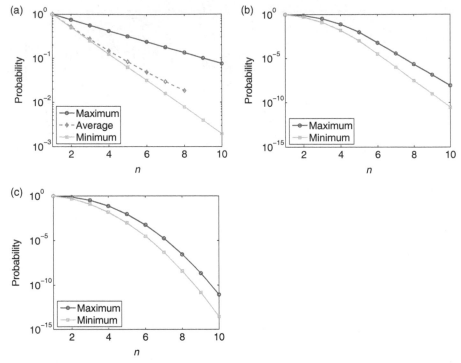

FIGURE 7.5   Probability that the stations collide n times before a message is sent. (a) $K = 1$; (b) $K = 5$; (c) $K = 10$.

that the probabilistic choice of backoff delay is over a discrete set of delays. The plots for the average case are smoother and, as expected, contained within the boundaries of the minimum and maximum values.

7.4.3.2 *Collision Probabilities*

Second, we consider the probability that n collisions occur before a single message is successfully sent. Results are shown in Figure 7.5, again for three values of the maximum backoff limit K, and for n ranging between 1 and 10. As before, we show both the minimum and maximum probability, computed by PRISM. Where possible, we also show the average case, as computed by APMC. However, in the majority of cases, computation of these values is not practical due to their small size. Recall that the number of samples required is quadratic in the inverse of the desired approximation. For the set of results corresponding to $K = 1$ shown in the figure, we had to use a precision of 10^{-3}, which required approximately 2×10^{9} samples. As is clear from the other graphs in Figure 7.5, larger values of K would require considerably greater precision and hence an infeasible number of samples.

Note that, since our model is constructed in such a way that the stations always collide initially, for K equals to 1, 5, and 10, the minimum and maximum probability of one collision occurring ($n = 1$) is 1. In all three cases, the results for $n = 2$ also agree, as do those for $n \leq 6$ where K is 5 or 10. This is to be expected since the stations' backoff counters cannot reach $n + 1$ until the stations have collided $n + 1$ times. Taking as an example the case where $n = 1$, we can illustrate the reasoning behind the results as follows:

- The minimum probability equals 0.5 and corresponds to the situation when the stations begin their first attempt at sending messages at the same time (with no constraint on the propagation delay). In this scenario, the stations will detect the first collision at the same time, and therefore, the probability that they collide a second time is the probability that the stations select the same number of slots to wait. Hence, since this is a random choice between waiting 1 or 2 slots, the stations collide a second time with probability 0.5.
- The maximum probability equals 0.75 and corresponds to the case when the propagation delay equals σ and the difference between when the stations initially try to send their messages is also σ time units. In this case, the second station to attempt transmission will detect this collision σ time units before the other, and therefore, the stations will collide a second time if either stations decide to wait the same number of slots, or the first station waits for two slots while the second station decides to wait one slot; that is, the probability of colliding a second time is 0.75.

In general, as n increases, and since the range over which a station selects its backoff grows exponentially each time the stations collide, while $n \leq K + 1$, we see that the probability that the station collide n times declines rapidly. However, once $n > K + 1$, the stations' backoff counters are no longer incremented after a collision (they have reached their maximum value K), and therefore, the range of values over which the stations choose to "backoff" remains the same. Hence, the chance that they collide no longer falls as rapidly.

7.4.3.3 Expected Costs Finally, we consider two properties that can be analyzed by augmenting our probabilistic models with costs. First, we assign a cost of 1 to each transition in our model, which corresponds to a collision and then compute the expected number of collisions that will occur for different values of the maximum backoff limit K. These results (again, minimum and maximum values, over all resolutions of nondeterminism) are shown in Figure 7.6a. Second, we assign a cost of 1 to each transition, which represents a discrete timestep and then compute the expected time required for message sending to complete. These results can be found in Figure 7.6b. In principle, it would certainly be possible to also generate average values for these properties using discrete event simulation and Monte Carlo methods, as described above. However, these techniques are not yet supported in APMC, and so, we do not include such results.

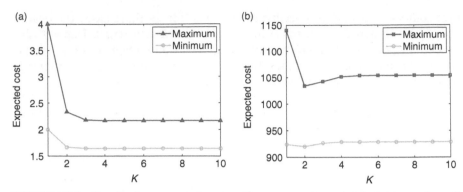

FIGURE 7.6   Results for expected cost until a message is sent. (a) Cost: number of collisions; (b) cost: elapsed time.

We see that both the expected number of collisions and expected time initially decrease as K increases. This results from the fact that, as K is incremented, there is less chance of the stations colliding when they attempt to retransmit and a message will be sent sooner. For the expected number of collisions, there is very little difference in the results once K is greater than 2. This is because the probability of colliding more than three times is very small (see Fig. 7.5). A similar situation exists for larger values of K in the graph for expected time. Note, though, that the expected time increases between $K = 2$ and $K = 4$ and is at its smallest for $K = 2$. This is because, although the probability of 3 or 4 collisions occurring is low, the larger amount of time spent in backoff in these cases increases the impact on the expected time.

7.5   DISCUSSION AND CONCLUSION

In this chapter, we have illustrated the applicability of formal verification to the analysis of communication protocols, in particular using PTA and probabilistic model checking, either with numerical solution methods or approximate techniques based on Monte Carlo simulation and sampling. We conclude with a discussion comparing these two approaches.

We first discuss the types of analysis that can be performed with each. The main strength of the numerical solution approach is that it is based on the full model, constructed via an exhaustive search of the state space. This means that it is possible to derive exact answers to temporal logic property queries (in fact, as discussed earlier, iterative numerical solution methods are usually used to construct an approximation up to the desired precision, but exact methods are always available). Furthermore, this exhaustive approach makes it possible to compute best- and worst-case results, for example, over all possible initial configurations for a model or all possible resolutions of nondeterminism (representing, e.g., concurrent scheduling between processes or multiple values for an unspecified model parameter).

By comparison, sampling-based techniques are inherently approximate, and the results represent a notion of average behavior. However, the methods are applicable to a far wider array of models and properties. Unlike numerical solution, which can only be used where tractable solution algorithms are available, sampling can be applied to any model on which a random simulation can be accurately performed. Similarly, any property that can be computed based on finite paths through the model can be analyzed in this way.

Another important area of comparison is the relative efficiency of the two approaches. Clearly, the improved accuracy and coverage of numerical solution comes at a cost. One of the principal advantages of sampling techniques is that the amount of memory required to execute them is fractional compared with exact approaches. This is because they can be performed on a succinct representation of the model (e.g., its description in some high-level modeling formalism), and the simulation process typically needs only to store a single state of the model at any time. This allows sampling to be performed on much larger models than numerical solution, where the exhaustive exploration and construction of the model could easily be infeasible. In the CSMA/CD case study presented earlier, for example, it would certainly be possible to consider larger model configurations with more than two stations.

A second advantage of the sampling is that it is significantly easier to implement in a parallel or distributed setting, which can of course dramatically improve the run time. This is because the computations of each individual sample are independent, unlike parallelizations of numerical solution, for which large amounts of process intercommunication are necessary. In fact, this performance advantage is rather important since, as we have seen earlier, to obtain accurate results, it may be necessary to generate an extremely large number of samples. In particular, this situation cannot be avoided when the actual values being computed are very small.

Overall, it is clear that both exact approaches to probabilistic model checking, based on exhaustive exploration of models followed by numerical solution, and approximate approaches based on discrete-event simulation and sampling, have contrasting advantages, disadvantages, and trade-offs. It is likely, therefore, that a successful analysis of large probabilistic system, such as a communication protocol, would make use of both types of technique.

ACKNOWLEDGMENTS

When this work was carried out, the authors were supported by the French project RNTL "Averroes" (Marie Duflot and Claudine Picaronny), FORWARD and EPSRC projects GR/S11107 and GR/S46727 (Marta Kwiatkowska, Gethin Norman, and David Parker), and MIUR-FIRB Perf (Jeremy Sproston). The authors also gratefully acknowledge the contributions of Laurent Fribourg, Thomas Hérault, Richard Lassaigne, Frédéric Magniette and Stéphane Messika, and EPITA for the use of their computing facilities.

REFERENCES

1. R. Alur and D. L. Dill. A theory of timed automata. *Theoretical Computer Science*, 126(2):183–235, 1994.

2. R. Alur and T. Henzinger. Reactive modules. *Formal Methods in System Design*, 15(1):7–48, 1999.

3. APMC web site. Available at: http://sylvain.berbiqui.org/apmc

4. J. Barnat, L. Brim, I. Cerna, M. Ceska, and J. Tumova. ProbDiVinE-MC: Multi-core LTL model checker for probabilistic systems. In *Proceedings of the 5th International Conference on Quantitative Evaluation of Systems (QEST'08)*, pp. 77–78, IEEE CS Press, 2008.

5. J. Berendsen, D. Jansen, and J.-P. Katoen. Probably on time and within budget—On reachability in priced probabilistic timed automata. In *Proceedings of the 3rd International Conference on Quantitative Evaluation of Systems (QEST'06)*, pp. 311–322, IEEE CS Press, 2006.

6. A. Bianco and L. de Alfaro. Model checking of probabilistic and nondeterministic systems. In P. Thiagarajan, ed. *Proceedings of the 15th International Conference on Foundations of Software Technology and Theoretical Computer Science (FSTTCS'95)*, *Volume 1026 of LNCS*, pp. 499–513, Springer, 1995.

7. P. Buchholz and P. Kemper. Numerical analysis techniques in the APNN toolbox. In Workshop on Formal Methods in Performance Evaluation and Applications, pp. 1–6, 1999.

8. F. Ciesinski and C. Baier. LiQuor: A tool for qualitative and quantitative linear time analysis of reactive systems. In *Proceedings of the 3rd International Conference on Quantitative Evaluation of Systems (QEST'06)*, pp. 131–132, IEEE CS Press, 2006.

9. C. Courcoubetis and M. Yannakakis. The complexity of probabilistic verification. *Journal of the ACM*, 42(4):857–907, 1995.

10. M. Duflot, L. Fribourg, T. Herault, R. Lassaigne, F. Magniette, S. Messika, S. Peyronnet, and C. Picaronny. Probabilistic model checking of the CSMA/CD protocol using PRISM and APMC. In M. Huth, ed. *Proceedings of the 4th Workshop on Automated Verification of Critical Systems (AVoCS'04), Volume 128 of ENTCS*, pp. 195–214, Elsevier Science, 2004.

11. M. Duflot, M. Kwiatkowska, G. Norman, and D. Parker. A formal analysis of bluetooth device discovery. *International Journal on Software Tools for Technology Transfer*, 8(6):621–632, 2006.

12. The Fortuna Model Checker. Available at: http://www.cs.ru.nl/J.Berendsen/fortuna/

13. T. Gonsalves and F. Tobagi. On the performance effects of station location and access protocol parameters in Ethernet networks. *IEEE Transactions on Communications*, 36(4):441–449, 1988.

14. G. Guirado, T. Herault, R. Lassaigne, and S. Peyronnet. Distribution, approximation and probabilistic model checking. In M. Leucker and J. van de Pol, eds. *Proceedings of the 4th International Workshop on Parallel and Distributed Methods in Verification (PDMC'05), Volume 135(2) of ENTCS*, pp. 19–30, Elsevier, 2005.

15. H. Hansson and B. Jonsson. A logic for reasoning about time and probability. *Formal Aspects of Computing*, 6(5):512–535, 1994.

16. T. Henzinger, X. Nicollin, J. Sifakis, and S. Yovine. Symbolic model checking for real-time systems. *Information and Computation*, 111(2):193–244, 1994.

17. T. Herault, R. Lassaigne, F. Magniette, and S. Peyronnet. Approximate probabilistic model checking. In B. Steffen and G. Levi, eds. *Proceedings of the 5th International Conference on Verification, Model Checking and Abstract Interpretation (VMCAI'04), Volume 2937 of LNCS*, pp. 73–84, 2004.

18. A. Hinton, M. Kwiatkowska, G. Norman, and D. Parker. PRISM: A tool for automatic verification of probabilistic systems. In H. Hermanns and J. Palsberg, eds. *Proceedings of the 12th International Conference on Tools and Algorithms for the Construction and Analysis of Systems (TACAS'06), Volume 3920 of LNCS*, pp. 441–444, Springer, 2006.

19. B. Jeannet, P. D'Argenio, and K. Larsen. RAPTURE: A tool for verifying Markov decision processes. In I. Cerna, ed. *Proceedings on Tools Day, Affiliated to 13th International Conference on Concurrency Theory (CONCUR'02), Technical Report FIMU-RS-2002-05*, pp. 84–98, Faculty of Informatics, Masaryk University, 2002.

20. J. Katoen. A semi-Markov model of a home network access protocol. In H. Schwetman, J. Walrand, K. Bagchi, and D. DeGroot, eds. *Proceedings of the International Workshop on Modeling, Analysis, and Simulation on Computer and Telecommunication Systems (MASCOTS'93)*, pp. 293–298, The Society for Computer Simulation, 1993.

21. J. Katoen, E. Hahn, H. Hermanns, D. Jansen, and I. Zapreev. The ins and outs of the probabilistic model checker MRMC. In *Proceedings of the 6th International Conference on Quantitative Evaluation of Systems (QEST'09)*, IEEE CS Press, 2009.

22. M. Kwiatkowska, G. Norman, and D. Parker. Stochastic games for verification of probabilistic timed automata. In J. Ouaknine and F. Vaandrager, eds. *Proceedings of the 7th International Conference on Formal Modeling and Analysis of Timed Systems (FORMATS'09), Volume 5813 of LNCS*, pp. 212–227, Springer, 2009.

23. M. Kwiatkowska, G. Norman, D. Parker, and J. Sproston. Performance analysis of probabilistic timed automata using digital clocks. *Formal Methods in System Design*, 29:33–78, 2006.

24. M. Kwiatkowska, G. Norman, and R. Segala. Automated verification of a randomized distributed consensus protocol using Cadence SMV and PRISM. In G. Berry, H. Comon, and A. Finkel, eds. *Proceedings of the 13th International Conference on Computer Aided Verification (CAV'01), Volume 2102 of LNCS*, pp. 194–206, Springer, 2001.

25. M. Kwiatkowska, G. Norman, R. Segala, and J. Sproston. Automatic verification of real-time systems with discrete probability distributions. *Theoretical Computer Science*, 286:101–150, 2002.

26. M. Kwiatkowska, G. Norman, and J. Sproston. Probabilistic model checking of the IEEE 802.11 wireless local area network protocol. In H. Hermanns and R. Segala, eds. *Proceedings of the PAPM/PROBMIV'02, Volume 2399 of LNCS*, pp. 169–187, Springer, 2002.

27. M. Kwiatkowska, G. Norman, and J. Sproston. Probabilistic model checking of deadline properties in the IEEE 1394 FireWire root contention protocol. *Formal Aspects of Computing*, 14(3):295–318, 2003.

28. M. Kwiatkowska, G. Norman, J. Sproston, and F. Wang. Symbolic model checking for probabilistic timed automata. *Information and Computation*, 205(7):1027–1077, 2007.

29. PRISM web site. Available at: http://www.prismmodelchecker.org

30. M. Riedl, J. Schuster, and M. Siegle. Recent extensions to the stochastic process algebra tool CASPA. In *Proceedings of the 5th International Conference on Quantitative Evaluation of Systems (QEST'08)*, pp. 113–114, IEEE CS Press, 2008.

31. A. Roy and K. Gopinath. Improved probabilistic models for 802.11 protocol verification. In K. Etessami and S. Rajamani, eds. *Proceedings of the 17th International Conference on Computer Aided Verification (CAV'05), Volume 3576 of LNCS*, pp. 239–252, Springer, 2005.

32. J. Rutten, M. Kwiatkowska, G. Norman, and D. Parker. *Mathematical Techniques for Analyzing Concurrent and Probabilistic Systems*. P. Panangaden and F. van Breugel, eds. Volume 23 of CRM Monograph Series. AMS, 2004.

33. R. Segala and N. A. Lynch. Probabilistic simulations for probabilistic processes. *Nordic Journal of Computing*, 2(2):250–273, 1995.

34. M. Tribastone. The PEPA plug-in project. In *Proceedings of the 4th International Conference on Quantitative Evaluation of Systems (QEST'07)*, pp. 53–54, IEEE Computer Society, 2007.

35. J. Wang and S. Keshav. Efficient and accurate Ethernet simulation. In *Proceedings of the 24th IEEE Conference on Local Computer Networks*, pp. 182–191, 1999.

36. H. Younes. Ymer: A statistical model checker. In *Proceedings of the 17th International Conference on Computer Aided Verification (CAV'05), Volume 3576 of LNCS*, pp. 429–433, Springer, 2005.

37. H. Younes and R. Simmons. Probabilistic verification of discrete event systems using acceptance sampling. In E. Brinksma and K. Larsen, eds. *Proceedings of the 14th International Conference on Computer Aided Verification (CAV'02), Volume 2404 of LNCS*, pp. 223–235, Springer, 2002.

38. S. Yovine. Kronos: A verification tool for real-time systems. *International Journal of Software Tools for Technology Transfer*, 1:123–133, 1997.

PART V

INTERNET AND ONLINE SERVICES

CHAPTER 8

DESIGN FOR VERIFIABILITY: THE OCS CASE STUDY

JOHANNES NEUBAUER
Chair Programming Systems, TU Dortmund University, Dortmund, Germany

TIZIANA MARGARIA
Chair Service and Software Engineering, University of Potsdam, Potsdam, Germany

BERNHARD STEFFEN
Chair Programming Systems, TU Dortmund University, Dortmund, Germany

8.1 INTRODUCTION

The Online Conference System (OCS) is an online manuscript submission and review service. It is part of a product line for the Springer Verlag that started in 1999 [20–21, 29] and evolved over time to include also journal and volume production preparation services. The OCS acts as a decision support system facilitating the process of approving and rejecting submissions. Therefore, the service follows a well-defined workflow that is customized for different application areas like conferences or journals. Its aim is to assist the efficient cooperation of the different participants in this collaborative process.

Since 2009, the OCS underwent a complete redesign and reimplementation, with the aim of making it more flexible and adaptable, and at the same time better suited to verification. Figure 8.1 sketches how we proceeded. We started with some local models describing, for example, the overall evaluation pattern for conference proceedings and the life cycle of papers from the user's perspective. These models can then be model checked for essential properties, comprising security aspects, progress properties, or simply the intended causality. Subsequently, these "local" models were semiautomatically combined and

Formal Methods for Industrial Critical Systems: A Survey of Applications, First Edition.
Edited by Stefania Gnesi and Tiziana Margaria.
© 2013 IEEE. Published 2013 by John Wiley & Sons, Inc.

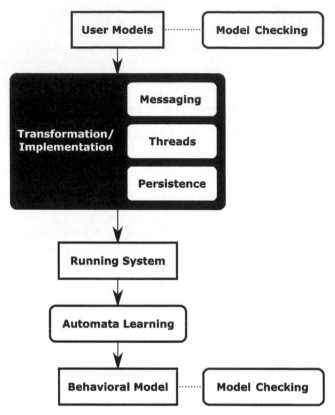

FIGURE 8.1   Procedure model for the model-driven development approach for the new OCS.

transformed to run on an enterprise platform using complex communication and synchronization primitives, like event handling and process creation. In particular, this means that we did not construct any global model of the OCS. Rather, we gave full freedom for the above-mentioned transformation, which we then complemented by automata learning techniques described in Section 8.4, to retrospectively infer a global model.

In this chapter, we focus on the verification, validation, and in particular the learning aspects, and treat the complex semiautomatic transformation process (highlighted in black), which takes care of

- process synchronization via messages,
- event handling via messages,
- parallelism via (dynamically created) threads (shared resources), and
- persistence of the process state and business objects,

as a "black box." More concretely, we will describe how the "local" models of the OCS are developed (Sections 8.2 and 8.3) and verified (Section 8.4), and how their combination to a system running on an enterprise platform can be validated (Section 8.5). Key to the global validation of the corresponding emergent behavior is the experimental exploration of and behavioral model construction for the system via automata learning. Subsequently, we will sketch how this approach might scale (Section 8.5.3), summarize related work (Section 8.6), and finally present our conclusions and perspectives (Section 8.7).

8.2 THE USER MODEL

Abstractly seen, the central purpose of the OCS is the adequate handling of a wealth of independent but often indirectly related user interactions. So seen, the OCS is a reactive system with a graphical user interface (GUI) provided as a web application. Users can decide when they execute their tasks, which typically consist of small workflows themselves, and, in case of multiple tasks, the order in which they want to process or perhaps reject them. In addition, this interaction potential strongly depends on the phase (submission phase, reviewing phase, discussion phase, etc.) of the evaluation process, which there-fore has a clear control-oriented character. However, the high degree of freedom in choosing individual tasks and the large number of involved actors excludes a direct modeling in terms of control-oriented graph structures (e.g., automata, transition systems) due to the state-explosion problem [6]. We therefore decided for a hybrid modeling in terms of

- a collection of individual models for each business entity (like conference, paper) organized and synchronized by means of events and resource sharing,
- individual models in terms of control-flow graph-like structures, express-ing the stepwise evolution of the individual processes for each of the involved business objects within the overall evaluation process, which consist of
- states embedding ECA rules* that declaratively express the alternative behaviors that the system offers in each state.

Whereas the individual models for the various business entities can be verified by means of techniques like model checking, as described in Section 8.4, we propose an alternative approach for dealing with the evaluation processes' overall correctness: the use of automata learning to learn (infer) the global behavioral model from the real implementation via guided experimentation

---

* ECA rules model the potential of user interactions as a set of rules that can be accessed concur-rently, and that are selected according to a current event and an associated condition.

(see Section 8.5). The charm of this approach is that it suppresses all the internal details of the complex design models as well as the difficulty of dealing with the complex communication and synchronization methods in modern enterprise architectures, and clearly focuses on the primary issue: the user-level correctness.

Figure 8.2 depicts the user model of a conference paper's behavior as such a hybrid graph. Syntactically, the first state is the "Start" node and the control flows along the edges. Edge labels represent events (either system events or user interactions) that trigger the transition to a successor state. System events occur for instance when a deadline expires, causing the system to transition to a different phase (state) with a different behavior.

The OCS is a role-based system [22], meaning that in a given state, different roles may have different action potentials. These different action potentials are therefore distinguished in our models, and modeled individually within a state, separated by vertical bars. For example, as soon as a conference is activated (right after the start node), the conference is in the "abstract submission" state and users with role submitter may submit abstracts while other roles cannot. In addition, there are pure control flow nodes without any internal structure that, for example, check a condition (like "reviewer assigned?") or do other system actions like escalating a problem to the person responsible (e.g., "escalate to pc chair").

The available actions in a given state are recognizably modeled as ECA rules. What of the rich control structure is best captured as control structure, and what as ECA rule is not uniquely determined and it is clearly a matter of design. In fact, if one wishes less states and more compact graphs, it is possible to introduce more preconditions than just those defined by the state and the role. Syntactically, a precondition of an ECA rule is denoted by a condition in square brackets followed by an implication sign ("$\rightarrow$"). For example, "[*docav ail*]$\rightarrow$*downloaddoc*" means that a document can be downloaded only after it is stored, that is, after an upload. Postconditions are defined analogously. All the actions in a state refer to ECA rules. If they have more sophisticated conditions, they are not modeled in the user model but in the ECA rule itself. For example, a document upload may be constrained to "PDF" files.

We use hierarchy to achieve simpler and better structured models. For example, in the phase "review" of Figure 8.2, the ECA rule for the reviewer has a boldface "review" action. This graphically indicates that there is a submodel for this rule, here shown in Figure 8.3. The submodel shows how to use subreviewers in the reviewing process. The use of hierarchy considerably simplifies the user model of Figure 8.2, and additionally, it shows that the subreviewing is a self-contained behavior. Indeed, some conferences do not allow subreviewing at all.

In Figures 8.2 and 8.3, the user model describes the workflow of a single paper. Thus, the roles "submitter" and "reviewer" are here related to the currently considered paper, whereas the roles "pc member" and "pc chair" act more globally as they are related to the conference service for the running

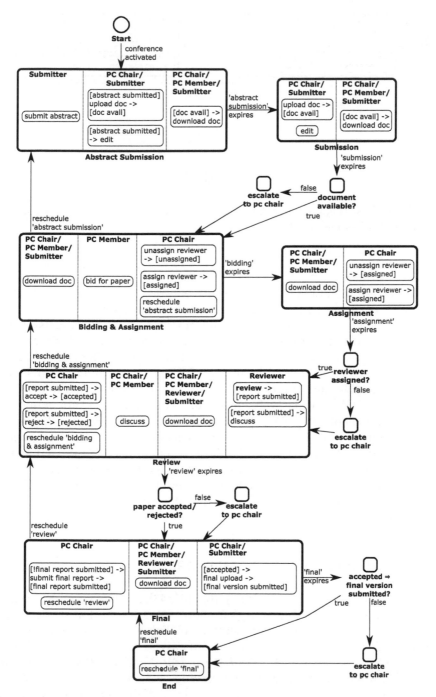

FIGURE 8.2   The hybrid user model of a paper's behavior in the new OCS.

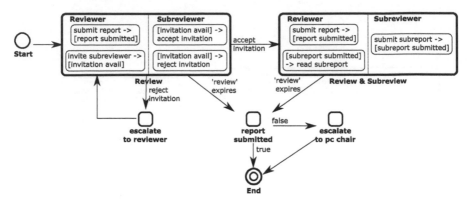

FIGURE 8.3   Workflow process of a review. This refers to the bold written ECA rule labeled "review" in Figure 8.2.

conference. For better readability, the figure only displays one reviewer for the considered paper together with one associated subreviewer.

This modeling style makes it easy and modular to define variants of the conference and paper workflows: Different conference workflows can be defined in separate user models and coexist in the same OCS system. The set of ECA rules in each state in the user model can also be interpreted as the currently available functions in the OCS. We use this information to dynamically build the GUI for the web application. At runtime, the system queries which conditions of the ECA rules evaluate to true and presents the corresponding action set to the user's GUI. This dynamic way of GUI construction is independent of the concrete workflow of the conference service and therefore applies to any variant of the (conference) service that may arise.

The graphs we just discussed are themselves formal models. They are modeled in the jABC (Section 8.3) and model checked as shown in Section 8.4.

8.3   THE MODELS AND THE FRAMEWORK

The OCS models are realized in the jABC [33, 48], a framework for service-oriented design and development that allows users to develop services and applications easily by composing reusable building blocks into (flow-) graph structures that are both formally sound and easy to read and to build. These building blocks are called *Service-Independent Building Blocks* (SIBs) in analogy to the telecommunication terminology [45], and in the spirit of the service-oriented computing paradigm [28, 35] and of the *One Thing Approach* [46], an evolution of the model-based lightweight coordination approach of Reference 32 specifically applied to services. The SIBs are parameterizable so that their behavior can be adapted depending on the current context of use.

Furthermore, each SIB has one or more outgoing branches, which specify the successor of the SIB. Which branch of the SIB is used is determined at runtime.

On the basis of a large library of such SIBs, the user builds models for the desired system in terms of hierarchical graphs called *Service Logic Graphs* (SLGs) [4]. In an SLG, a SIB may represent a single functionality or a whole subgraph (i.e., another SLG), thus serving as a macro that hides more detailed process models. This feature grants a high reusability not only of components, but also of whole (sub-) models, within larger applications.

SLGs are semantically interpreted as Kripke Transition Systems (KTS), a generalization of both Kripke structures and labeled transition systems [38] that allows labels both on nodes and edges. Nodes in the SLG represent activities (or services/components, depending on the application domain). The edges directly correspond to SIB branches: They describe how to continue the execution depending on the result of the previous activity.

An extensible set of jABC plug-ins provides additional functionality that adequately supports the activities needed along the development life cycle, like animation, rapid prototyping, formal verification, debugging, code generation, and change management.

The Tracer plug-in provides the execution layer for SLGs within jABC. The Tracer interprets an SLG as an executable directed control flow graph, which can be traced, like in a standard debugger, in run mode or step mode and using breakpoints or pause to interrupt the execution. It can be used throughout the development cycle to test the runtime behavior, from a quick animation of the initial models to a more thorough simulation in later stages.

Once the SLG of a jABC application is fully designed and the SIBs are all implemented, the graph is ready for code generation and deployment. This is the task of Genesys [19], a jABC plug-in that provides highly specialized code generators for different target platforms and languages like Java, C#, BPEL, and Android.

The interpretation of an SLG as KTS is, however, the central feature to enable formal verification of these models, and to ensure at design time that they comply to a set of properties. This is important not only during the initial development phase, but in particular also during the system's evolution, in order to support change management in a property-oriented way.

8.4 MODEL CHECKING

We use model checking during the whole development process to ensure that specific properties hold on the models for the individual business objects. From the system's point of view, this activity can be regarded as subsystem-level verification. There is no global design model. Rather, the global system behavior only emerges through the actual implementation-level interaction between the process instances realizing the various subsystems. As we will see in Section 8.5, the global behavior can be validated on models extrapolated using specifically adapted automata learning technology.

The properties we want to verify for the models of the subsystems presented as SLGs are expressed in Computational Tree Logic (CTL) [6], enhanced with the parameterized box and diamond operator of Hennessy–Milner Logic (HML) [12]:

$$\Phi ::= AP \mid (\neg\Phi) \mid (\Phi \wedge \Phi) \mid (\Phi \vee \Phi) \mid AG\Phi \mid A(\Phi U\Phi) \mid [a]\Phi \mid \langle a\rangle\Phi. \quad (8.1)$$

The semantic interpretation is as follows:

- AP represents the atomic propositions, in particular *tt* and *ff*, the constants true and false.
- $\neg$, $\wedge$, and $\vee$ are the usual Boolean operators.
- $AG\Phi$ means "Φ holds on each path at each state."
- $A(\Phi U\Psi)$ means "on each path, Φ holds until Ψ is true. Ψ is required to hold (at least) at one state along each path. Where Ψ is true, Φ might be true or not."
- $[a]\Phi$: "Φ holds on all 'a'-successor nodes."
- $\langle a\rangle$ Φ: "Φ holds on at least one 'a'-successor node."

CTL is a widely used formalism to express properties of systems that are modeled as automata, as in this case. In this book, it is also used by Siminiceanu and Ciardo (Chapter 5) to reason about properties of avionics systems.

The user model shown in Figure 8.2, which we already sketched in Section 8.2, describes the control flow of handling paper submissions during the whole life cycle of a conference service, which is organized in several phases (like "abstract submission," "submission," "bidding," "review," "final"), each with dedicated actions. For example, a document upload for a paper should only be allowed in the "abstract submission" and the "submission" phases, a property that can be expressed in our version of CTL:

$$AG([`\text{submission}´ \text{expires}](AG(\neg\text{upload doc}))). \quad (8.2)$$

This formula, which expresses that upload doc is prohibited after the edge labeled with 'submission' expires is traversed, can then be easily checked for the SLG describing the paper handling via model checking. Surprisingly, it turns out that the property does not hold. This is due to some "feature interaction" [17–18] with a (popular) OCS feature that allows to reschedule the submission phase (see the edge reschedule 'abstract submission' pointing to the 'abstract submission' phase in Fig. 8.2). As we do not want to sacrifice this popular feature, we must relax the property to tolerate the additional behavior, for example, in the following fashion:

$$AG(['\text{submission}' \text{expires}](A((\neg\text{upload doc})U(\text{Abstract Submission})))). \quad (8.3)$$

8.5 VALIDATING EMERGING GLOBAL BEHAVIOR VIA AUTOMATA LEARNING

Characteristic for our approach to verify global system properties is the clear cut between the "traditional" treatment of subsystems, as sketched above, and the learning-based investigation of global behavior. Like for many practical systems, extending the local modeling of the subsystems to a formal model of the global behavior of the OCS (as we did in Reference 22 for the role-based aspects) would be very tedious, as it involves various communication and synchronization paradigms, like event handling, shared resources, and even process creation, and all this for quite a number of running process instances. We therefore adopted a different view: The primary concern is only the global user process, and only effects visible there are essential. Automata learning (see Chapter 11 and also References 16 and 41) has the potential to infer or extrapolate approximations and views of this user process via systematic experimentation with the application running on an enterprise platform. Being experimentation/test based, this approach has the following advantages:

- the otherwise inevitable state-explosion problem does not arise,
- the investigation bases on the real enterprise system with all its complex communication and synchronization mechanism,
- the modeling can be fine-tuned via abstraction, suppressing detail, and projection, focusing on certain activities,
- the precision of the modeling can be improved along the systems' life cycle: Discrepancies between the extrapolated model and the real system revealed during model-based monitoring can directly be used to refine the model.

The arising models can then be used for test generation, in particular for regression testing, verification via model checking (see the procedure model in Fig. 8.1), as well as for some manual inspection. In the following, we will illustrate this approach by first learning some abstract views of the global user behavior, before we indicate how domain knowledge can be used to make this approach scale to larger, eventually realistic system models.

8.5.1 The Learning Setup

In this section, we show how the learning approach presented in Chapter 11 can be applied to the OCS. This requires in particular to identify an adequate alphabet, which allows us to steer the experimentation and to observe the essential system structure. Due to the flexibility of the LearnLib [39–41], we can directly infer models in terms of specific SLGs, which, structurally, very much resemble Mealy machines [30, 43], that is, the model structure specifically supported by the LearnLib [30]. The corresponding input alphabet, the

FIGURE 8.4 Input alphabet: A set of user-level atomic actions.

basis for dynamically defining the test cases for the learning-based interrogation of the system, is given by the application programming interface (API) of the OCS for the web client. The reactions to these test cases constitute the output alphabet. The SLG shown in Figure 8.6 is an example of a small learned model. It has four states, indicated by the circular nodes, and 25 transitions, represented by the squares. The labels of these squares are taken from the input alphabet (see Fig. 8.4 for the initial input alphabet considered later), and the edges leaving the squares are labeled with symbols of the output alphabet (here `default` and `error`). The next section provides an intuitive account of this kind of modeling.

This SLG representation is quite verbose, but it has two advantages:

- as the square nodes directly correspond to API calls to OCS, these models are directly executable within the jABC, and
- it can also be used to represent the test cases dynamically created during the learning process, with the effect that the jABC immediately becomes a corresponding test environment.

Before the SIBs displayed in Figure 8.4 can be used in test cases, they must be fully instantiated. For example, the login SIB must be filled in with a user/password combination, and, typically, one would need at least one correct and one incorrect such combination in order to explore the system to be learned.

The learning process itself also requires some preparation:

- As the dynamically created test cases must be independent, it is important to start each of them on a "fresh" system. According to the abstraction technique for *resetting* as described in Chapter 11, we solve this by creating a new conference in the OCS for each test case.
- The learning process iteratively produces so-called hypothesis models, that is, intermediate models that are consistent with the observations made so far. So-called *equivalence queries* then check whether these hypotheses match already the desired models. For the OCS, we provide enhanced input symbols (cf. Fig. 8.5) that allow us to pinpoint potential differences more easily between hypotheses and the system to be learned.

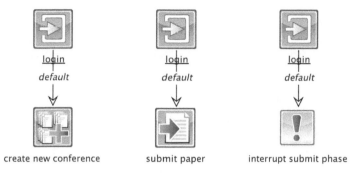

login

default

login

default

login

default

create new conference   submit paper   interrupt submit phase

FIGURE 8.5   Input sequences as an enhancement to the alphabet.

The following still quite elementary treatment of the OCS is based on these prerequisites.

8.5.2   Learning Behavioral Models

Once the alphabet shown in Figure 8.4 is fully instantiated, the automata learner generates the SLG in Figure 8.6. This SLG, which is itself executable on the real OCS, describes the behavior of the OCS at a level of abstraction implicitly defined by the chosen set of input symbols.

In this SLG, the SIBs labeled State <number> correspond to the states of the underlying Mealy machine. Outgoing edges from these states reach the SIBs corresponding to the OCS input symbols. For example, in State 0, the user can log in or log out. We see this because we can go from State 0 to another state over SIBs labeled with those actions and with a positive verdict (their default outgoing edge). On the other hand, in this state, the user can neither submit a paper nor create a new conference, because these actions lead to negative verdicts (the outgoing edges error), and thus are not feasible in the underlying OCS.

The SLG shown in Figure 8.6 was obtained with a standard approximation of an equivalence oracle, that is, an oracle designed to detect discriminating runs, which are runs in the symmetric difference of the hypothesis model and the real system. This simple oracle simply looks for discrepancies with a look-ahead of one around each state of the hypothesis automaton. As equivalence oracles are in practice typically not realizable (cf. Chapter 11), the LearnLib offers a collection of different approximations for them. A very simple extension to the "one look-ahead" version is to enhance the input alphabet with sequences of elementary input symbols, like the ones shown in Figure 8.5 for the OCS. This alphabet enhancement directly leads to the refined five-state model displayed in Figure 8.7. The slight extension of the look-ahead caused by the three combined alphabet symbols is, for example, sufficient for our simple approximation of the equivalence query to detect that in the hypothesis,

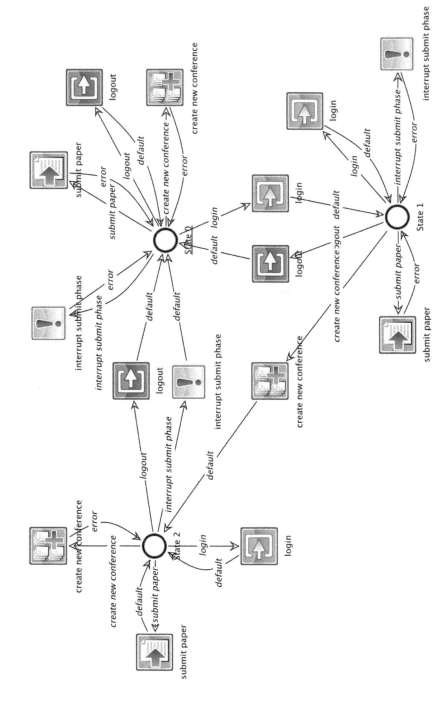

FIGURE 8.6 Learned Mealy machine with atomic alphabet only (Fig. 8.4).

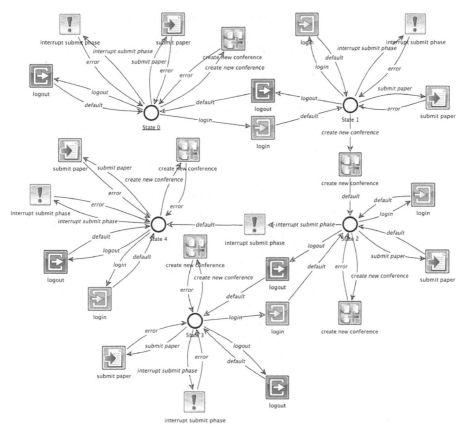

FIGURE 8.7   Learned Mealy machine with symbol sequences (Fig. 8.5).

it is not possible to submit a paper once you have logged out, even though it should be possible, after you have logged in again.

Section 8.5.3 indicates how learning can be enhanced to obtain truly realistic behavioral models. In fact, using the LearnLib, we were already able to learn models with thousands of states [40]. One of the main obstacles in practice is the realization of an adequate equivalence oracle, that is, one that detects discriminating runs very quickly [13]. In fact, manual guidance may be very handy here. This is supported by the SLGs for the hypothesis models being executable: Their execution is automatic for square SIBs, and whenever a (circular) state SIB is executed, a dialog pops up and offers the user the choice of the next input symbol and therefore allows the user to guide the search for discriminating runs.

More elaborate is the possibility of a model-checking-based search for discriminating runs. As the SLGs can readily be model checked, you may formulate temporal formulas that are assumed to hold for the OCS. If such a formula fails to hold for the hypothesis model, it is a concrete candidate to be tested on the OCS. If this test succeeds, a discriminating run is found. In fact, a refinement of the model of Figure 8.6 toward the model of Figure 8.7 could have also been obtained via a formula that expresses the fact that it is always possible to eventually submit a paper until the submission phase is interrupted.

8.5.3 Automata Learning Facilitating Domain Knowledge

Learning requires the execution of a large number of tests on a system to be learned. Even without any test that checks for conformance of hypotheses and the actual system, at least kn^2 test runs (called "membership queries" in the learning literature) are required, where n is the number of states and k is the number of inputs. A model with 30 states and 12 inputs requires already more than 10,000 tests. In a simulated environment or in scenarios where there is only local computation involved in the execution of one query, this is no problem. On systems like the OCS, such huge numbers of queries cannot be conducted. The test driver for learning the OCS triggers a real installation of the system similar to the setup in a productive environment. The queries are sent over a network via Remote Method Invocation (RMI). Every parameter and each return value has to be serialized and deserialized in this process. This results in execution times per symbol of up to several seconds. Hence, learning—which may easily comprise hundreds of thousands of test cases— turns out to be a long-lasting activity.

In References 14, 15, and 31, filters have been introduced to reduce the number of required test cases on the basis of domain knowledge as also explained in Chapter 11. For the OCS, we constructed the setup displayed in Figure 8.8, where the actual test execution is guarded by five filters. A filter evaluates an incoming query. If it can answer the whole query without running new tests, it will return that answer and avoid the redundant experimental effort. Some filters modify the query and pass only a prefix to the next filter and return a concatenated answer using domain knowledge for adding the suffix, for example. The order of the filters may change the outcome significantly [31]. A filter may also delegate a query unmodified to the next filter. The following list describes the filters mentioned in Figure 8.8. They are used for learning a bigger automaton presented hereafter:

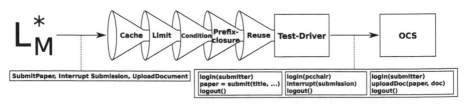

FIGURE 8.8 The learn setup with filters for the OCS.

Cache. The learning algorithm produces redundant queries at some points, especially during handling counterexamples. The cache filter maintains all the computed results and answers duplicates directly.

Limit. The limit filter limits the number of occurrences of a symbol in a test. If the filter is, for example, set to 1 and the symbol occurs twice, the filter discards the suffix of the word and produces the output symbol error.

Condition. The condition filter truncates the suffix of a word that misses a necessary symbol as a precondition or that has a preceding symbol that is prohibited, and returns the output symbols error for the remaining suffix.

Prefix-closure. The OCS uses a transaction manager. If an error occurs, the active transaction is rolled back without changing the system state. The prefix-closure filter facilitates this property and cuts the suffix of a failed query, and returns the output symbol error.

Reuse. The reuse filter saves resets and symbol executions by reusing existing conference services. If a prefix of a test has already been requested, the reuse filter will execute the suffix on the corresponding conference service and return the concatenation of the output symbols of the already executed prefix and the newly executed suffix.

Figure 8.9 depicts the correspondingly learned model for the alphabet shown in Figure 8.10 in terms of a deterministic automaton with partial transition function, where all states are accepting, and where the input symbols are abbreviated (but still uniquely identifiable). This representation is possible because the automaton is prefix-closed and, after eliminating all error branches, only possesses one output symbol. The model, learned in 1 hour and 58 minutes, has 29 states and 107 transitions. Figures 8.11 and 8.12 show the effect of the different filters. In short, the L_M^* algorithm uses 31,971 queries and 432,558 symbols. Applying the filters reduces the tests to 1518, and only 8418 symbols are executed on the system under test (SUT). This means that the treatment of 95.25% of the queries and 98.05% of the symbols have been suppressed by the filters.

While learning this model, we detected a flaw in the system that escaped our traditional testing effort: Interrupting the submission and upload phase before a paper is submitted immediately leads to the end state, as seen in the highlighted error trace in Figure 8.9. At the concrete level of the OCS implementation, this error corresponds to a deadlock after the interruption mentioned above. That this deadlock is identified with the state in which the model terminated is due to the fact that in both situations the only continuation is the empty word. Thus, they are Nerode equivalent.

At the same time, the learned model is still incorrect, because our approximative equivalence oracle was too weak to reveal all observable states. For example, the highlighted reflexive edges for accepting and rejecting a paper in states 2, 11, 16, 23, and 28 should lead to new states, analogously to

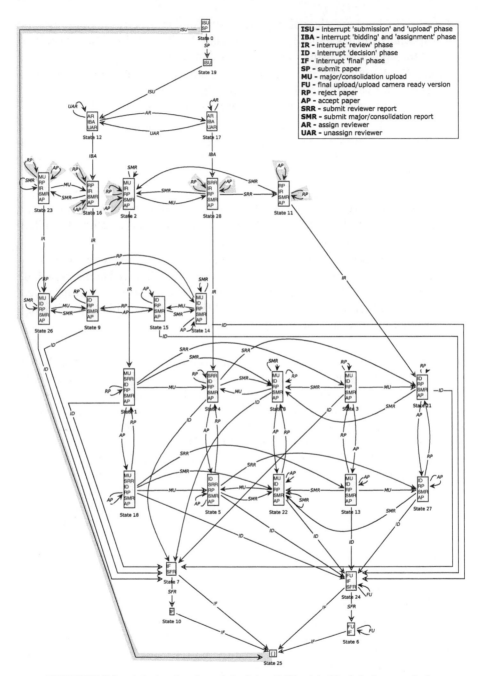

FIGURE 8.9   A behavioral model of the OCS with 12 alphabet symbols.

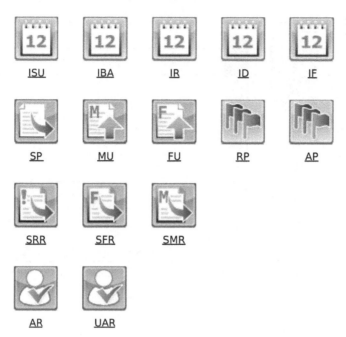

FIGURE 8.10   Alphabet with 12 symbols. The authentification is integrated into the alphabet symbols.

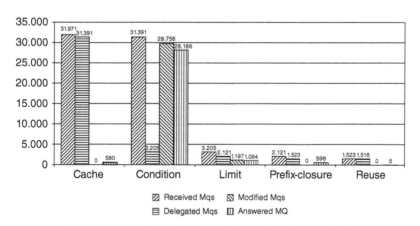

FIGURE 8.11   Filter statistics (membership queries).

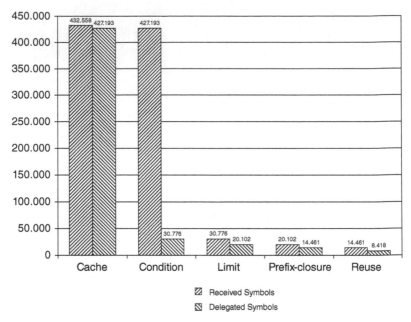

FIGURE 8.12   Filter statistics (symbols).

the situation for states 1 and 4. We are currently improving our approximative equivalence oracle to automatically resolve such problems.

8.6   RELATED WORK

The approach of using automata learning to bridge the gap between local feature models and their combined emerging behavior on an enterprise platform with complex state-of-the-art communication and synchronization facilities is new, and to our knowledge, there is no literature on a similar application of such techniques.

Related work can be found, however, on the three aspects of (1) verifying feature-based systems, (2) verifying aspects of online conference systems, and (3) verifying policies in general.

8.6.1   Feature-Based Systems

Feature-based systems have their longest history in the telecommunication domain, where they have been successfully in use on a global scale since the late 1980s. These systems can be seen as the precursors of the more modern concept of product lines, and are still the most challenging, ubiquitous, and large-scale implementations of this category of systems. In the traditional telephony setting, features are understood as modifiers of a basic telephony service [5]. Features are typically executed sequentially, each of them departing and returning to the base service, in the so-called daisy or sequential model of execution [44]. In web-based applications, the proportion between base system and features is more extreme: Web-based applications have a minimal skeleton service and are almost completely constituted of features. The modeling and verification of such feature-based systems has been studied in depth for quite a while: For example, advanced compositional model-checking techniques have been proposed in References 3 and 26 to deal efficiently with the specification of properties of feature-based systems. The goal there is to be able to partition both the functionality and the requirements and to achieve automatic property composition at checking time. In the original OCS as well as in the new OCS described here, in order to account for the necessary complex evolution of services and for their flexible adaptation, we allow a *multilevel organization* of features, whereby specialized features are built on the availability of other, more basic, functionalities. In order to keep this structure manageable and the resulting behaviors easily understandable, we restrict us to *monotonic features*, which are guaranteed to add behavior. Restricting behavior, which is also done via features in other contexts (e.g., in a feature-based design in Reference 11) and similarly in aspect-oriented design [24], is done in an orthogonal way in our setting: via constraints at the requirements level. The redefinition of behavior via features, which is a mechanism considered, for example, in Reference 11 with a clear influence by the overwriting practices of object-oriented design, is not allowed in our setting. This is a clear design choice, because attempts to define and analyze interactions in the presence of redefining features have clearly shown that it is very hard to deal with feature models that allow modification and inhibition. Because we wish the behavior to be as compositional as possible, and the composition to be as intuitive and explicit as possible, we prefer to avoid any modeling trait that could mask transparency and lead to incongruences or unexpected interferences.

In contrast to Reference 5, we distinguish the description of the feature's behavior from that of a feature's legal use. Restrictions of behaviors are in fact expressed at a different level, that is, at the requirements level (via temporal logic constraints), and are part of an aspect-oriented description of properties that we want to be able to check automatically, using formal verification methods. All the properties mentioned earlier in Section 8.4 are requirements expressible in this logic, and they are instances of the classes of safety and consistency requirements identified in Reference 1 to be characteristic of computer-supported collaborative work platforms. They are specific instantiations of role-based access control (RBAC) models [42]. Being able to automatically verify such properties via model checking is a clear advantage of the jABC, and it is essential in order to guarantee the safety of the kind of applications we build.

8.6.2 Aspects of Online Conference Systems

Concerning online conference systems, surprisingly little is published in scientific conferences about these tools, given that many originate directly in the community of computer scientists and that they are an excellent domain for the application and validation of the design and verification methods put forward by the community and even by their respective authors themselves. There were early papers on Cyberchair [49] and Continue [25], but very little is found on the concrete information of what and how is verified of these systems. After all, such submission systems treasure the still unpublished intellectual property of entire communities, so it would be reasonable to expect a high interest of the communities to know how their intellectual property is guarded.

Concerning verification, Continue has been used as case study in a number of papers on modeling and verification [9, 27, 36]. They concern the use of abstract state machines to model the dynamic aspects of policies [9], ensuring that the navigation in the browser does not undermine the policies that enforce restricted access [27, 36], and the model checker for policy verification Margrave [8]. The dynamic aspects considered in this work are just the normal phase-oriented switch of rights for each role, which we elegantly capture as SLG (as shown in Fig. 8.2) without the need to resort to any additional and more technical formalism. The formal verification of the OCS has been described in several papers [21–23], in particular concerning the treatment of roles and rights and a comparison with other policy description languages.

8.6.3 Policies

Access to sensible data via complex online services requires an adequate mechanism to define, verify, and enact policy compliance that ensures the trustability of a service [7]. In Reference 23, we described and compared the XML-based description languages XACML [10, 37] and WS-Policy [2] with the constraint and graph-based approach for modeling access control as used by the OCS. In a perspective of change management and evolution, a structured and flexible policy model is needed to handle dynamism, particularly when handling rights in systems with many users that hold different roles. While XACML and WS-Policy can be sufficient to describe local role/rights models, adequate to express static policies, for the OCS, we need to express process-oriented policies: Such policies embed local policies in a temporal component, in the sense of linear time temporal logics or as in our case branching time temporal logics. This is elegantly covered by the jABC-based capabilities, but neither covered by XACML nor WS-Policy, which are purely propositional. Furthermore, the model-based validation of policy constraints via model checking is an important key to warrant the reliability of service control mechanisms. This enables the continuous compliance checking along the incremental refinement and evolution along the entire lifetime of the service, this way adequately supporting the alignment between a service and its policy set. For the moment, this is provided in the jABC, but not by XACML and WS-Policy, which are therefore still insufficient for our needs.

8.7 CONCLUSION AND PERSPECTIVES

We introduced a new hybrid modeling approach aimed at overcoming the gap between intuitive user-level modeling and complex applications running in an enterprise environment. Prerequisite of our approach is to model the essential business entities, like in case of the OCS, conferences, papers, and other business objects, in terms of control-flow graph-like structures. These structures express the stepwise evolution of the business entities within the overall evaluation process, which consist of states embedding ECA rules that declaratively express the alternative behaviors that the system offers in each state, and help to semiautomatically combine these "local" models into a global system. The global system runs on an enterprise platform using complex communication and synchronization primitives, like event handling and process creating. This way the individual models for the various business entities can be verified by means of techniques like model checking, but the global system cannot, as there is no corresponding global model. We have indicated how this shortcoming can be overcome using automata learning to infer global behavioral models from the real implementation via guided experimentation, in order to support validation and verification at the system level. The entire development is consistent with the principles of *incremental formalization* [47] and *continuous model-driven engineering* [34] that we advocate for a gradual but consistent form of design support via formal methods, applied not only initially at design time, but throughout the system's lifetime and evolution.

The OCS covers many different applications areas. It is currently used for conferences, journals, and other variants of submission and review processes, but it can be easily customized to support other instances of committee-based distributed decision support. The complexity supporting the needs of all variations is handled by introducing product lines, organized at the modeling level. All conference, journal, or other services can coexist in one OCS instance. This way, resources are saved and all services can depend on one consistent user database.

So far, we have learned only a small portion of the OCS. The next goal is to learn larger parts, which requires advances in the following dimensions:

- enhance the alphabet of considered actions,
- optimize the learn process:
  - further reduce the really executed membership queries via filters that utilize the available domain knowledge;
  - establish views on the behavioral model, in order to concentrate on specific aspects of the model;

     ◦ elaborate on the level of abstraction for the learn process, in order to get a reasonable model (e.g., constrain the count of papers in a conference, or the count of reviewers for a paper).

Fortunately, the development of the LearnLib, our learning framework, goes exactly in these directions. We are therefore confident that we will be able to demonstrate the impact of these improvements soon, by providing expressive models of the OCS's global behavior that comprise causal relations and policies, security aspects, and progress properties.

REFERENCES

1. T. Ahmed and A. R. Tripathi. Static verification of security requirements in role based cscw systems. SACMAT, pp. 196–203. ACM, 2003.

2. S. Bajaj, et al. Web services policy 1.2-framework (WS-policy). W3C Member Submission, 25, 2006.

3. C. Blundell, K. Fisler, S. Krishnamurthi, and P. Van Hentenryck. Parameterized interfaces for open system verification of product lines. In *ASE 2004, 19th IEEE International Conference on Automated Software Engineering, Linz, Austria*, pp. 258–267. IEEE Computer Society, 2004.

4. V. Braun, N. Kalt, B. Steffen, and T. Margaria. Hierarchical service definition. In Annual Review of Communication, pp. 847–856. International Engineering Consortium Chicago (USA), IEC, 1997.

5. J. Bredereke. On feature orientation and on requirements encapsulation using families of requirements. In M. D. Ryan, J.-J. Ch. Meyer, and H.-D. Ehrich, eds. *Objects, Agents, and Features, Volume 2975 of Lecture Notes in Computer Science*, pp. 26–44. Springer, 2003.

6. E. M. Clarke, O. Grumberg, and D. A. Peled. *Model Checking*. MIT Press, 2001.

7. K. Fisler, S. Krishnamurthi, and D. J. Dougherty. Embracing policy engineering. In G.-C. Roman and K. J. Sullivan, eds. *FoSER*, pp. 109–110. ACM, 2010.

8. K. Fisler, S. Krishnamurthi, L. A. Meyerovich, and M. C. Tschantz. Verification and change-impact analysis of access-control policies. In G.-C. Roman, W. G. Griswold, and B. Nuseibeh, eds. *ICSE*, pp. 196–205. ACM, 2005.

9. C. Gordon, L. Meyerovich, J. Weinberger, and S. Krishnamurthi. Composition with Consistent Updates for Abstract State Machines. 2008.

10. P. Griffin. Introduction to XACML. Technical Report, Bea Systems, 2004.

11. H. Harris and M. Ryan. Theoretical foundations of updating systems. In *ASE*, pp. 291–294. IEEE Computer Society, 2003.

12. M. Hennessy and R. Milner. On observing nondeterminism and concurrency. In J. W. de Bakker and J. van Leeuwen, eds. *ICALP, volume 85 of Lecture Notes in Computer Science*, pp. 299–309. Springer, 1980.

13. F. Howar, B. Steffen, and M. Merten. From zulu to rers—Lessons learned in the zulu challenge. In *Proceedings of the ISoLA 2010 (1)—Leveraging Applications of Formal Methods, Verification, and Validation—Heraklion, Crete, Greece, Oct. 2010,*

Proceedings, Part I, volume 6415 of Lecture Notes in Computer Science, pp. 687–704. Springer, 2010.

14. H. Hungar, T. Margaria, and B. Steffen. Test-based model generation for legacy systems. In *IEEE International Test Conference (ITC), Charlotte, NC, September 30–October*, pp. 971–980. IEEE Computer Society, 2003.

15. H. Hungar, O. Niese, and B. Steffen. Domain-specific optimization in automata learning. In *Proceedings of the CAV 2003, 15th International Conference on Computer Aided Verification, Boulder, CO, volume 2725 of Lecture Notes in Computer Science*, pp. 315–327. Springer, 2003.

16. H. Hungar and B. Steffen. Behavior-based model construction. *STTT, International Journal on Software Tools for Technology Transfer*, 6(1):4–14, 2004.

17. B. Jonsson, T. Margaria, G. Naeser, J. Nyström, and B. Steffen. Incremental requirement specification for evolving systems. In *FIW, Feature Interactions in Telecommunications and Software Systems VI, May 17–19, 2000, Glasgow, Scotland, UK*, pp. 145–162. IOS Press, 2000.

18. B. Jonsson, T. Margaria, G. Naeser, J. Nyström, and B. Steffen. Incremental requirement specification for evolving systems. *Nordic Journal of Computing*, 8(1):65–87, 2001.

19. S. Jörges, T. Margaria, and B. Steffen. Genesys: Service-oriented construction of property conform code generators. *ISSE*, 4(4):361–384, 2008.

20. M. Karusseit and T. Margaria. Feature-based modelling of a complex, online-reconfigurable decision support service. WWV '05, 1st International Workshop on Automated Specification and Verification of Web Sites, March 2005. ENTCS 1132.

21. M. Karusseit and T. Margaria. Feature-based modelling of a complex, online-reconfigurable decision support service. *Electronic Notes in Theoretical Computer Science*, 157(2):101–118, 2006.

22. M. Karusseit and T. Margaria. A web-based runtime-reconfigurable role management service. In *Automated Specification and Verification of Web Systems, 2006. WWV'06. 2nd International Workshop*, pp. 53–60. IEEE, 2007.

23. M. Karusseit, T. Margaria, and H. Willebrandt. Policy expression and checking in xacml, ws-policies, and the jabc. In *TAV-WEB 2008, Proceedings of the Workshop on Testing, Analysis, and Verification of Web Services and Applications, held in conjunction with the ISSTA 2008, Seattle, Washington, USA*, pp. 20–26. ACM, 2008.

24. S. Katz and G. Joseph. Aspects and superimpositions. In A. M. D. Moreira and S. Demeyer, eds. *ECOOP Workshops, volume 1743 of Lecture Notes in Computer Science*, pp. 308–309. Springer, 1999.

25. S. Krishnamurthi. The continue server (or, how I administered PADL 2002 and 2003). In V. Dahl and P. Wadler, eds. *PADL, volume 2562 of Lecture Notes in Computer Science*, pp. 2–16. Springer, 2003.

26. H. C. Li, S. Krishnamurthi, and K. Fisler. Verifying cross-cutting features as open systems. In SIGSOFT FSE, pp. 89–98, 2002.

27. D. R. Licata and S. Krishnamurthi. Verifying interactive web programs. In ASE, pp. 164–173, 2004.

28. T. Margaria. Service is in the eyes of the beholder. *Computer*, 40:33–37, 2007.

29. T. Margaria and M. Karusseit. Community usage of the online conference service: An experience report from three cs conferences. In *I3E 2002, 2nd IFIP Conference on E-Commerce, E-Business, E-Government (I3E 2002), towards the Knowledge*

Society: eCommerce, eBusiness, and eGovernment, Lisbon, Portugal, volume 233 of IFIP Conference Proceedings, pp. 497–511. Kluwer, 2002.

30. T. Margaria, O. Niese, H. Raffelt, and B. Steffen. Efficient test-based model generation for legacy reactive systems. In *HLDVT '04: Proceedings of the High-Level Design Validation and Test Workshop, 2004. Ninth IEEE International*, pp. 95–100, IEEE Computer Society, Washington, DC, 2004.

31. T. Margaria, H. Raffelt, and B. Steffen. Analyzing second-order effects between optimizations for system-level test-based model generation. In *IEEE International Test Conference (ITC), Austin, TX (USA), November*, p. 467, 2005.

32. T. Margaria and B. Steffen. Lightweight coarse-grained coordination: A scalable system-level approach. *STTT*, 5(2–3):107–123, 2004.

33. T. Margaria and B. Steffen. Agile it: Thinking in user-centric models. In *Leveraging Applications of Formal Methods, Verification and Validation, Proceedings of the ISoLA 2008, volume 17 of Communications in Computer and Information Science*, pp. 490–502. Springer Verlag, 2009.

34. T. Margaria and B. Steffen. Continuous model-driven engineering. *IEEE Computer*, 42(10):106–109, 2009.

35. T. Margaria, B. Steffen, and M. Reitenspieß. Service-oriented design: The roots. In *ICSOC 2005: 3rd ACMSIGSOFT/SIGWEB International Conference on Service-Oriented Computing, LNCS N.3826*, pp. 450–464, Springer Verlag, Amsterdam, December 2005.

36. J. McCarthy and S. Krishnamurthi. Interaction-safe state for the web. Scheme and Functional Programming, 2006.

37. T. Moses, et al. Extensible access control markup language (XACML) version 2.0. Oasis Standard, 200502, 2005.

38. M. Müller-Olm, D. A. Schmidt, and B. Steffen. Model-checking: A tutorial introduction. SAS, pp. 330–354, 1999.

39. H. Raffelt, B. Steffen, and T. Berg. LearnLib: A library for automata learning and experimentation. In *Proceedings of the 10th International Workshop on Formal Methods for Industrial Critical Systems (FMICS '05)*, pp. 62–71, ACM Press, Lisbon, Portugal, 2005.

40. H. Raffelt, M. Merten, B. Steffen, and T. Margaria. Dynamic testing via automata learning. *STTT*, 11(4):307–324, 2009.

41. H. Raffelt, B. Steffen, T. Berg, and T. Margaria. LearnLib: A framework for extrapolating behavioral models. *STTT*, 11(5):393–407, 2009.

42. R. Sandhu, E. Coyne, H. Feinstein, and C. Youman. Role-based access control models. *Computer*, 29(2):38–47, February 1996.

43. M. Shahbaz and R. Groz. Inferring mealy machines. In FM, pp. 207–222, 2009.

44. M. Shaw and D. Garlan. *Software Architecture: Perspectives on an Emerging Discipline*. Prentice Hall, 1996.

45. B. Steffen and T. Margaria. Metaframe in practice: Design of intelligent network services. In *Correct System Design—Correct System Design, Recent Insight and Advances, volume 1710 of Lecture Notes in Computer Science*, pp. 390–415. Springer, 1999.

46. B. Steffen and T. Margaria. Business process modeling in the jABC: The one-thing approach. In J. Cardoso and W. van der Aalst, eds., *Handbook of Research on Business Process Modeling*, pp. 1–26. IGI Global, 2009.

47. B. Steffen, T. Margaria, A. Claßen, and V. Braun. Incremental formalization: A key to industrial success. *Software—Concepts and Tools*, 17(2):78, 1996.

48. B. Steffen, T. Margaria, R. Nagel, S. Jörges, and C. Kubczak. *Model-Driven Development with the jABC, Volume 4383 of LNCS*, pp. 92–108. Springer Berlin/Heidelberg, 2006.

49. R. Van De Stadt. Cyberchair: A web-based groupware application to facilitate the paper reviewing process, 2001. Available at: http://www.cyberchair.org

CHAPTER 9

AN APPLICATION OF STOCHASTIC MODEL CHECKING IN THE INDUSTRY: USER-CENTERED MODELING AND ANALYSIS OF COLLABORATION IN *THINKTEAM*®

MAURICE H. TER BEEK
ISTI-CNR, Pisa, Italy

STEFANIA GNESI
ISTI-CNR, Pisa, Italy

DIEGO LATELLA
ISTI-CNR, Pisa, Italy

MIEKE MASSINK
ISTI-CNR, Pisa, Italy

MAURIZIO SEBASTIANIS
Focus PLM srl, Ferrara, Italy

GIANLUCA TRENTANNI
ISTI-CNR, Pisa, Italy

9.1 INTRODUCTION

In this chapter, we describe a general methodology for modeling and analyzing industrial software systems in their design phase, that is, prior to their implementation, by means of (stochastic) model checking [1–3].

One of the difficulties in the domain of formal modeling and verification is that detailed models tend to generate very large state spaces, due to, for example, many interleaving activities. Our approach is therefore of a different

Formal Methods for Industrial Critical Systems: A Survey of Applications, First Edition.
Edited by Stefania Gnesi and Tiziana Margaria.

nature. We develop and study rather limited, abstract formal models that are intended to address specific issues, and use these models to verify properties that provide insight in the dependencies of various aspects of the models and their effect on system performance from an easy to understand user perspective. This way of using model checking is in support of a prototyping-like modeling technique. The focus is on obtaining in a relatively fast way an informed, but perhaps somewhat approximate, understanding of the consequences— both qualitative and quantitative—of adding specific features to an existing system (design). This is quite different from the traditional use of model checking as a technique to develop rather complete specifications, with the aim of reaching a maximal level of confidence in the correctness of complicated distributed algorithms. In this sense, our proposed use of model checking is somewhat resembling the idea of extreme programming [4]: generating simple ad hoc models of new features that are meant to be added to a system (design). In close cooperation with our industrial partner think3, we have used our methodology to model and analyze proposed extensions of their product data management (PDM) system *thinkteam*. Our approach thus implicitly forms a *hands-on* practical experience to illustrate the potential of (stochastic) model checking for the analysis of user aspects of software systems in the industry and also of its current limitations. The challenge is to introduce this technique in the industry, where model checking is currently not part of software engineering practice.

Product life cycle management (PLM) is the activity of managing a company's product across its life cycle—from conception, through design and manufacturing, to service and disposal—in the most effective way [5]. think3's PLM is a suite of integrated PLM applications built on *thinkteam*, which is think3's PDM application catering the document management needs of design processes in the manufacturing industry. *thinkteam* allows enterprises to capture, organize, automate, and share engineering information in an efficient way. The *thinkteam* setting, on which our research was performed, consisted of a number of users that all interact with one centralized relational database management system (RDBMS). This RDBMS controls the storage and retrieval of data (like CAD files) in a file-system-like repository, called the vault, with a file's editing rights being exclusive. The adopted file access mechanism by designers is based on a *retry* policy: There is no queue (or reservation system) handling the user's requests for editing rights on a file.

In previous works [6, 7], our focus was on *qualitative* model checking to verify the properties of *thinkteam* extended with a notification system for users based on a publish/subscribe paradigm. We analyzed a number of qualitative correctness properties addressing concurrency control, correctness, usability, and user awareness. This research has led to the inclusion of a notification mechanism in *thinkteam*. Some usability issues, influenced more by a system's performance than by its functional behavior, however, cannot be analyzed by qualitative model checking alone. One such issue was raised in References 6 and 7: We showed that a user can be excluded from obtaining a file simply because competing users are more "lucky" in their attempts to obtain the same file. Such behavior is explained by the fact that users are only provided with a retry-based file access mechanism. User satisfaction depends both on qualitative and quantitative aspects. For instance, frequent retrying could be very frustrating and should therefore be avoided.

Analyses with qualitative model checking can show a problem exists, but not quantify its effect on usability. In our case, the number of retries (i.e., of repeated requests) a user has to perform before obtaining a file is an important usability measure. If the number is high, a waiting list policy should be considered rather than the simpler retry policy. We analyzed the trade-off between these design options in Reference 8 by means of stochastic model checking, an extension of qualitative model checking allowing the analysis of qualitative and performance- and dependability-related—that is, quantitative—system properties [3, 9–12].

One of the problems of model-based approaches is that of scalability: how to deal with the state explosion that arises through attempts to model the interleaving activity that comes with many asynchronously operating clients. In Reference 13, we explored a recently proposed *scalable* model-based technique, fluid flow analysis [14]. This technique supports the analysis of many replicated entities with autonomous behavior that collaborate by means of forms of synchronization. It builds upon a process algebraic approach and adds techniques for quantitative analysis to those for behavioral analysis. Formally, the technique consists of deriving automatically a set of ordinary differential equations (ODEs) from a specification defined using the Performance Evaluation Process Algebra (PEPA) [15]. The solution of the set of ODEs, by means of standard numerical techniques, provides insight into the dynamic change over time of aggregations of components that are in particular states. The approach abstracts away from the identity of the individual components. The derivation of sets of ODEs from PEPA specifications, the algorithms to solve ODEs, and the generation of the numerical results are supported by the PEPA workbench [16].

In Reference 17, finally, we used qualitative and quantitative model checking to evaluate *thinkteam*, and three proposed extensions, to assist the design phase of this industrial collaborative system. In this chapter, we illustrate the general methodology underlying all of the aforementioned experiences. To illustrate this methodology, we also revisit one of the analyses reported in Reference 17, namely the one using *stochastic* model checking to verify an extension with multiple replicated vaults. This verification is meant to quantify the time (which is not logged) that designers waste on down/uploading and on retrying in the presence of multiple replicated vaults. To do so, we will use the same structure of the stochastic model as in Reference 17, but vary the parameters. More in particular, we use the *realistic* parameter values that we obtained from analyzing the *thinkteam* log file of the actual usage of *thinkteam* by one of think3's clients. The analysis was performed using the statistical software package SPSS [18]. As the values are obtained from real data, this chapter thus presents an improvement of the part of Reference 17 in which rather generic assumptions on editing and down/uploading times were made. Our contribution thus shows that model checking can be of great help in an exploratory design phase, both for comparing different design options and for refining and improving the description of the proposed extensions.

This chapter starts with detailed descriptions of *thinkteam* in Section 9.2 and of the log-file analysis in Section 9.3. In Section 9.4, we describe the proposed *thinkteam* extension and its stochastic model, after which relevant correctness and performance properties are formalized and verified, and the outcome is interpreted. Section 9.5 contains the lessons we learned from this industrial case study. Finally, we draw some conclusions in Section 9.6.

9.2   *THINKTEAM*

This section contains an overview of think3's PDM application *thinkteam*. For details, see http://www.think3.com.

Design activities produce and consume information—both documental (CAD drawings, models, and manuals) and nondocumental (bill of materials, reports, and workflow trails). The composition of this information eventually activates the process that produces a physical object. Information mismanagement can—and often does—have direct impact on the cost structure of the manufacturing phase. An important part of the design office's work is to maintain and update projects that have been previously released: A historical view of past information is an absolute must for this. This is where PDM applications come into play.

9.2.1   Technical Characteristics

thinkteam is a three-tier data management system running on Wintel platforms. A typical installation scenario is a network of desktop clients interacting with one centralized RDBMS server and one or more file servers. In this setting, components resident on each client node supply a graphical interface, metadata management, and integration services. Persistence services are achieved by building on the characteristics of the RDBMS and file servers. In the following, we provide a brief overview of the operations of the (logical) *thinkteam* subsystems relevant to the purpose of this chapter.

9.2.1.1   Metadata Management   *thinkteam* allows its users to manage representations of concrete entities (e.g., documents and components). These representations (often called business items or business objects) are described using an object model or meta-object model that can be customized by the end users, for example, by changing the attributes pertaining to various types of objects or by adding object types. Metadata management refers to operations on object instances and to the rules these operations obey to, as they are

TABLE 9.1 *thinkteam* **User Operations**

Operation	Effect
get	Extract a read-only copy of a document from the vault
import	Insert an external document into the vault
checkOut	Extract a copy of a document from the vault (exclusive)
unCheckOut	Cancel the effects of the preceding checkOut
checkIn	Replace an edited (previously checked out) document in the vault
checkInOut	Replace an edited document in the vault (retaining editing rights)

implemented in *thinkteam*. Typical operations are creation, attribute editing (e.g., adding/changing description, price), revising, changing state, connecting with other objects, and deletion. *thinkteam* uses an RDBMS to persist and retrieve both its object model and the objects that are created during operation. RDBMS interactions are fairly low level in nature and are completely transparent to end users.

9.2.1.2 Vaulting Controlled storage and retrieval of document data in PDM applications is traditionally called vaulting, the vault being a file-system-like repository. The two main functions of vaulting are (1) to provide a single, secure, and controlled storage environment in which the documents controlled by the PDM application are managed and (2) to prevent inconsistent updates or changes to the document base, while still allowing the maximal access compatible with the business rules. While the first function is subject to the implementation of the vaulting system's lower layers, the second is implemented in *thinkteam*'s underlying protocol by a set of operations (listed in Table 9.1) that are available to the users.

Note that document access (through a *checkOut*) is based on a *retry* policy: There is no queue or reservation system handling the requests for editing rights on a document.

9.2.2 *thinkteam* at Work

thinkteam supports CAD designers in various design phases of the overall industrialization part of a given project. Vaulting capabilities are most frequently used by CAD designers during the modeling phases, briefly described next.

9.2.2.1 Geometry Information Retrieval The most usual design work in the manufacturing industry (*thinkteam*'s prime target) involves the production of components that are part of more complex goods. The CAD models describing these products are called *assemblies* and are structured as composite documents referring to several (sometimes thousands) individual model files. Most of the geometry data a designer deals with thus consist of reference material, that is, parts surrounding the component he or she is actually creating or modifying. The designer needs to interact with this material in order to position, adapt, and mate to the assembly the part he or she is working on. Most reference parts are production items subjected to PDM, whose counterparts (model files) reside in the vault. The logical operation by which the designer gains access to them is the *get* operation, which is performed automatically when viewing a file. This is the most frequently used type of activity, and it is involved in all other activities listed below, as well as in many others not explicitly mentioned (e.g., visualization, printing).

9.2.2.2 *Geometry Modification*

Modifying an existing part is the second most used operation a designer performs. As it is an already existing and managed part (i.e., present in the vault), the designer must express the intent to modify it with an explicit *checkOut* operation that prevents modification attempts by other users (exclusive lock). When ready to publish his or her work, the designer releases it to the system via the explicit *checkIn* operation, which makes the model available again for modification by other users. Were the designer to change his or her mind while modifying a model, then he or she may use the *unCheckOut* operation, which unlocks the model but discards any changes that occurred since the *checkOut*. Finally, he or she may use the *checkInOut* operation to release to the vault an intermediate version of the model, retaining exclusive modification rights.

9.2.2.3 *Geometry Creation*

Lastly, a designer may create a completely new component model and insert it into the system. As the model will initially be created outside the system vault, an *import* operation is required to register it in *thinkteam*.

9.3 ANALYSIS OF THE *THINKTEAM* LOG FILE

thinkteam handles a few hundred thousand files for some 20–100 users. To obtain realistic data on the particular use that clients make of *thinkteam*, think3 provided us with a cleaned-up log file to analyze, comprising all activity (in terms of the operations listed in Section 9.2.1.2) of one of the manufacturing industries using *thinkteam* from 2002 to 2006. In order to fine-tune certain parameters of the model of *thinkteam* that we will present in the next section, we are interested in the following usage-centered info: the average duration of editing sessions, the average duration of periods during which files are not used for editing sessions, and the average number of times users unsuccessfully retry to obtain files for editing sessions. The aim of the analysis we describe in this section is thus to obtain some insight on the timing issues concerning the duration of editing sessions and the occupancy of files.

Even though this log file was cleaned up (i.e., logged information that was not related to the aforementioned operations was removed), for our specific purposes, it has been necessary to perform some further "cleaning." Due to the huge amount of data, the particular format used, and the specific kind of usage-centered quantitative information we were interested in, it turned out that developing specialized scripts was the most efficient way to perform this "cleaning" (most multirelational data mining methods require loading the entire data in the main memory, which makes them unsuitable for mining a log file with a huge amount of data). Developing these scripts also helped to spot a number of irregularities in the log and automatically correct them. These mainly consisted of incorrect orderings of some of the operations that were caused by the log's granularity with an accuracy in seconds. A higher precision (e.g., up to the nearest millisecond) would have been needed to avoid having to correct these orderings. We used the same scripting technique to simplify the log file (e.g., filtering useless user actions and so on) and to transform it into a format accepted by the statistical analysis software package SPSS [18].

The resulting log file contains, for each operation, its time stamp (in the format day-month-year and hour-minute-second), the name of the user who performed it, and the file in the vault the operation refers to. In this way, each line in the log file represents an atomic access to the vault. The format of the log file is easy to handle, but it contains a really huge amount of data (792,618 vault accesses by 104 users with respect to 183,492 files). Moreover, think3 has improved its logging mechanism during the years, meaning that different years are difficult to compare and also that 2006 is the most complete. For these reasons, we restricted our analysis to the year 2006.

The data of 2006 concerns 83 users collaborating on a total of 181,535 files, 23,134 of which were checked out at least once during the year. The remaining files were used exclusively as reference material, for example, downloaded in read-only fashion by means of *get* operations. A total of 65 users were found to be involved in editing sessions. We present the analysis of a subset of the data that has direct relevance for the model analyzed in the next section. These concern the duration of editing sessions (i.e., the time that passes between a *checkOut* and a *checkIn* of a file by the same user) and the duration of periods in which files were not locked (i.e., the time that passes between a *checkIn* and *checkOut* of the same file by possibly different users). Instead, the number of times a user unsuccessfully tries to *checkOut* a locked file (i.e., checked out by another user) is not explicitly logged, so little can be said about that in a direct way. It is however possible to obtain an indirect approximation of the number of users that compete for access to the same file by analyzing the number of users that modify the same file during the investigated period. To give an idea, Figure 9.1 shows 1 week of editing activity on a particular file. We see that four users are responsible for 20 editing sessions that week to the same file.

Figures 9.2 and 9.3 present data obtained after removing irrelevant operations from the log file, like numerous *get* operations (recall that this is the most frequently used operation), operations originating from system administrator interventions, and several anomalous log operations. The graphs were drawn

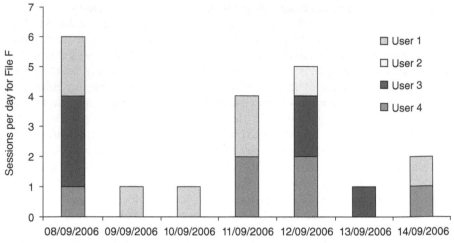

FIGURE 9.1   A week of *checkOut* sessions on a file.

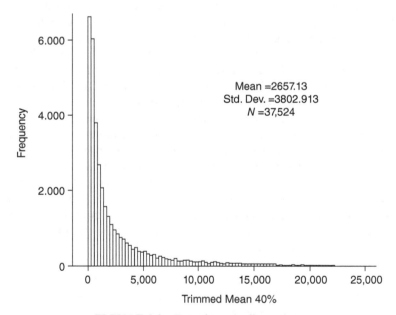

FIGURE 9.2   Duration of edit sessions.

by SPSS v15.0 [18] after computing the *mean trimmed 40%* (i.e., discarding the lower and higher 20% scores and taking the mean of the remaining scores). In statistics, the trimmed mean is known to be a more robust estimator than the mean in the presence of *outliers* in the data (i.e., extreme scores), because it is less sensitive to outliers but will still give a reasonable estimate of central tendency or mean. Figure 9.2 shows a histogram of the distribution of the

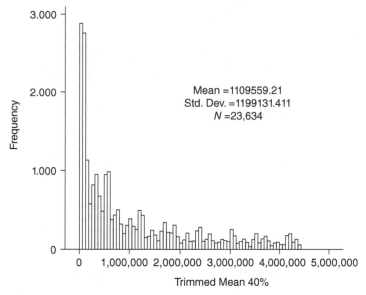

FIGURE 9.3 Duration of file interaccess time.

duration of $N = 37{,}524$ editing sessions. On the x-axis, time is presented in seconds, such that each bar contains the scores in the data set that lie in the corresponding interval of almost 5 minutes (278 seconds) that it presents. The histogram shows all sessions except for 20% of the shortest and 20% of the longest sessions, in practice meaning that sessions of less than 111 seconds (i.e., ca. 2 minutes) and more than 22,256 seconds (i.e., ca. 370 minutes) have been removed. We see that the mean duration trimmed 40% of an edit session is 2,657 seconds, so ca. 44 minutes. It is easy to see that most sessions tend to be rather short.

In Figure 9.3, a histogram is shown of the duration of intervals during which all $N = 23{,}634$ files that were involved in at least two editing sessions were *not* locked (i.e., taken in *checkOut*). These data give an impression of the time that passes between vault accesses to the same file by possibly different users. Time is represented, in seconds, on the x-axis, such that each bar contains the scores in the data set that lie in the corresponding interval of about 17 hours (62,500 seconds) that it presents. Many of the durations fall into the first few intervals, indicating that there are many cases in which files were used rather intensively.

We have extracted an ordered list of session durations from the cleaned-up log file. Since there are 21,365 different sessions durations, the table in Figure 9.4 shows only an extract of this ordered list (the full table contains 21,365 rows). This extract, however, clearly illustrates the presence of outliers in this list of session durations. At one extreme, we have 3,926 file modifications of less than a second, while at the other extreme, we have several file modifications

#	Session Duration (Seconds)	Session Duration (dd/hh/mm/ss)	Frequency	Percentage	Cumulative Percentage
1	0	00d 00h 00' 00"	3926	6.2751%	6.2751%
2	1	00d 00h 00' 01"	1553	2.4822%	8.7574%
3	2	00d 00h 00' 02"	248	0.3963%	9.1538%
4	3	00d 00h 00' 03"	98	0.1566%	9.3104%
5	4	00d 00h 00' 04"	64	0.1022%	9.4127%
...	...	...	...	...	...
1064	1063	00d 00h 17' 43"	8	0.0127%	49.960%
1065	1064	00d 00h 17' 44"	4	0.0063%	49.966%
1066	1065	00d 00h 17' 45"	9	0.0143%	49.980%
1067	1066	00d 00h 17' 46"	4	0.0063%	49.987%
1068	1067	00d 00h 17' 47"	9	0.0143%	50.001%
1069	1068	00d 00h 17' 48"	12	0.0191%	50.020%
1070	1069	00d 00h 17' 49"	4	0.0063%	50.027%
1071	1070	00d 00h 17' 50"	8	0.0127%	50.039%
1072	1071	00d 00h 17' 51"	12	0.0191%	50.059%
...	...	...	...	...	...
21361	23733879	274d 16h 44' 39"	1	0.0015%	99.993%
21362	24787896	286d 21h 31' 36"	1	0.0015%	99.995%
21363	25150004	291d 02h 06' 44"	1	0.0015%	99.996%
21364	25484279	294d 22h 57' 59"	1	0.0015%	99.998%
21365	25900836	299d 18h 40' 36"	1	0.0015%	100.00%

FIGURE 9.4 Ordered list of session durations.

TABLE 9.2 Number of Files Edited by at Least Two Users

Number of files	5077	1407	301	79	24	22	8	8	6	10	3	1	1	1
Number of users	2	3	4	5	6	7	8	9	10	11	12	13	14	17

that lasted for almost 300 days. The extremely short sessions in fact do not correspond to real user editing sessions, but rather to automatic system operations that were also logged and that feature in the log file as very short *checkOut–checkIn* sessions. The extremely long sessions, on the other hand, are the result of files that have been unlocked by the intervention of a system administrator (for instance, due to users who forgot to *checkIn* a file). Both extremes clearly do not correspond to typical user operations, which justifies our choice for the trimmed mean.

Finally, Table 9.2 shows the number of files that in 2006 were edited by more than one user. A further analysis of these files shows that it is quite common that multiple users are editing the same file on the same day (cf. Fig. 9.1) and that there are even days in which up to eight users are accessing the same file. We are aware of the fact that the log-file analysis is only covering 1 year of data collected at one particular client of think3, and might therefore be not completely representative of a general *thinkteam* use. However, the logged data are real observations and as such do provide information on an example use of *thinkteam*, which can help to put our modeling results in a proper perspective. On the other hand, this log-file analysis has also shown that some data that would have been useful for a further evaluation of usability issues is not currently collected in *thinkteam*'s log files. Hence, our cooperation has also served to develop further ideas about which data to log in the future.

9.4 *THINKTEAM* WITH REPLICATED VAULTS

The outcome of the research we will describe in the remainder of this chapter has been used by think3 for a recent extension of *thinkteam*, namely the addition of multiple replicated vaults. These vaults reside in a number of geographically distributed locations (cf. Fig. 9.5, where document *checkIn/Out* is represented by dotted arrows and metadata operations by solid ones). However, *thinkteam* is aware of the status of the replicated vaults and of all files, that is, whether a file is currently checked out by a designer or available for modification.

When a designer queries *thinkteam* in this new setting, for example, for a copy of a file, *thinkteam* typically responds by assigning the "best possible" vault location. Ideally, this is the designer's preferred vault location (with a good connection in terms of bandwidth), while a second-best location is

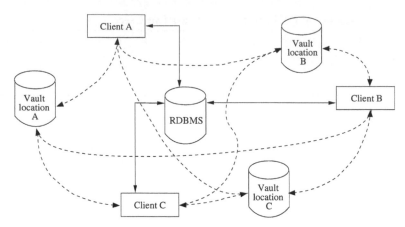

FIGURE 9.5   *thinkteam* with replicated vaults.

assigned if the preferred location is down or has a too high workload. If, on the other hand, *thinkteam* notices that the most recent *checkIn* of the requested file was performed by the same designer, then he or she is told to use the local version of the file on his or her desktop (thus saving a *checkOut*).

When a designer has obtained a vault address, he or she may *checkOut* the file, edit it, and eventually *checkIn* the file, again with a strong preference for his or her preferred vault location. After each *checkIn*, the respective location informs *thinkteam* that the file has been uploaded. Afterward, *thinkteam* updates the file's status, that is, removes the lock and makes it available for other designers. This communication also transfers the status information of the vault locations to *thinkteam*. Neither the communications between the vault locations needed to keep them consistent nor those between the vault locations and *thinkteam* are represented in Figure 9.5. In the model of *thinkteam* we will consider in this chapter, we do not explicitly address the communications between vaults but assume that they are kept consistent using suitable algorithms. The communication between the vaults and *thinkteam* will be modeled explicitly.

9.4.1   A Stochastic Model of *thinkteam*

We consider a model composed of three vault locations (Va, Vb, and Vc) containing identical file repositories, three explicitly modeled clients (CA, CB, and CC) competing for the same file, and the *thinkteam* application TT. Each vault location is connected to TT, and they communicate their status regularly to TT. Interesting aspects of a vault location's status for performance analysis purposes are, for example, its workload, availability (i.e., being up or down), and the bandwidth offered to the various clients. TT keeps a record of the status of all files, like whether a file is locked (i.e., checked out by a client) or available for download and modification.

9.4.1.1 *Assumptions* The model is taken from Reference 17, and it is based on the following assumptions:

1. The bandwidth between a client and a vault is constant, and each client prefers down- and uploading files from the vault to which it has the best connection. At times, this connection may be down, however, in which case a client will use the next preferred vault.
2. Each client has a static preference list indicating the preferred vault order.
3. The three explicitly modeled clients do not influence significantly the overall performance of the full system (including many active clients modeled implicitly by the responsiveness characteristics of the various vaults). Our aim is to analyze a number of correctness and usability aspects of the system from these three clients' viewpoint.
4. We only consider a subset of the operations available to *thinkteam* clients, namely the most important ones: *checkOut* and *checkIn*. This keeps the model relatively simple. Further operations could easily be added.
5. We currently do not enable TT to inform a client that he or she can use the local version of the file on his or her desktop if TT notices that the most recent *checkIn* of the requested file was performed by that client.

These assumptions originate from discussions with think3 on reasonable client behavior (1), from the need for modeling an abstract model of *thinkteam* (2, 4, and 5) and from rigorous and logically informed reasoning (3).

9.4.1.2 *Model* The model is specified with PEPA [15], which we will not explain in detail. The complete PEPA specification is given in the appendix of Reference 17. For a compact presentation, we depict the clients, vaults, and TT as a kind of stochastic automata in Figures 9.6–9.8, which have also been used in discussions with our colleagues from think3. The labels of the states and transitions play an important role in the next section, when the analyses of the model are discussed. The transition labels are of the general form "from_to_

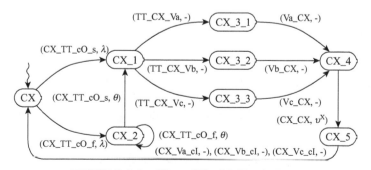

FIGURE 9.6 Client CX with X = A, B, C.

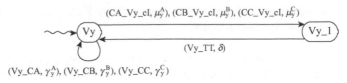

FIGURE 9.7   Vault Vy with y = a, b, c.

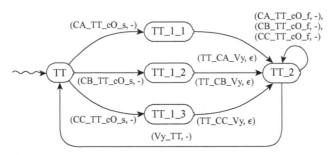

FIGURE 9.8   TT with y = a, b, c.

action," in which the "from_to" part indicates the direction of the information flow between processes (e.g., CA_TT denotes a communication from CA to TT), while the "action" part indicates a specific action (e.g., cO_s for successful *checkOut*, cO_f for unsuccessful *checkOut*, and cI for *checkIn*).

9.4.1.3 *Client Process*   The behavior of a client CX, with X = A, B, C, is modeled as follows (cf. Fig. 9.6). Initially, in state CX, with rate* λ, client CX performs a request to TT to download a file for modification. This request to TT is successful when the file is available (CX_TT_cO_s, λ) and fails when the file is currently being edited by another client (CX_TT_cO_f, λ). If the request is successful, TT provides the address of the "best possible" vault location to the CX (e.g., TT_CX_Va means that CX receives the address of vault A).

The policy to assign a vault location is kept very simple in the current model: Each client receives the address of his or her preferred vault location (the first on his or her preference list) with highest static probability and the addresses of different vault locations with lower probabilities. This models the fact that the preferred vault location is not always available, be it due to a high workload or due to temporary unavailability. These probabilities can be tuned so as to better match the performance characteristics of the system. Indications for such probabilities could, in theory, be obtained from an analysis of log files of the performance characteristics of the single vault currently used in

---

* A rate *r* of an action defines a duration Δt while the average duration is given by $1/r$ since, by definition, Δt is an exponentially distributed random variable with rate *r*.

thinkteam. The specific log files that we have analyzed, however, did not register such information.

When client CX has obtained the address of a vault location, he or she can *download* (e.g., by (Va_CX, -) from Vault A) the requested file (which is usually part of a document composed of the file to be edited and of files of the parts surrounding the component that are not to be edited), then *edit* the file while in state CX_4, leaving that state (by (CX_CX, v^X)) with rate v^X corresponding to an average time $1/v^X$ for editing for this specific client and, finally, *upload* the file to a vault by means of a *checkIn* (e.g., by (CX_Va_cI, -) to Vault A), following a preference list as for downloading, and return to initial state CX. Actions with a rate indicated by "-" are passive, that is, the rate value is established during synchronization—in this case between the client and the vault process, the latter determining its value.

If the client's request for a file fails, it starts a series of retry actions (in state CX_2) to obtain the file at a later moment. This essentially means that the client continues to make requests (by (CX_TT_cO_f, θ)) but at a higher rate θ. After a number of successive failed requests, the client eventually makes a successful request and moves to state CX_1.

9.4.1.4 Vault Process

The behavior of a vault Vy, for y = a, b, c, is modeled as follows (cf. Fig. 9.7). A vault (location) can receive *download* operations from a client (by (Vy_CX, γ_y^X)) with rate γ_y^X corresponding to the average download time $1/\gamma_y^X$ for that specific client and vault, alternated with *checkIn* operations (CX_Vy_cI, μ_y^X) with rate μ_y^X. After each *checkIn*, the vault informs TT (by (Vy_TT, δ)) that the file has been *uploaded*. In this way, TT can update the status of the file, that is, remove the lock and make it available for other clients. The same communication also models the transfer of status information of the vaults to TT.

9.4.1.5 TT Process

The behavior of TT is modeled as follows (cf. Fig. 9.8). Initially, TT waits for file requests from clients to handle (e.g., from client A by action (CA_TT_cO_s, -)). In case of a successful file request, TT assigns a vault to the client, using the assignment policy described above.

This policy can be modeled stochastically by a race condition between the different assignments as follows. If client A should be assigned vault A on average in ca. 50% of the cases, vault B in ca. 33% and vault C in ca. 16% of the cases, one can choose suitable rates to reflect this. State TT_1_1, for example, has three outgoing transitions, labeled by (TT_CA_Va, 300), (TT_CA_Vb, 200), and (TT_CA_Vc, 100). The total exit rate from state TT_1_1 is thus 300 + 200 + 100 = 600 and the probability of client A being assigned vault A is then 300/600 = 0.5. Such relatively high exit rates model the fact that vault assignment is very fast compared with other activities. As a result, modeling preferences will not significantly influence the model's performance analysis. (For reasons of space and readability, these details are abstracted from in Fig. 9.8: Only a nominal indication ε of the relevant rates is given.) Actions

TABLE 9.3 Rate Values

λ	$\gamma_a^A = \mu_a^A$	$\gamma_a^B = \mu_a^B$	$\gamma_a^C = \mu_a^C$	$\gamma_b^A = \mu_b^A$	$\gamma_b^B = \mu_b^B$	$\gamma_b^C = \mu_b^C$
0.1	8	4	6	6	8	4

(TT_CX_Vy, ε) model assigning a vault, locking the file, and sending a client a vault address.

Any further request for the same file is explicitly denied (e.g., to client A by (CA_TT_cO_f, -)) until TT has received a message from a vault indicating that the file has been uploaded (e.g., for vault Y by (Vy_TT, -)). TT is then back in its initial state, ready to accept further requests for the file.

9.4.1.6 Full Specification   The specification of *thinkteam* is completed by the parallel composition, by means of the PEPA cooperation operator (here denoted as ||), of the three client processes, the three vault processes, and the TT process, as follows:

$$\text{USERS} \parallel _{\text{CX\_TT\_cO\_z, TT\_CX\_Vy, CX\_Vy\_cI, Vy\_CX}}\text{SYSTEM}$$

with USERS = CA $\parallel$ CB $\parallel$ CC, X = A, B, C, y = a, b, c, z = f, s and SYSTEM = TT $\parallel_{\text{Vy\_TT}}$ (Va $\parallel$ Vb $\parallel$ Vc).

Note that the analysis is restricted to a model with three clients competing for the same file during approximately the same period. The model can easily be extended with a limited number of explicitly modeled clients, as in our earlier work addressing a *thinkteam* model with one centralized vault [8]. A larger number of clients could be analyzed using simulation-based model checking [19], but at a higher computational cost and producing less accurate results.

9.4.2 Analysis of the Stochastic Model

In this chapter, we use the probabilistic symbolic model checker PRISM [11, 20], which supports, among others, the verification of continuous stochastic logic (CSL) properties over continuous-time Markov chains (CTMCs) [21]. CTMCs can be generated by high-level description languages, among which PEPA, for which PRISM provides a front end. The complete PEPA specification with three clients (given in the appendix of Reference 17) leads to a CTMC with 104 states and 330 transitions. All analyses reported in this section were performed with PRISM v3.1.1 and took a negligible amount of CPU time. The iterative numerical method used for the computation of probabilities was Gauss–Seidel and the accuracy 10^{-6}. See http://www.prismmodelchecker.org and Reference 20 for details.

$\gamma_c^A = \mu_c^A$	$\gamma_c^B = \mu_c^B$	$\gamma_c^C = \mu_c^C$	$\nu^A = \nu^B = \nu^C$	θ	$\delta = \varepsilon$	$\varepsilon_2 = 2\varepsilon$	$\varepsilon_3 = 3\varepsilon$
4	6	8	1.35	6	100	200	300

While we use a stochastic model with the same structure as the one proposed in Reference 17, we verify a variation of properties for new assumptions on important parameters, namely the edit and download rates. These assumptions have been empirically obtained from a real usage of *thinkteam*: We use the outcome of the analysis of the log file described in Section 9.3 of actual *thinkteam* usage by a particular industry and detailed discussions thereof with think3. Note that this analysis refers to only one client's *thinkteam* use during one specific year. The remaining rate values, such as the retry rate, were estimated by *think3*, but not covered by the log files used in our experiments. All rate values are listed in Table 9.3. The download rates should be read considering the letters in the subscripts (superscripts) to refer to the names of the vaults (clients). Hence γ_b^A, for example, is the download rate between vault B and client A.

We choose the unit of time of our model to be 1 hour. Rate $\gamma_b^A = 6$, for example, models that on average the download time between vault B and client A is 60/6 = 10 minutes. This may seem much at first but, as explained in Section 9.2.2, CAD designers use *thinkteam* to share assemblies, that is, composite documents referring to several (sometimes thousands) individual model files. Hence, when a client has to modify one file, many other files (forming the context of this file) need to be downloaded. Rate $\nu^A = 1.35$, for example, models that on average client A spends $60/1.35 \approx 44$ minutes editing the file in his or her possession, which indeed corresponds to the mean duration of editing sessions reported in Section 9.3 (cf. Fig. 9.2).

9.4.2.1 *Analyses of Qualitative Properties*

Prior to analyzing a model's performance, it is important to gain confidence in its functional correctness. We verified qualitative properties like deadlock absence, progress properties, and mutual exclusion of editing rights on a file. Stochastic model checking of PEPA models with PRISM is performed by first translating the PEPA model into an equivalent PRISM model, using the PRISM front-end facilities, and then verifying CSL formulae on the latter. The variables in these formulae refer to states in the PRISM model.

The probability should be (at most) zero that eventually a deadlock is encountered. This property can be formalized in CSL by using the predefined PRISM label "deadlock," which labels each absorbing state (i.e., a state from which there is a zero probability of exiting) in the following way:

$$\mathbf{P}_{<0}([\text{true } U \text{ "deadlock"}]),$$

which PRISM verification confirmed to hold for our model.

Whenever client X succeeds to *checkOut* a file from vault A, he or she eventually performs a *checkIn* of that file. This property is captured by the following CSL formula:

$$\mathbf{P}_{\geq 1}([\text{true } U \text{ "CXcheckIn" } \{\text{"CXcheckOut"}\}]),$$

where label "CXcheckIn" is defined as CX_STATE = CX_5 and "CXcheckOut" as CX_STATE = CX_3_1. Verification with PRISM confirmed the above formula to hold for our model.

The probability should be (at most) zero that two clients will eventually obtain permission to modify the same file at the same time. This property can be formalized in CSL as

$$\mathbf{P}_{\leq 0}([\text{true} U(\text{"OkAB" OR "OkAC" OR "OkBC"})]),$$

in which, for XY = AB, AC, BC, label

"OkXY" ≡ (CX_STATE = CX_1) AND (CY_STATE = CY_1),

meaning that two clients (X and Y) have obtained permission to edit the file (i.e., are in state CX_1 and CY_1, respectively). PRISM confirmed that this formula holds for our model.

9.4.2.2 *Analyses of Quantitative Properties* In this section, we show performance issues of our model, in particular usability issues seen from a client's perspective.

Swiftness of Releasing Files The second formula in the previous section only shows that a client eventually uploads the file (after downloading it). The following CSL formula can be used to quantify this issue:

$$\mathbf{P}_{=?}([\text{true } U^{\leq 1} \text{ "CXcheckIn" } \{\text{"CXcheckOut"}\}]),$$

that is, what is the probability that within 1 hour after downloading (by a *checkOut*) the file (state CX_3_1), client X is in state CX_5 ready to upload (by a *checkIn*) the file? The results are presented in Figure 9.9 for edit rate v^X varying from 0.75 to 5, that is, from an average of 12–80 minutes editing the file (corresponding to values within half the standard deviation of the mean in the distribution in Fig. 9.2). As expected, the less time a client spends editing, the higher the probability that he or she returns it within 1 hour.

Behavior on the Long Run A parameter influencing the clients' use of *think-team*, and thus also the time spent on different activities, is the average time that passes between accesses to the same file. The change in average time spent on different activities by a typical client when varying this interaccess time is

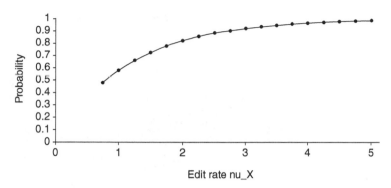

FIGURE 9.9 Probability for a client to *checkIn* a file within 1 hour after the *checkOut*.

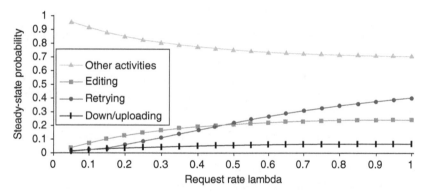

FIGURE 9.10 Time a client spends on different activities for various file interaccess times.

visualized in Figure 9.10: For each activity, we see the percentage of time client X spends on it, for various values of λ, which has a strong impact on the request rate.

We see that when λ is very low, most time is spent on activities other than editing, retrying and down/uploading. This pattern changes considerably as λ increases. The time spent waiting for the file (retrying) rapidly increases, and a client thus spends much less time on other activities. He or she also spends more time editing, but this increase is less rapid. It is interesting to note that from a certain point onward (when $\lambda \approx 0.45$), a client spends more time retrying to obtain the file than he or she does actually editing it.

The properties analyzed to obtain the results of Figure 9.10 are simple steady-state properties formalized in CSL as

$$\mathbf{S}_{=?}([\text{“ClientXinStateZ”}]),$$

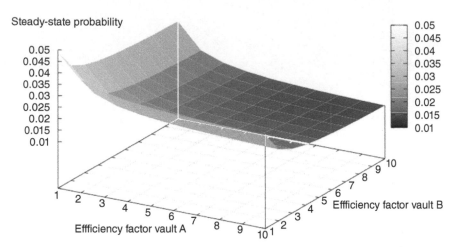

FIGURE 9.11   Steady-state probability for a client to be down- or uploading files.

where label "ClientXinStateZ" is replaced by the state indicating the specific activity of interest, for example, CX_STATE = CX_2 to indicate that client X is retrying to obtain a file.

Time Spent Down- and Uploading Files   The time clients spend down- and uploading files depends largely on the bandwidth of their connection to the vaults, the file sizes, and the workload of the vaults. Figure 9.11 shows the effect that a change in workload of vaults A and B has on the percentage of time client A spends down- and uploading files.

The x-axis shows an efficiency factor, ranging from 1 to 10, that multiplies the download rates γ_a^X, for X = A, B, C, of vault A for clients A, B, and C, initially set to 2, 1, and 1.5, respectively. Likewise on the y-axis, multiplying the download rates of vault B for clients A, B, and C, initialized at 1.5, 2, and 1, respectively. All other rates are as in Table 9.3.

Hence, the higher the efficiency factor, the faster the vaults perform. Indeed, as expected, we see that the probability that client A spends time down- and uploading on the long run is smallest when both vaults (A and B) are working optimally. We also observe that if only vault B has a high workload, and thus performs slower, then this influences the time client A spends down- and uploading. This is because part of the time client A downloads from (and uploads to) vault B. Another observation is that this percentage does not decrease much after a certain performance of the vaults has been reached: This occurs more or less at efficiency factor 5, for the parameter settings chosen for the analysis. The results in Figure 9.11 have been obtained by verifying the above formula for client A being in either of the states CA_3_1, CA_3_2, CA_3_3, or CA_5.

Number of Retries per Success   The perceived usability of *thinkteam* also depends on how often a client is unable to obtain a file he or she intends to modify. Failing to obtain a file means the client needs to spend time on either keep trying to obtain it at a later stage or change his or her work plan. If this situation occurs frequently, it might be perceived as annoying by the client and as a waste of time. Moreover, it may lead to the introduction of errors (the client may forget to edit the file later, or forget what modifications to make) or to problems in the overall workflow plan, and result in a delay in the delivery of the final product. It would therefore be useful to be able to quantify this problem under various conditions and for different user profiles of *thinkteam* clients. For instance, the different design phases may induce a different use of *thinkteam*: Initially, clients may need more time to modify a file because of a completely new design, but closer to the deadline, there might be a phase in which many clients need to frequently make small modifications in order to obtain a fine-tuning of the various components (cf. Fig. 9.1).

Figure 9.12 shows the results of one such an analysis. It shows how the average number of retries needed by client A to obtain the permission to modify a file changes with the simultaneous increase of all clients' edit and retry rates (leading to shorter average editing times and more frequent retrying attempts) and an increase in the frequency with which clients need the file, that is, modeling the aforementioned client behavior close to a deadline.

The chosen edit and retry rates were initialized at 0.5 and 1, respectively, which have been multiplied with a factor ranging from 1 to 10, while the request rate (whose inverse gives the average time that passes between a *checkIn* of a file and the following request to modify the same file) ranges from

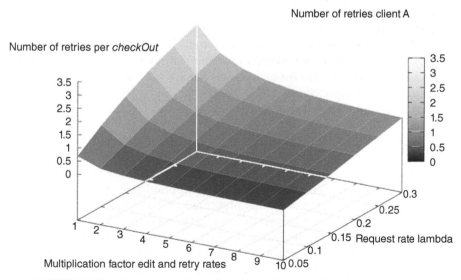

FIGURE 9.12   Average number of retries a client performs to obtain a file.

0.05 to 0.3. We thus consider, on the one hand, average client behavior ranging from editing the file for 2 hours and retrying to *checkOut* the file once every hour (*x*-axis' left end) to editing the file for only 12 minutes and retrying to *checkOut* the file as much as every 6 minutes (*x*-axis' right end) and, on the other hand, the time that passes between a file's *checkIn* and a subsequent request to *checkOut* that same file to range from only roughly once a day (*y*-axis' left end) to as often as once every 3 hours (*y*-axis' right end).

Figure 9.12 was obtained by extending the PRISM specification of our model with a reward structure to count the number of successful requests and another to count the number of retries. Reward structures defined over a CTMC define which actions need to be counted. The model can then be analyzed with respect to a number of reward-based properties. We use the steady-state reward formula that calculates the average reward on the long run. This is formalized in PRISM as

$$\mathbf{R}\{\text{``label''}\} = ?[S],$$

in which "label" is a reward structure and S denotes that the steady-state reward is calculated. The number of repeated failed requests per successful request shown in Figure 9.12 was thus obtained by dividing the outcome of this formula for label = NrFailedRequestsClientA by that for label = NrSuccessfulRequestsClientA.

We see in Figure 9.12 that the number of retries a client needs to perform to obtain the file increases when, on average, clients spend a longer time editing the file while their attempts to retry to *checkOut* the file are not so frequent (toward the *x*-axis' left end), in particular if the time between a file's *checkIn* and subsequent *checkOut* request simultaneously decreases (toward the *y*-axis' right end).

Having more detailed data on a particular usage context allows a more accurate stochastic analysis using the same model. The specific usage characteristics of *thinkteam* in the studied environment show that the number of retries per successful *checkOut* on average is quite acceptable, also when edit and retry rates go up close to a deadline period during which many clients need to frequently make small modifications to the file (toward the *x*-axis' right end).

Analyses of the same model in Reference 17, for less favorable situations assuming much longer editing sessions (ca. 200 rather than 44 minutes) and much faster down/uploading (ca. 1 rather than 10 minutes), show that the number of retries per success may become unacceptably high (roughly a factor 10 worse than the number of retries presented in Fig. 9.12). In such cases, a waiting list policy can be shown more suitable than a retry policy, reducing the time clients waste retrying to obtain the files. A similar observation has been confirmed by the analysis performed in Reference 13 with a different analysis technique, allowing one to consider the dynamic effects of the presence of a much larger number of clients.

9.5 LESSONS LEARNED

During interactive design sessions with think3, which included both physical meetings and meetings by means of collaborative systems like teleconferencing and electronic mail, think3 has acquired a basic knowledge of the main techniques and tools underlying our modeling and verification methodology. In fact, we have been able to use our formal models in various ways to discuss the behavior of *thinkteam* and its proposed extensions. Examples include simulations, message sequence charts, and counterexamples produced by model checkers. This has helped to detect a number of ambiguities and unclear aspects of the designs that think3 had in mind regarding the proposed *thinkteam* extensions. think3 furthermore has used our model of *thinkteam* extended with a publish/subscribe event notification service as a basis for their implementation of this extension, which of course provided increased confidence on the usefulness of the system design. For think3, the experience with model-checking specifications of concurrent systems, before actually implementing them, has been a true eye opener. They have recognized the inherent concurrency aspects of collaborative systems like *thinkteam*, as well as their intricate behavior. Furthermore, the relatively simple, lightweight, and abstract high-level models that we have developed during our cooperation have turned out to be of great help to focus on the key issues of the development of the interface aspects of *thinkteam*, before turning to the more detailed design and implementation issues.

9.6 CONCLUSIONS

We performed formal analyses of qualitative and quantitative properties of a small, yet relevant industrial case study concerning usability aspects of think3's PDM application *thinkteam*. We modeled the added functionality of replicated vaults with the stochastic process algebra PEPA and verified properties expressed in the stochastic temporal logic CSL over the model with the stochastic model checker PRISM. The verified properties include functional properties like vault assignment, mutual exclusion of editing rights and absence of deadlocks, and, in particular, performance properties providing information on the usability aspects of *thinkteam* under different assumptions on the quality of service of connections, vault availabilities, and work patterns of users.

Our graphical representation of the PEPA specification helped to develop and discuss the model with our think3 colleagues from the industry. Moreover, *thinkteam* is used by many important manufacturing industries that nowadays have several dislocated design departments, each of which needs reliable and efficient software systems to cooperate in an efficient way. The many inherent concurrency aspects that think3 needs to face when producing their software, and their awareness of the difficulties this implies when assessing the quality of their products, made it easier to raise their interest for the use of model-checking techniques in the early phases of software design.

The fact that we have developed the *thinkteam* model in close collaboration with think3 has shown that the activity was worthwhile to obtain precise and unambiguous specifications and has helped to provide better documentation of *thinkteam*. On the other hand, the model and the results have benefited considerably from the information that we have managed to obtain by analyzing the log file of the actual use of *thinkteam*. Still further analyses of such data can be of help to obtain models that can also be used to analyze *thinkteam* when used under different usage patterns. We believe this to be an interesting topic for further technology study. The models and results in their turn have also generated ideas for improved logging of *thinkteam*'s user activities, in order to get more insight into the usability aspects of *thinkteam* at work.

ACKNOWLEDGMENTS

The work described in this chapter was partially funded by the Italian projects TOCAI (MIUR/FIRB) and XXL (CNR/RSTL). *thinkteam*, think3, and think-PLM are registered trademarks of think3 Inc.

REFERENCES

1. E. Clarke, E. Emerson, and A. Sistla. Automatic verification of finite-state concurrent systems using temporal logic specifications. *ACM Transactions on Programming Languages and Systems*, 8:244–263, 1986.

2. E. M. Clarke, Jr., O. Grumberg, and D. A. Peled. *Model Checking*. MIT Press, 1999.

3. M. Kwiatkowska, G. Norman, and D. Parker. Stochastic model checking. In *Formal Methods for the Design of Computer, Communication and Software Systems: Performance Evaluation, Lecture Notes in Computer Science 4486*, pp. 220–270. Springer, 2007.

4. D. Wells. Extreme Programming: A Gentle Introduction, 2006. Available at: http://www.extremeprogramming.org

5. J. Stark. *Product Lifecycle Management: 21st Century Paradigm for Product Realisation*. Springer, 2005.

6. M. H. ter Beek, M. Massink, D. Latella, S. Gnesi, A. Forghieri, and M. Sebastianis. Model checking publish/subscribe notification for *thinkteam*. In *Proceedings FMICS'04, Electronic Notes in Theoretical Computer Science 133*, pp. 275–294. Elsevier, 2005.

7. M. H. ter Beek, M. Massink, D. Latella, S. Gnesi, A. Forghieri, and M. Sebastianis. A case study on the automated verification of groupware protocols. In *Proceedings ICSE'05*, pp. 596–603. ACM Press, 2005.

8. M. H. ter Beek, M. Massink, and D. Latella. Towards model checking stochastic aspects of the *thinkteam* user interface. In *Proceedings DSVIS'05, Lecture Notes in Computer Science 3941*, pp. 39–50. Springer, 2006.

9. P. Buchholz, J. Katoen, P. Kemper, and C. Tepper. Model-checking large structured Markov chains. *Journal of Logic and Algebraic Programming*, 56:69–96, 2003.

10. H. Hermanns, J.-P. Katoen, J. Meyer-Kayser, and M. Siegle. A tool for model-checking Markov chains. *International Journal on Software Tools for Technology Transfer*, 4(2):153–172, 2003.

11. M. Kwiatkowska, G. Norman, and D. Parker. Probabilistic symbolic model checking with PRISM: A hybrid approach. In *Proceedings TACAS'02, Lecture Notes in Computer Science 2280*, pp. 52–66. Springer, 2002.

12. H. Younes and R. Simmons. Probabilistic verification of discrete event systems using acceptance sampling. In *Proceedings CAV'02, Lecture Notes in Computer Science 2404*, pp. 223–235. Springer, 2002.

13. M. Massink, D. Latella, M. H. ter Beek, M. D. Harrison, and M. Loreti. A fluid flow approach to usability analysis of multi-user systems. In *Proceedings HCSE'08, Lecture Notes in Computer Science 5247*, pp. 166–180. Springer, 2008.

14. J. Hillston. Fluid flow approximation of PEPA models. In *Proceedings QEST'05*, pp. 33–43. IEEE Press, 2005.

15. J. Hillston. *A Compositional Approach to Performance Modelling*. Cambridge University Press, 1996.

16. M. Tribastone. The PEPA Plug-In Project. In *Proceedings QEST'07*, pp. 53–54. IEEE Press, 2007.

17. M. H. ter Beek, S. Gnesi, D. Latella, M. Massink, M. Sebastianis, and G. Trentanni. Assisting the design of a groupware system—Model checking usability aspects of *thinkteam*. *Journal of Logic and Algebraic Programming*, 78:191–232, 2009.

18. R. Levesque. *SPSS Programming and Data Management*. SPSS, 2007. Available at: http://www.spss.com

19. T. Hérault, R. Lassaigne, F. Magniette, and S. Peyronnet. Approximate probabilistic model checking. In *Proceedings VMCAI'04, Lecture Notes in Computer Science 2937*, pp. 307–329. Springer, 2004.

20. D. Parker, G. Norman, and M. Kwiatkowska. *PRISM 2.0—Users' Guide*, February 2004. Available at: http://www.cs.bham.ac.uk/~dxp/prism

21. V. Kulkarni. *Modeling and Analysis of Stochastic Systems*. Chapman & Hall, 1995.

PART VI

RUNTIME: TESTING AND MODEL LEARNING

CHAPTER 10

THE TESTING AND TEST CONTROL NOTATION TTCN-3 AND ITS USE

INA SCHIEFERDECKER and ALAIN-GEORGES VOUFFO-FEUDJIO
Fraunhofer FOKUS, Berlin, Germany

10.1 INTRODUCTION

The TTCN-3 language was created [1] due to the imperative necessity to have universally understood language syntax able to describe test behavior specifications. Its development was imposed by industry and science to obtain a single test notation for all black-box and gray-box testing needs. In contrast to earlier test technologies, TTCN-3 encourages the use of a common methodology and style, which leads to a simpler maintenance of test suites and products. With the help of TTCN-3, the tester specifies the test suites at an abstract level and focuses on the test logic to check a test purpose itself rather than on the test system adaptation and execution details. A standardized language provides a lot of advantages to both test suite providers and users. Moreover, the use of a standard language reduces the costs for education and training, as a great amount of documentation, examples, and predefined test suites are available. It is obviously preferred to use always the same language for testing than learning different technologies for distinct testing kinds. Constant use and collaboration between TTCN-3 vendors and users ensure a uniform maintenance and development of the language.

TTCN-3 is the successor of the Tree and Tabular Combined Notation (TTCN) that was originally developed by the International Organization for Standardization (ISO) from 1984 to 1997 as part [2] of the widely used Open Systems Interconnection (OSI) Conformance Testing Standard and Methodology.

Formal Methods for Industrial Critical Systems: A Survey of Applications, First Edition.
Edited by Stefania Gnesi and Tiziana Margaria.
© 2013 IEEE. Published 2013 by John Wiley & Sons, Inc.

TTCN has been a rather static test specification language in tabular format that emphasized the tree structure in testing of pairs of stimulus and several responses. TTCN was further evolved into TTCN-2 and TTCN-2++ [3] by the European Telecommunication Standards Institute (ETSI) adding modularization, concurrent tests, and support for Abstract Syntax Notation One (ASN.1 [4, 5]). The development toward TTCN-3 started at ETSI 1998. The first version of TTCN-3 was published in 2000. Since then, TTCN-3 was continuously updated and extended. The most recent version is v4.2.1 [4, 6–17] from 2010.

TTCN-3 enables systematic, specification-based testing for various kinds of tests including, for example, conformance, interoperability, regression, robustness, performance, and scalability testing. The TTCN-3 is a language to define test procedures to be used for black-box and gray-box testing of distributed systems. It allows an easy and efficient description not only of simple centralized, but also of complex distributed test behaviors in terms of sequences, alternatives, and loops of stimuli and responses. The test system can use a number of test components to perform test procedures in parallel. The TTCN-3 language is characterized by a well-defined syntax and operational semantics, which provide a precise understanding of TTCN-3 test specifications and their execution.

For testers, the task of specifying tests consisting of test data, test configurations, and test behaviors is easy to perform. A test system can communicate with a system under test (SUT) synchronously or asynchronously. The data transmitted between the test system and the SUT can be defined by templates, which can make use of powerful matching mechanisms to define the precise set of used or expected data. A verdict handling mechanism is provided to assess the reactions of the SUT. The types and test data can be either described directly in TTCN-3 or imported from other data type languages. Moreover, various forms of parameterization for templates, test cases, or functions and even for TTCN-3 modules are supported to enable the flexible reuse and adaptation of test specifications within different test campaigns. The selection of test cases to be executed can be either controlled directly by the user during a test run or specified in the control part of a module.

Figure 10.1 shows an overview of the TTCN-3 language. The TTCN-3 metamodel defines the various concepts of TTCN-3 and their relations [18]. The concepts can be presented in textual [6], tabular [7], graphical [8], or another proprietary presentation format. In addition, the TTCN-3 supports the import of data types and values specified in ASN.1, Interface Definition Language (IDL [12, 19]), and Extended Markup Language (XML [13, 20]). Also, other data formats such as Structured Query Language (SQL [19]) or Web Services Description Language (WSDL [21]) can be supported [22].

The ETSI standard for TTCN-3 comprises 10 parts that are grouped in the "Methods for Testing and Specification; the Testing and Test Control Notation Version 3" set of documents:

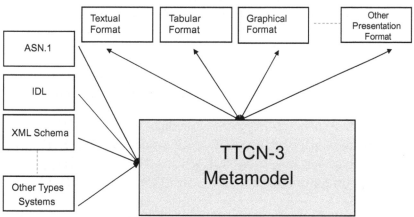

FIGURE 10.1 Basic structure of the TTCN-3 technology.

1. The TTCN-3 Core Language [6]. This document specifies the syntax of the TTCN-3 language and how test suites are defined by a set of TTCN-3 modules.

2. The Tabular Presentation Format (TFT [7]). TTCN-3 offers other presentation formats than the textual one. The tabular format is similar in appearance and functionality to earlier versions of TTCN-2 [20]. It was designed for users that prefer the previous TTCN-2 style of writing test suites. A TTCN-3 module is presented in TFT as a collection of tables. This format, however, did not find many users and has its latest release in 2007.

3. The Graphical Presentation Format (GFT [8]). It is the second presentation format of TTCN-3 that is based on message sequence charts (MSCs [19]). In GFT, TTCN-3 behavior definitions are represented by sequence diagrams. GFT has been used a lot up until the Unified Modeling Language™ (UML) Testing Profile [23] became more and more in use as another front end for TTCN-3.

4. The operational semantics [9]. Part 4 describes the meaning of TTCN-3 behavior constructs and provides a state-oriented view of the execution of a TTCN-3 module.

5. The TTCN-3 Runtime Interfaces (TRI [10]). A TTCN-3-based test system requires a platform-specific adaptation to the SUT to handle communication and timing matters. TRI defines a set of interfaces to adapt a test system to an SUT, which is realized by a system adapter.

6. The TTCN-3 Control Interfaces (TCI [11]). In addition, a TTCN-3-based test system requires an adaptation to the test platform addressing test management, test component handling, external data encoding/decoding, and logging. The set of interfaces for that defined by TCI is realized by a test adapter.

Additional parts of the standard concerning the language mappings and other language features have been developed and encompass the following:

7. The language mapping from ASN.1 modules to TTCN-3 [4].

8. The language mapping from IDL specifications to TTCN-3 [12].

9. The language mapping from XML schemata to TTCN-3 [13].

10. The support for documentation tags in TTCN-3 modules [14].

In 2010, extension packages have been added to TTCN-3. An extension package defines an additional but optional set of concepts for TTCN-3 useful in dedicated application domains. For example, real-time concepts are useful to test embedded or time-critical systems, but are not needed for testing in general. The extension packages for TTCN-3 include the following:

11. The support for static configuration and deployment [15].

12. The support for advanced parameterization including, for example, type parameterization [16].

13. The support for behavior types to allow, for example, the dynamic assignment of functions [17].

14. The support for TTCN-3 performance and real-time testing [24].

The TTCN-3 is a continuously maintained test technology to which new standard parts are added when needed by the industrial users. Up-to-date information is available at the TTCN-3 home page hosted by ETSI [25].

10.2 THE CONCEPTS OF TTCN-3

The TTCN-3 core language is a test specification and test implementation language, which has the look and feel of a modern programming language. Besides typical programming constructs, the TTCN-3 contains all the important features necessary to specify test data and test procedures for various kinds of tests including test verdicts, data templates, timer handling, test components, synchronous and asynchronous communication, logging, and alike. A

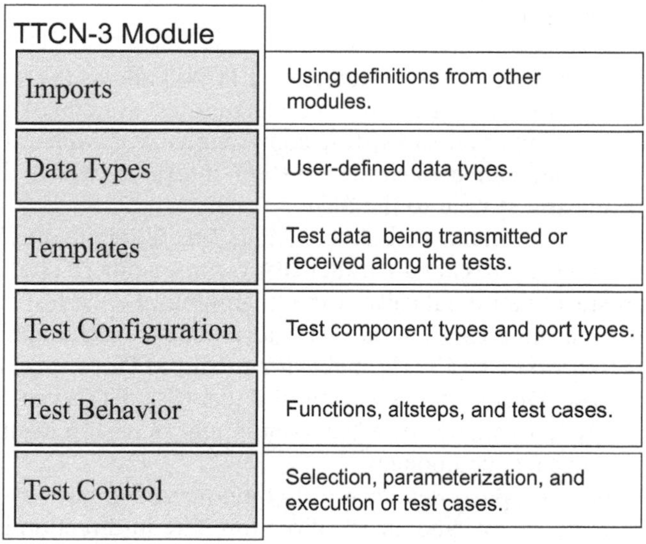

TTCN-3 Module	
Imports	Using definitions from other modules.
Data Types	User-defined data types.
Templates	Test data being transmitted or received along the tests.
Test Configuration	Test component types and port types.
Test Behavior	Functions, altsteps, and test cases.
Test Control	Selection, parameterization, and execution of test cases.

FIGURE 10.2   TTCN-3 module structure.

TTCN-3 test specification can import definitions from other modules; define types and test data; specify test behavior in functions, altsteps, and test cases; and define the selection, parameterization, and execution of test cases in a control part (see Fig. 10.2).

10.2.1 Modules

The top-level building block of a TTCN-3-based test specification is a `module`. A module contains all other TTCN-3 constructs but cannot contain submodules. It can import completely or partially definitions of other modules. The modules can be parameterized with values that are supplied by the test environment at runtime. For parameters, default values can be specified in addition.

A TTCN-3 module has two parts: the module definition part and the module control part. The definition part contains the data defined by that module (functions, test cases, components, types, templates), which can be used throughout the module and can be imported from other modules. The control part is the main program of a module and describes the execution sequence of the test cases or functions. It can access the verdicts delivered by test cases, and, according to them, it can decide the next steps of test execution. The test behaviors in the TTCN-3 are defined within functions, altsteps, and test cases. The control part of a module may call any test case or function defined in or imported by the module to which it belongs.

10.2.2   Test System

A test case is executed by a test system. The TTCN-3 allows the specification of static nondistributed and of dynamic concurrent test systems. A test system consists of a set of interconnected test components with well-defined communication ports and an explicit test system interface, which defines the boundaries of the test system to the SUT.

Within every test system, there is one Main Test Component (MTC). All other test components are called Parallel Test Components (PTCs). The MTC is created and started automatically at the beginning of each test case execution. A test case terminates when the MTC terminates, which implies also the termination of all other PTCs. The behavior of the MTC is specified by the body of a test case. During the execution of a test case, PTCs can be created, started, and stopped dynamically. A test component may stop itself or can be stopped by another test component.

For communication purposes, each test component can have a set of local ports. Each port has an in- and an out-direction. The in-direction is modeled as an infinite first in, first out (FIFO) queue, which stores the incoming information until it is processed by the test component owning that port. The out-direction is directly linked to the communication partner being another test component or the SUT; that is, outgoing information is not buffered.

During test execution, the TTCN-3 distinguishes between connected and mapped ports. Connected ports are used for the communication with other test components. If two ports are connected, the in-direction of one port is linked to the out-direction of the other and vice versa. A mapped port is used for the communication with the SUT. The mapping of a port owned by a test component to a port in the abstract test system interface can be seen as pure name translation defining how communication streams should be referenced. The TTCN-3 distinguishes between the abstract and the real test system interface. The abstract test system interface is modeled as a collection of ports that defines the abstract interface to the SUT. The real test system interface is the application specific part of a TTCN-3-based test environment. It implements the real interface of the SUT and is defined in the TRI (part 5 of TTCN-3).

In the TTCN-3, connections and mappings are created and destroyed dynamically at runtime. There are no logical restrictions on the number of connections and mappings a component may have, but only limitations of the used test device(s). A component (and even a port) may be connected to itself. One-to-many connections are allowed. These can be used for one-to-one communication, where during test execution the communication partner has to be specified uniquely and for one-to-many communication by means of multicasting and broadcasting. For the communication among test components and between test components and the SUT, TTCN-3 supports message-based and procedure-based communication. Message-based communication is based on an asynchronous message exchange where sender and receiver proceed independently of each other (except that a message can only be received after being sent).

Procedure-based communication is based principally on calling procedures in remote entities synchronously. In procedure-based communication, the calling component is principally blocked up until receiving a response or exception to its call. In TTCN-3, both the client side, that is, calling procedures and awaiting responses or exceptions, and the server side, that is, accepting calls and issuing responses or raising exceptions, can be specified for testing purposes.

10.2.3   Test Cases and Test Verdicts

Test cases define test behaviors that have to be executed to check whether the SUT passes the test or not. Like a module, a test case is considered to be a self-contained and complete specification of a test procedure that checks a given test purpose. The result of a test case execution is a test verdict.

The TTCN-3 provides a special test verdict mechanism for the interpretation of test runs. This mechanism is implemented by a set of predefined verdicts, local and global test verdicts, and operations for reading and setting local test verdicts. The predefined verdicts are `pass`, `inconc`, `fail`, `error`, and `none`. They can be used for the judgment of complete and partial test runs. A pass verdict denotes that the SUT behaves according to the test purpose; a fail indicates that the SUT violates its specification. An inconc (inconclusive) describes a situation where neither a pass nor a fail can be assigned. The verdict error indicates an error in the test devices. The verdict none is the initial value for local and global test verdicts; that is, no other verdict has been assigned yet. During test execution, each test component maintains its own local test verdict. A local test verdict is an object that is instantiated automatically for each test component at the time of component creation. A test component can retrieve and set its local verdict. The verdict error is not allowed to be set by a test component. It is set automatically by the TTCN-3 runtime environment, if an error in the test equipment occurs. When changing the value of a local test verdict, special overwriting rules are applied. The overwriting rules only allow a test verdict to become worse; for example, a pass may change to inconc or fail, but a fail cannot change to a pass or inconc.

In addition to the local test verdicts, the TTCN-3 runtime environment maintains a global test verdict for each test case. The global test verdict is not accessible by the test components. It is updated according to the overwriting rules when a test component terminates. The final global test verdict is returned to the module control part when the test case terminates.

10.2.4   Alternatives and Snapshots

A special feature of the TTCN-3 semantics is the snapshot. Snapshots are related to the behavior of components. They are needed for the branching of behavior due to the occurrence of time-outs, the termination of test components, and the reception of messages, procedure calls, procedure replies, or exceptions. In the TTCN-3, this branching is defined by means of alt statements.

An alt statement describes an ordered set of alternatives, that is, an ordered set of alternative branches of behavior. Each alternative has a guard. A guard consists of several preconditions, which may refer to the values of variables, the status of timers, the contents of port queues, and the identifiers of components, ports, and timers. The same precondition can be used in different guards. An alternative becomes executable, if the corresponding guard is fulfilled. If several alternatives are executable, the first executable alternative in the list of alternatives will be executed. If no alternative becomes executable, the alt statement will be executed again.

The evaluation of several guards needs some time. During that time, preconditions may change dynamically. This will lead to inconsistent guard evaluations, if a precondition is verified several times in different guards. The TTCN-3 avoids this problem by using snapshots. Snapshots are partial module states, which include all information necessary for the evaluation of alt statements. A snapshot is taken, that is, recorded, when entering an alternative. For the verification of preconditions, only the information in the current snapshot is used. Thus, dynamic changes of preconditions do not influence the evaluation of guards.

10.2.5   Default Handling

In the TTCN-3, defaults are used to recurring sets of alternatives, which are often used to handle unexpected responses or absent responses. Default behavior can be specified by `altsteps` and activated as defaults. For each test component, the defaults, that is, activated altsteps, are stored in a default list in the order of their activation. The TTCN-3 operations `activate` and `deactivate` operate on that default list. An activate operation appends a new default to the end of the list, and a deactivate operation removes a default from that list.

The activated defaults are invoked at the end of each alt statement, if due to the current snapshot none of the alternatives in the alt match. Like the alternatives in an alt, activated defaults and their alternatives are evaluated one by one. If one of the alternatives matches, it is being executed. If none of the alternatives of an activated default match, a new snapshot is taken and the alt statement is being executed again.

In case of a successful match in a default, the default may stop the test component by means of a `stop` statement, it may `repeat` the alt statement to be executed once more, or it may continue the main control flow of the test component immediately after the alt statement from which the default has been invoked.

The TTCN-3 uses altsteps to specify default behaviors or to structure sets of alternatives. The semantics of altsteps is closely related to alternatives and snapshots. Like an alt statement, an altstep defines an ordered set of alternatives. The difference is that no snapshot is taken when entering an altstep. The evaluation of the altstep alternatives is based on the current snapshot from the alt statement, from which it is invoked. Conceptually, the alternatives of the altstep are inserted at the end into the set of alternatives of the alt statement. It is also possible to invoke an altstep like a function. In this case, the altstep is interpreted as an alt statement that only invokes the altstep; that is, the altstep alternatives are the only alternatives of that alt statement.

10.2.6 Communication Operations

Communication operations are important for the specification of test behaviors. The TTCN-3 supports message-based and procedure-based communication. The communication operations can be grouped in two parts: stimuli, which send information to SUT, and responses, which are used to describe the reaction of the SUT.

Message-based communication in the TTCN-3 is asynchronous communication meaning that the sending of messages is nonblocking; after sending the message, the system does not wait for a response. A receive operation blocks the execution until a matching message is received at the specified port. A receive operation defines a matching part for valid messages to be received. Optionally, an address can be specified to identify the connection from which the message is being expected. The following operations are defined for message-based communication:

- `send` to direct a message to the SUT or another PTC,
- `receive` to accept a message from the SUT or another PTC, and
- `trigger` to ignore incoming messages up until the expected one arrives.

Procedure-based communication in the TTCN-3 is synchronous communication meaning that the invocation of calls is basically blocking. For synchronous communication, the following operations are defined:

- `call` to invoke a remote procedure,
- `getcall` to accept a call from,
- `reply` to provide a reply to a call,
- `getreply` to accept a reply to a call,
- `raise` to provide an exception to a call, and
- `catch` to accept an exception to a call.

10.2.7 Test Data Specification

A test system needs to exchange data with the SUT and between PTCs. The communication with the SUT can be either asynchronous, by sending/receiving messages to/from the SUT, or synchronous, by calling procedures of the SUT or accepting procedure calls from the SUT. In these cases, the test data have to be defined by the test system according to the SUT specification. The TTCN-3 offers different constructs to describe the test data: types, templates, variables, procedure signatures, and so on. They can be used to express protocol message, service primitives, procedure invocations, exception handling, and alike. Besides these, the TTCN-3 also offers the possibility to import data described in other languages such as ASN.1, IDL, or XML.

The TTCN-3 provides a number of basic and predefined types, based on which user-defined types can be specified. Most of the types are similar to the types of well-known programming languages such as Java or C. Some of them, however, are test domain specific:

- `port` types define types of messages or procedures that can be communicated via port (instances) of a given port type in a communication between PTCs or with the SUT.
- `component` types define the local ports, variables, constants, and timers of MTCs or PTCs of a given component type.
- The `verdicttype` is an enumeration of the possible verdicts that can be the result of a test case.
- The `anytype` is a union of all known TTCN-3 types and is used to specify generic data that are evaluated when the concrete data is known.
- The `default` type is used for handling default alternatives.

The TTCN-3 also supports ordered structured types such as `record`, `record of`, `set`, `set of`, `enumerated`, and `union`. For procedure-based communication, procedure signatures can be defined. Signatures are characterized by their name, optional list of parameters, optional return values, and optional list of exceptions.

A `template` represents test data of a given type used to define messages to be sent or received. Templates define either distinct values that are to be transmitted or sets of values (by use of wildcards or other matching mechanisms) against which received messages are evaluated to match or not. When comparing a received message with a template, the template matches if the message is one of the values in the value set defined by the template. Templates can be specified for basic types, user-defined types, or procedure signatures. They can be parameterized and reused or modified in other template definitions.

As not all details of the TTCN-3 can be given here, please refer to the standard series [4, 6–17], further papers [25–27], and tools [22] to get a deeper insight into the test technology.

10.3   AN INTRODUCTORY EXAMPLE

In the following, a small test specification in TTCN-3 is given in order to give an insight into this technology. The well-known triangle testing example by G. J. Myers [28] for the classification of triangles is used. A triangle is defined by its side lengths and has to be classified into scalene, isosceles, and equilateral triangles. In addition, the data used to characterize a triangle can be incorrect, or the data are correct but do not define a triangle.

When testing software that classifies triangles, the question of typing of the SUT has to be posed. In TTCN-3, you are explicitly defining the SUT-type system—in this case, by defining type `Triangle` to consist of three `integer` values of unlimited size and by defining type `Classification` to specify the possible triangle classifiers:

```
type integer Triangle[3] (0..infinity);
// whole numbers to characterize a triangle
type enumerated Classification {
// properties of a triangle
  syntacticallyIncorrect,
  noTriangle,
  scaleneTriangle,
  isoscelesTriangle,
  equilateralTriangle
}
```

Subsequently, the interface `DetermineTriangle` to the SUT can be defined in terms of a message-based port that transmits values of `Triangle` in the in-direction and values of `Classification` in the out-direction. A test component for the SUT uses that port as defined by the test component type `TriangleTester`:

```
type port DetermineTriangle message
  { out Triangle; in Classification }
// Interface to SUT
type component TriangleTester
  { port DetermineTriangle b }
// Test Component
```

These definitions are sufficient to define concrete tests for the SUT as demonstrated by the test case `Simple` that checks for a concrete equilateral triangle:

```
testcase Simple() runs on TriangleTester {
// a simple test case
    b.send(Triangle: {2,2,2});
    // the triangle to be checked
    b.receive(Classification: equilateralTriangle);
    // the expected response
    setverdict(pass); // a successful test
}
```

This test specification given above is wiring the test data firmly with the testing activity, which is neither useful nor easy to maintain. Another method would be to separate the test data from the test behavior. In order to so, we define an additional type `TestVector` that pairs triangle integer triples and their classifications. Concrete triangle triples and classifiers are then defined in form of templates valid1, valid2, and so on:

```
type record TestVector {
 // combination of inputs and expected outputs
   Triangle input,
   Classification output
 }
 template TestVector valid1:= {{2,2,2},
isoscelesTriangle};
 // valid triangle
 template TestVector valid2:= {{2,2,1},
equilateralTriangle};
 // etc.
 template TestVector invalid1:= {{1,0,3}, noTriangle };
 // invalid triangle
 template TestVector invalid2:= {{1,2,3}, noTriangle };
 // etc.
```

In addition, a test specification should define how unexpected or no responses from the SUT are to be evaluated. Unexpected responses are handled by a receive any statement (second alternative in the alt statement), which is evaluated only after the alternative for the correct response (first alternative in the alt statement). In order to identify no responses from the SUT, the local timer noResponse is defined, started, and observed for time-out whenever a triangle classification query is given to the SUT:

```
testcase Extended(TestVector tv) runs on TriangleTester
{
 // a parameterised test
   timer noResponse:= 1.0;
   // timer with 1 second timeout duration
   b.send(tv.input); noResponse.start;
   alt {
       [] b.receive(tv.output) {setverdict(pass);}
         // expected correct response
       [] b.receive {setverdict(fail);}
         // unexpected incorrect response
         [] noResponse.timeout {setverdict(fail);}
         // no response at all
   }
}
```

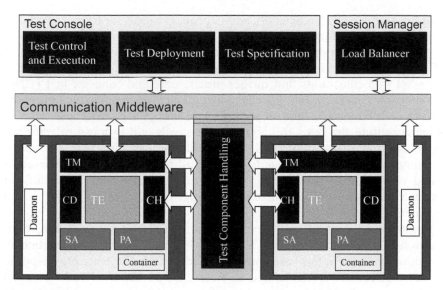

FIGURE 10.3   A TTCN-3 integrated development environment based on Eclipse.

We could further extend the examples by, for example, using parameterization to have additional flexibility in the test data or by giving queries with two parallel testing components to the SUT to check concurrent usages.

By using TTCN-3 tools [22], TTCN-3 test specifications as those defined for the triangle example can be developed, implemented, and executed efficiently (Fig. 10.3).

10.4 TTCN-3 SEMANTICS AND ITS APPLICATION

The semantics of TTCN-3 is defined by an operational semantics [9], which defines the meaning of TTCN-3 behaviors in an intuitive and unambiguous manner. It is not in itself a formal semantics, so that the abilities for formal verification and validation are limited. In fact, the operational semantics of TTCN-3 provides a state-oriented view on the execution of TTCN-3 modules. It defines solely the meaning of behavior in TTCN-3, that is, functions, altsteps, test cases, module control, and behavioral statements like communication operations or control flow statements.

The operational semantics uses flow graphs of the TTCN-3 module to be executed. A flow graph is a directed graph that consists of labeled nodes and labeled edges, which describe the possible flow of control during the execution of the behavior represented by the flow graph. The operational semantics is used to construct runtime environments (see the following section), to test solutions (see, e.g., References 29), and to provide a basis for formal semantics definitions for additional validation and verification purposes.

A major research direction is on analyzing and improving the quality of TTCN-3 test suites. Herein, the operational semantics of TTCN-3 has been extended with constraints that further precise data and behavior in TTCN-3 test suites. An overview on optimizing test quality for maintenance purposes is given in Reference 30: metrics, patterns, and antipatterns have been defined, which constitute the basis to identify code smells and propose refactorings for an assessment and automated restructuring of test suites [31]. The use of guidelines for improved test suite design and maintenance and their automated verification is presented in Reference 32. Reference 33 presents an approach to analyze and optimize the coverage of test data in TTCN-3-based test suites.

Furthermore, verification of test behavior in TTCN-3 has been subject to research. In particular, behavioral anomalies like inconsistencies in test behavior within and across test cases have been identified. For example, response inconsistencies have been defined in Reference 34 and analyzed by model checking.

Another major research direction along formalized testing based on TTCN-3 is on testing real-time, embedded systems: In Reference 35, the authors provided a semantics for host-based testing with simulated time and a simulated-time solution for distributed testing with TTCN-3. Reference 36 defines a formal semantics based on timed automaton for testing of real-time systems with an extended version of TTCN-3. Some of these concepts became later part of the real-time concepts for TTCN-3 in Reference 24. Reference 35 provides concepts for testing continuous behavior of embedded systems and a formal semantics based on stream processing functions as used by the time partition test (TPT) method. This was further extended into a semantics definition based on hybrid automata and is now being considered for addition to real-time concepts for TTCN-3 in Reference 24 too.

10.5   A DISTRIBUTED TEST PLATFORM FOR THE TTCN-3

The full potential of the TTCN-3 can be realized by a test platform that supports test execution across multiple, potentially heterogeneous test interfaces and devices. By that, not only a potentially distributed and heterogeneous configuration of an SUT can be reflected by the test system by use of interconnected test devices, but also performance and scalability issues of the test system can be addressed.

We have developed such a distributed test platform for the TTCN-3 (depicted in 0) by using a Common Object Request Broker Architecture (CORBA [37]) middleware. We use this platform in particular not only for performance, scalability, and load and stress tests, but also for nondistributed functional tests or for cases were single test devices and/or interface are needed only. We do not intend to make an exhaustive presentation of all implementation details; rather, we provide an overview of the most important aspects (Fig. 10.4).

The test console is the control point of our platform and is an integrated development environment (IDE), which provides support to specify TTCN-3 test cases, create test sessions, deploy test suites into containers, and control the test execution.

Daemons are stand-alone processes installed on any test device. They manage the containers that belong to different sessions. Containers intercede between the test console and components, providing services transparently to both, including transaction support and resource pooling. From the test view point, containers are the target operational environment and comply with the TCI standard for a TTCN-3 test execution environment. Within a container, the following specific test system entities exist:

- TTCN-3 engine (TE) executes the compiled TTCN-3 code. This entity manages different subentities for test control, behavior, components, types, values, and queues realizing the TTCN-3 semantics.
- Component handler (CH) handles the communication between test components. The CH interface contains operations to create, start, and stop test components; establish the connection between test components (map, connect); handle the communication operations (send, receive, call, reply); and manage the verdicts. The information about the created components and their physical locations is stored in a repository inside the containers.
- Test management (TM) manages the test execution. This entity implements operations to execute tests and provide and set module parameters and external constants. The test logging is also tracked by this component.
- Encoding/decoding (CD) encodes and decodes values according to assumed or given types. Every TTCN-3 value is encoded into bitstrings for communication with the SUT. The received data are decoded into abstract TTCN-3 types and values.

The container subentities are functionally bound by the TRI and TCI and communicate with each other via the CORBA platform. The session manager coordinates test components (and their behaviors) chosen at test deployment (and not in the test specification). The TRI system adapter realizes SUT-specific communication and timing. It is typically provided by the test developer. The TCI test adapter realizes the adaptation to the test management environment and to the test devices. It is typically provided by the test vendor.

The whole execution platform is implemented in Java JDK1.4 [38]. For the communication between containers, we used the CORBA implementation provided with JDK1.4. Following the standard specification helped us to optimize our execution environment for common operations across the test

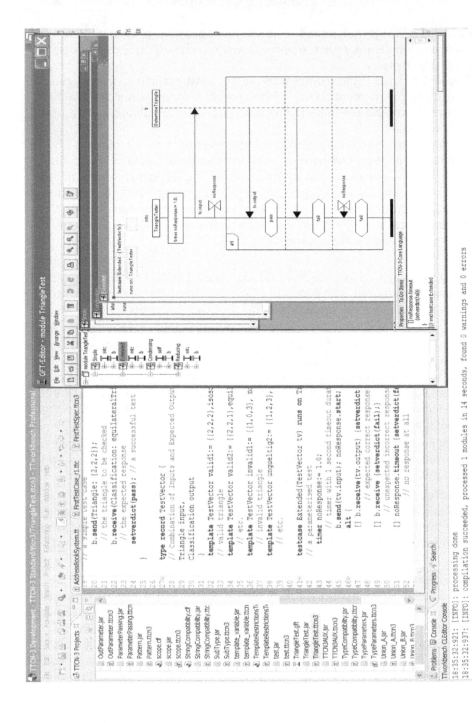

FIGURE 10.4 A distributed test platform architecture for the TTCN-3.

execution. The advantage of adopting a pure Java solution for our TTCN-3 platform gave us hardware and operating systems independence, so that we are able to run tests in various scenarios and deployment configurations for different SUTs.

10.6 CASE STUDY I: TESTING OF OPEN SERVICE ARCHITECTURE (OSA)/PARLAY SERVICES

In the following, we describe different case studies that demonstrate the application of the TTCN-3 to test various target systems. The first case study is on testing OSA/Parlay [39] services. OSA/Parlay defines a set of standard Application Programming Interfaces (APIs) jointly developed by the Mobile Systems 3rd Generation Partnership Project (3GPP), ETSI, and the Parlay Group to ease the creation of telecom services. The APIs provide a common interface to the underlying network, offering software developers major support to implement their telecom applications.

The TTCN-3 is particularly suited for testing client–server applications when the communication interfaces between client and server are well specified; that is, an interface definition language like IDL or WSDL is given. Based on these specifications, functional tests for operations the server provides to its clients as well as of functional tests for client-side applications that use the server features can be generated.

The architecture of OSA/Parlay is depicted in Figure 10.5. OSA/Parlay defines three types of components: applications, service capability servers, and a framework:

- `Applications` represent any business application that uses the core network. The application connects and authenticates to the framework. After successful authentication, the application uses the framework for service discovery.
- The `services` that the network can provide and the applications can request are called service capability features (SCFs). An application can use an SCF via calls to its interfaces, which are described in the OSA technical specifications.
- A `framework` provides applications with directory services and connection factories, and mediates between the SCFs and the applications. The only thing the application needs to know is where to find the factory, and what features it is looking for.

The aim of this case study was to realize a TTCN-3-based test framework for the testing of OSA/Parlay-based services and applications. The TTCN-3 is used to specify tests for the operations of the framework, the services, and/or the application APIs. The test system can be in two different roles:

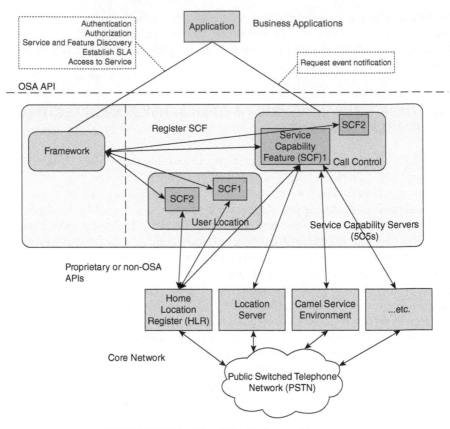

FIGURE 10.5   The OSA/Parlay architecture.

- the role of a service consumer that communicates via the OSA/Parlay API with the framework or with the services, or
- the role of the framework or of a service that validates the behavior of the application.

The application tested in the case study was a small application that uses OSA/Parlay to establish a call between two users connected to the network. The test system emulates the behavior of the SCFs, which are used to establish calls between two users.

The tool environment for testing the OSA/Parlay application with TTCN-3 uses the TTCN-3 to Java compiler TTthree provided by Testing Technologies [22] and an IDL-to-TTCN-3 plug-in and a test adaptor for CORBA provided by Fraunhofer FOKUS [40].

In a first step, the OSA/Parlay IDL specifications have been compiled to TTCN-3 using the IDL-to-TTCN-3 plug-in based on the standardized mapping rules [12]. As a result of this step, the data types and structural information of the OSA/Parlay interfaces are available in TTCN-3. In a second step, the functional behavior of the application along selected scenarios has been specified in TTCN-3. The scenarios contain operations to be called at the OSA/Parlay interfaces, time-outs, default behaviors, and so on. Each test case consists of a preamble, a test body, a postamble, and the assignment of a final verdict. In a last step, the concrete test data for each of the method calls and messages to be sent and received has been specified.

A hybrid approach for the test tools has been selected due to the complex behavior of the test preamble: To emulate the complex behavior of the entire OSA/Parlay framework with the test tools (in TTCN-3) would not have been feasible for this case study. Thus, a Java implementation of the OSA/Parlay framework has been integrated into the test tool chain for handling the test preamble (in particular, authentication and service discovery). The actual test bodies reflecting the main concerns of the test scenarios have been implemented in TTCN-3.

This case study demonstrated how TTCN-3 can be used to develop test automation for systems and services that use a synchronous communication scheme following request–response scenarios. In addition, it showed that the language mappings (in this case for IDL) provide good means to generate the interface-related test structures efficiently. Last but not least, the case study demonstrated that TTCN-3 only solutions are not always practical, but that the open system architecture of TTCN-3 enables an easy integration with non-TTCN-3 components. This case study has been further elaborated and lead to the definition of test patterns often used in test solutions for communication services infrastructures [35].

10.7 CASE STUDY II: TESTING OF IP MULTIMEDIA SUBSYSTEM (IMS) EQUIPMENT

The purpose of this case study is to apply TTCN-3 for the definition of performance tests for IMS [41] equipment. The IMS is an open, standardized, operator-friendly, multimedia network architecture for mobile and fixed Internet Protocol (IP) services. IMS supports a rich set of services available to end users on either wireless or wired user equipment, which are provided via a uniform interface.

The IMS reference architecture is presented in Figure 10.6. IMS defines that traffic between a User Equipment (UE) and the Proxy-Call/Session Control Functions (P-CSCF) is carried by an IPSec tunnel (i.e., via secure IP) corresponding to the UE. A P-CSCF is a Session Initiation Protocol proxy (the SIP, being a protocol, e.g., for the control of multimedia sessions in the Internet [42]) that is the first point of contact for an IMS terminal. It is assigned to an IMS terminal during registration, and does not change for the duration of the registration. The Interrogating Call/Session Control Functions (I-CSCF) queries the Home Subscriber Server (HSS) to retrieve the user location, and

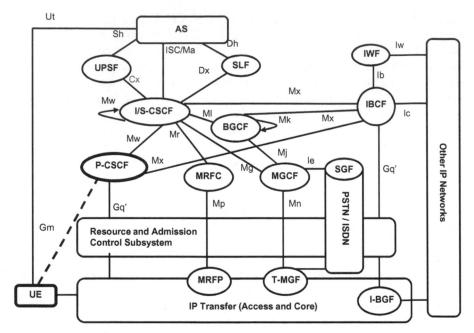

FIGURE 10.6   IMS reference architecture (from 3GPP).

then routes the SIP request to its assigned Serving Call/Session Control Functions (S-CSCF). S-CSCF is the central node of the signaling plane, which decides to which application server(s) the SIP message will be forwarded to, in order to provide their services.

The aim of this case study was to develop IMS performance tests in TTCN-3 that define the input stimulus to the SUT along precise transaction types and contents, statistical distributions for transaction types, arrival rates, and other relevant parameters. The tests specify how the traffic is to be provided to the SUT, define the measurements that have to be taken, and how the results are to be reported.

The performance tests measure the capacity of the control plane of an IMS system. This consists of the components that perform SIP-based signaling to each other and the database accessed by those components.

A call is a relationship between one or more subscribers, signaled and managed through the IMS system. The intent of a subscriber when using IMS is to make calls, so the obvious way to obtain realistic behavior in an IMS test is to model the behavior of calls. We use a voice call model describing the behavior of a call established for a conventional audio or multimedia conversation. Figure 10.7 depicts the sequence of messages through which a voice call passes.

The realization of the call scenario is based on the SIP conformance test suite by ETSI [43] and on the SIP specification by IETF [42]. The type system

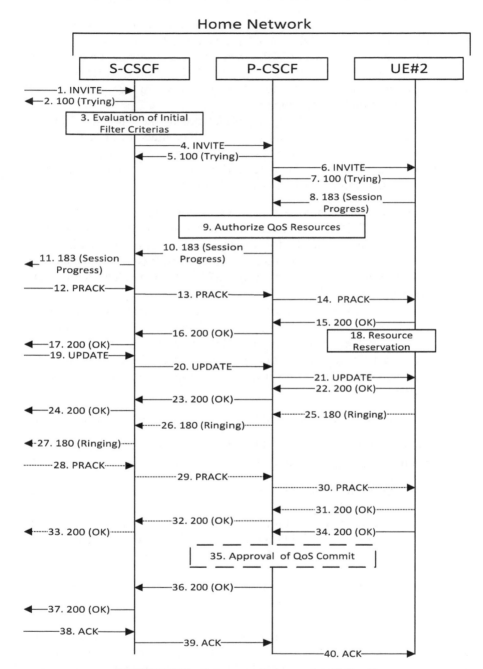

FIGURE 10.7 Sequence diagram of an IMS call.

and template definitions of the conformance tests are reused in the performance test specification for creation of inputs to the IMS system.

The call scenario uses two UEs that establish a call session. One of them plays the role of CALLER by sending the INVITE message to the IMS network and another one plays the role of CALLEE by accepting the call invitation and responding accordingly.

The performance tests scale by a parallel run of the call establishment procedure. The UEs (callers and callees) are implemented in TTCN-3 as PTCs that interact with the SUT via the system component. The case study implements two techniques to realize load test, where the SUT is put under increasing load while its responsiveness is being measured and analyzed:

1. *Use of PTC.* This technique is the obvious method to implement parallel activities in TTCN-3. The callers and callees are implemented as PTCs and executed in parallel. Unfortunately, this technique has the disadvantage that the creation of too many test components may consume too many hardware resources (memory, CPU), which may lead to an overloading of the test system.

2. *Reuse of Test Components after Call Establishment.* This technique is used together with the first one implying that once a test component finished a call establishment procedure, it is reused for a next call (of course with new identifiers and sets of data). Thus, only one test component may establish several calls in a second increasing the overall workload.

The key performance parameters evaluated within the case study have been

- the number of invitations (INVITE messages) per second and
- delays of the reaction of the SUT measured under load.

Figure 10.8 displays the number of INVITES per second applied for a period of 80 seconds.

Figure 10.9 shows the evolution of the delays in the reactions of the SUT when applying a load of 35 INVITES/second. Reading the two graphs in parallel, one can identify when the IMS system needs more time for internal computations.

This case study has demonstrated the power of TTCN-3 to specify and execute not only functional tests, but also performance and load tests. It uses the capabilities of TTCN-3 to specify distributed and concurrent test setups by using PTCs, which can be assigned different test behaviors. In addition, the case study shows the abilities of the TTCN-3 logging format defined in Reference 11 to enable test reports that contain graph-based evaluations of the test execution and SUT timing.

This case study has been further extended and led to the evaluation of concrete IMS equipment provided by a hardware vendor. Additional results are described in Reference 44.

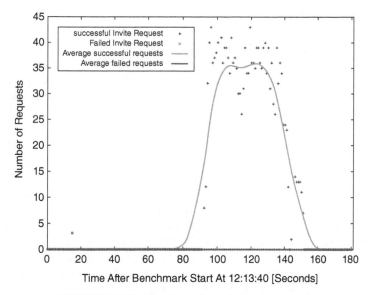

FIGURE 10.8   Number of requests per second.

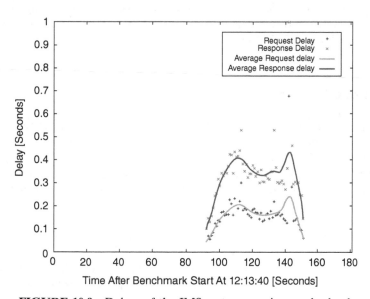

FIGURE 10.9   Delays of the IMS system reactions under load.

10.8 CONCLUSION

TTCN-3 is the only standardized test specification and implementation technology being applicable to a wide range of test kinds for various system technologies. It has progressed a lot in the past: A plethora of tools is available that support TTCN-3 in a different scale. Various test solutions are based on TTCN-3. There are plans to apply TTCN-3 in additional domains such as scientific computing or cloud computing.

Still, more needs to be done. In particular, people need to be trained in order to enable an efficient use and adoption of this test technology. The established TTCN-3 Certificate [45] provides a good basis—however, more reading and training material and training courses should be provided.

Also, TTCN-3 is rarely lectured at universities—although free tools help in this. In particular, it is not enough to spread the knowledge about TTCN-3 and its success stories, but a thorough methodology including guidelines and best practices for the application of TTCN-3 should also be provided.

A strong basis for the further adoption of TTCN-3 will be an ongoing maintenance and evolution of TTCN-3. Although already a quite exhaustive and powerful set of testing concepts is supported by TTCN-3, still more requirements appear—for example, to have native support for object-oriented data types when interacting with the SUT. However, like in the past, every new concept is very critically reviewed and discussed before being added to the core language and its execution interfaces or to one—if not to a new— extension package of TTCN-3.

REFERENCES

1. J. Grabowski, D. Hogrefe, G. Rethy, I. Schieferdecker, A. Wiles, and C. Willcock. An introduction into the testing and test control notation (TTCN-3). *Computer Networks Journal*, 42(3):375–403, 2003.

2. ISO/IEC 9646-3. Information Technology—Open Systems Interconnection— Conformance Testing Methodology and Framework—Part 3: The Tree and Tabular Combined Notation (TTCN), 1998.

3. ETSI TR 101 666. Information Technology Open Systems Interconnection Conformance Testing Methodology and Framework; the Tree and Tabular Combined Notation (TTCN) (Ed. 2++), May 1999.

4. ETSI ES 201 873-7. Methods for Testing and Specification (MTS); the Testing and Test Control Notation Version 3; Part 7: Using ASN.1 with TTCN-3, April 2012.

5. ISO/IEC 9075. Database Language SQL (Structure Query Language), July 30, 1992.

6. ETSI ES 201 873-1. Methods for Testing and Specification (MTS); the Testing and Test Control Notation Version 3; Part 1: TTCN-3 Core Language, April 2012.

7. ETSI ES 201 873-2. Methods for Testing and Specification (MTS); the Testing and Test Control Notation Version 3; Part 2: Tabular Presentation Format, April 2012.

8. ETSI ES 201 873-3. Methods for Testing and Specification (MTS); the Testing and Test Control Notation Version 3; Part 3: Graphical Presentation Format, April 2012.

9. ETSI ES 201 873-4. Methods for Testing and Specification (MTS); the Testing and Test Control Notation Version 3; Part 1: TTCN-3 Operational Semantics, April 2012.

10. ETSI ES 201 873-5. Methods for Testing and Specification (MTS); the Testing and Test Control Notation Version 3; Part 5: TTCN-3 Runtime Interface (TRI), April 2012.

11. ETSI ES 201 873-6. Methods for Testing and Specification (MTS); the Testing and Test Control Notation Version 3; Part 6: TTCN-3 Control Interface (TCI), April 2012.

12. ETSI ES 201 873-8. Methods for Testing and Specification (MTS); the Testing and Test Control Notation Version 3; Part 8: The IDL to TTCN-3 Mapping, April 2012.

13. ETSI ES 201 873-9. Methods for Testing and Specification (MTS); the Testing and Test Control Notation Version 3; Part 9: Use XML with TTCN-3, April 2012.

14. ETSI ES 201 873-10. Methods for Testing and Specification (MTS); the Testing and Test Control Notation Version 3; Part 10: TTCN-3 Documentation Comment Specification, April 2012.

15. ETSI ES 202 781. Methods for Testing and Specification (MTS); the Testing and Test Control Notation Version 3; TTCN-3 Language Extensions: Configuration and Deployment Support, April 2012.

16. ETSI ES 202 784. Methods for Testing and Specification (MTS); the Testing and Test Control Notation Version 3; TTCN-3 Language Extensions: Advanced Parameterization, April 2012.

17. ETSI ES 202 785. Methods for Testing and Specification (MTS); the Testing and Test Control Notation Version 3; TTCN-3 Language Extensions: Behavior Types, April 2012.

18. I. Schieferdecker and G. Din. A metamodel for TTCN-3. In *1st International Workshop on Integrated Test Methodologies. Colocated with 24th International Conference on Formal Description Techniques (FORTE 2004)*, Toledo, Spain, September 2004.

19. IETF RFC 2616. Hypertext Transfer Protocol (HTTP/1.1), June 1999.

20. ITU-T X.680. Data Networks and Open System Communications. OSI Networking and System Aspects—Abstract Syntax Notation One (ASN.1), July 2002.

21. W3C. Web Services Description Language (WSDL) 1.1, 2001. Available at: http://www.w3.org/TR/wsdl [accessed March 15, 2001].

22. Testing Technologies. TTworkbench—A TTCN-3 tool Set, 2012. Available at: http://www.testingtech.com

23. OMG. UML Testing Profile (UTP) Specification, Version 1.0, July 2005.

24. ETSI ES 202 782. Methods for Testing and Specification (MTS); the Testing and Test Control Notation Version 3; TTCN-3 Language Extensions: TTCN-3 Performance and Real Time Testing, July 2010.

25. ETSI TTCN-3. Home Page, 2012. Available at: http://www.ttcn-3.org

26. I. Schieferdecker and J. Grabowski. The graphical format of TTCN-3 and its rela-
    tion to UML and MSC. In *3rd International Workshop on SDL and MSC—
    Telecommunication and Beyond, SAM 2002*, Aberystwyth, UK, June 2002.

27. I. Schieferdecker and T. Vassiliou-Gioles. Realizing distributed TTCN-3 test systems
    with TCI. In *IFIP 15th International Conference on Testing Communicating
    Systems—TestCom 2003*, Cannes, France, May 2003.

28. G. J. Myers. *The Art of Software Testing*. John Wiley & Sons, 2004.

29. P. Xiong, R. L. Probert, and B. Stepien. An Efficient Formal Testing Approach for
    Web Service Testing with TTCN-3, 2005. Available at: http://www.site.oottawa.ca/
    bernard/softcom paper.pdf

30. I. Schieferdecker, E. Bringmann, and J. Grossmann. Continuous TTCN-3: Testing
    of embedded control systems. In *Proceedings of the 2006 International Workshop
    on Software Engineering for Automotive Systems (SEAS '06)*, pp. 29–36. ACM, New
    York, 2006.

31. H. Neukirchen, B. Zeiss, J. Grabowski, P. Baker, and D. Evans. Quality assurance
    for TTCN-3 test specifications. *Software Testing, Verification and Reliability*, 18:71–
    97, 2008.

32. B. Zeiß. Quality assurance of test specifications for reactive systems. PhD thesis,
    Universität Göttingen, June 2010.

33. G. Din, D. Vega, and I. Schieferdecker. Automated maintainability of TTCN-3 test
    suites based on guideline checking. In *6th IFIP Workshop on Software Technologies
    for Future Embedded and Ubiquitous Systems (SEUS 2008)*, Capri Island, Italy,
    October 2008.

34. D. Vega, G. Din, and I. Schieferdecker. TTCN-3 test data analyser using constraint
    programming. In *19th International Conference on Systems Engineering (ICSENG
    2008)*, Las Vegas, NV, August 2008.

35. J. Grossmann, D. Serbanescu, and I. Schieferdecker. Testing embedded real time
    systems with TTCN-3. In *2nd International IEEE Conference on Software Testing,
    Verification, and Validation (ICST 2009)*, Denver, CO, April 2009.

36. S. C. C. Blom, T. Deiß, N. Ioustinova, A. Kontio, J. C. van de Pol, A. Rennoch, and
    N. Sidorova. TTCN-3 for distributed testing embedded software. In Perspectives of
    Systems Informatics, June 27–30, 2006, Novosibirsk, Russia, 2007.

37. OMG. Common Object Request Broker Architecture (CORBA) Specification,
    Version 3.1, January 2008.

38. Oracle. Java 4 SE Development Kit Version 4, JDK1.4, Documentation, 2005. Avail-
    able at: http://www.oracle.com/technetwork/java/index.html

39. ETSI ES 203 915. V1.1.1: OSA/Parlay Specification, April 2005.

40. Z. R. Dai. An Approach to Model-Driven Testing—Functional and Real-Time
    Testing with UML 2.0, U2TP and TTCN-3, Promotion, TU Berlin, Fakultät Elek-
    trotechnik und Informatik, June 2006.

41. 3GPP TS 23.228. Technical Specification Group Services and System Aspects: IP
    Multimedia Subsystem (IMS), Stage 2, 2006.

42. IETF RFC 3261. Session Initiation Protocol (SIP), June 2002.

43. ETSI TS 102 027-3. Ver. 3.2.1: Methods for Testing and Specification (MTS), Conformance Test Specification for SIP (IETF RFC 3261), Part 3: Abstract Test Suite (ATS) and Partial Protocol Implementation eXtra Information for Testing (PIXIT) proforma, 2005.

44. G. Din. A workload realization methodology for performance testing of telecommunication services. PhD thesis, TU Berlin, Fakultät Elektrotechnik und Informatik, September 2008.

45. GTB TTCN-3 Certificate. The TTCN-3 Syllabus and Certificate, 2008. Available at: http://german-testing-board.info/de/ttcn3_certificate.shtm

CHAPTER 11

PRACTICAL ASPECTS OF ACTIVE AUTOMATA LEARNING

FALK HOWAR
Chair Programming Systems, TU Dortmund University, Dortmund, Germany

MAIK MERTEN
Chair Programming Systems, TU Dortmund University, Dortmund, Germany

BERNHARD STEFFEN
Chair Programming Systems, TU Dortmund University, Dortmund, Germany

TIZIANA MARGARIA
Chair Service and Software Engineering, University of Potsdam, Potsdam, Germany

11.1 INTRODUCTION

Most systems in use today lack adequate specification or make use of under-specified or even unspecified components. In fact, the much propagated component-based software design style typically leads to underspecified systems, as most libraries only provide very partial specifications of their components. Moreover, typically, revisions and last-minute changes hardly enter the system specification. We observed this dilemma in the telecommunication area: Specifications of telecommunication protocols are usually provided as natural language text documents with no formal link to the actual implementation. This hampers the application of any kind of formal validation techniques like model-based testing [14] or model checking [17], and it makes it hard to keep documentation up to date. In fact, in practice, very often these specifications are not updated at all, turning the systems all too soon into legacy systems. Automata learning techniques have been proposed to overcome this situation, by allowing to construct and later update behavioral models

Formal Methods for Industrial Critical Systems: A Survey of Applications, First Edition.
Edited by Stefania Gnesi and Tiziana Margaria.

automatically [33–35, 44]. This has been illustrated a long time ago in the concrete setting of computer telephony integrated (CTI) systems [27–28]. There we observed the system's behavior in its reaction to test sequences. In this setting, behavior is understood as sequences comprising test stimuli and the corresponding reactions as words of a language over an alphabet consisting of symbols denoting the stimuli and the reactions, respectively. Automata learning aims at constructing finite automata for describing/approximating this language.

Figure 11.1 shows the general scheme of the learning process, modeled as eXtended Process Description Diagrams (XPDD), introduced in Reference 38. There we see that the learning process requires an abstract inference alphabet and test drivers for the system under learning (SUL, on the left) and produces a number of hypothesis automata before delivering the final model (on the right). The alphabet and a suitable test driver are all the previous knowledge needed about the system, which is a much lower requirement than otherwise popular trace-based approaches. The learning process itself is depicted in the center: Automata learning generates models by alternating local exploration (establishing closedness and consistency) and testing (approximative) equivalence (e.g., by means of conformance testing). Counterexamples resulting from failing equivalence tests are used to steer the next round of local exploration. This technique works well for reactive systems, whenever the chosen interpretation of the stimuli and reactions leads to a deterministic language. For such systems, automata learning can be regarded as *regular extrapolation*, that is, as a technique to construct the "best" regular model that is consistent with the observations made. This is similar to the well-known polynomial interpolation, where polynomials are used instead of finite automata, and functions instead of reactive systems. And like there, the quality, not the applicability, of extrapolation depends on the structure of the considered system behavior. However, due to the enormous degree of freedom inherent in reactive systems, automata learning is computationally much more expensive than polynomial interpolation. Thus, the success of automata learning in practice very much depends on the optimizations employed to exploit the specific profile of the system to be learned. See References 42 and 44 for a successful application scenario.

Figure 11.2 gives a high-level overview on what learning setups look like in practice: A learning algorithm (right-hand side of the picture) is connected to a SUL instance (left-hand side) via a test driver, which employs system instrumentation (e.g., provided by an interface description) to execute actual system invocations during learning. The test driver also mediates between abstract symbols in the realm of the learning algorithm and concrete invocations in the realm of the SUL. Details are given in Section 11.4.

In this chapter, we review the essence of practical automata learning, its major challenges, its variants, possible solutions, and illustrative case studies. These suggest that the theoretically quite well-studied active learning technology can be a specifically enhanced application and become a powerful tool

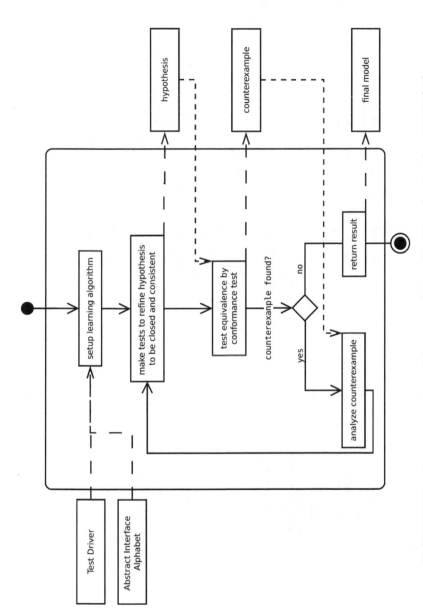

FIGURE 11.1 Common structure of the extrapolation algorithms (modeled as XPDD [38]).

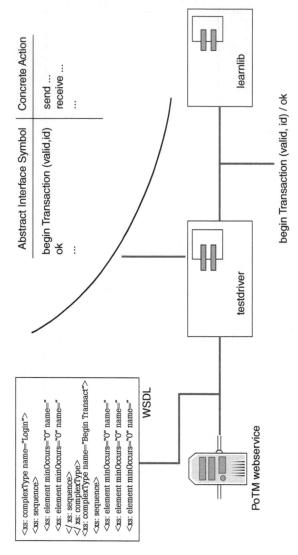

FIGURE 11.2 Schematic view of an experimental setup.

for practical system development. This requires application-specific optimizations to increase scalability, the adequate treatment of parameters and data flow, tailored abstraction mechanisms, and an adequate adaptation of testing technology.

Particularly promising are restricted application scenarios like in the case of the Connect project [37], which focuses on connectors and protocols, that is, on systems whose behavior has limited data dependencies. Section 11.4 reports on a case study where a behavioral model with more than 20.000 states has successfully been extrapolated from a router of similar profile. In another real-life case study, it is shown how a currently still very small behavioral view of Springer's editorial system Online Conference System (OCS) could be extrapolated from the running enterprise implementation (see Chapter 8). All this indicates that active learning has the potential to support the control of emerging behavior in such scenarios.

In the following, Section 11.2 sketches the principle of regular extrapolation in its basic form and for Mealy machine models. In Section 11.3, we sketch the major challenges of learning/extrapolating models for realistic (reactive) systems and subsequently discuss them in Sections 11.4–11.7. The chapter continues with a presentation of the Next Generation LearnLib (NGLL), our framework for flexible modeling of application-specific learning algorithms, then Section 11.9 presents the conclusions and perspectives.

11.2 REGULAR EXTRAPOLATION

Regular extrapolation attempts to construct a deterministic finite automaton (DFA) that matches the behavior of a given target automaton on the basis of observations of the target automaton and perhaps some further information on its internal structure. Here, we only summarize the basic aspects of our realization, which is based on Angluin's learning algorithm L^* from Reference 4.

Definition 1 A DFA is a tuple

$$A = \langle Q, q_0, \Sigma, \delta, F \rangle$$

where

Q is a finite nonempty set of states,
$q_0 \in Q$ is the initial state,
Σ is a finite alphabet,
$\delta: Q \times \Sigma \to Q$ is the transition function, and
$F \subseteq Q$ is the set of accepting states.

Intuitively, a DFA evolves through states $q \in Q$. Whenever one applies an input symbol (or action) $a \in \Sigma$, the automaton moves to a new state according to $\delta(q,a)$. A word $w \in \Sigma^*$ is accepted by the DFA if and only if the DFA reaches an accepting state $q_i \in F$ after processing w starting from its initial state. We write $q \xrightarrow{a} q'$ to denote that on input symbol a, the DFA moves from state q to state q'.

L^* is also referred to as an *active* learning algorithm as it learns DFAs by actively querying the *SUL*. It poses *membership queries* that test whether certain strings (potential runs) are contained in the *SUL*'s language (its set of runs), and *equivalence queries* that compare intermediately constructed hypothesis automata for language equivalence with the *SUL*. Learning terminates successfully as soon as an equivalence query signals success.

From a practical perspective, this approach may be regarded as an algorithmic pattern based on a simple interface to the target system for posing membership and equivalence queries. Usually, membership queries are then realized via testing, while equivalence queries must typically be approximated on the basis of membership queries. This means that the target automaton to be learned is defined by exactly this discipline: It is the smallest deterministic automaton defined by the results of the queries. In particular, it is not guaranteed to be correct or complete. Rather, its precision strongly depends on the quality of the approximation of the equivalence query. In the case where equivalence queries are perfect and the target system is regular, automata learning is guaranteed to terminate with the smallest deterministic automaton specifying the language of the target system.

In its basic form, L^* starts with a hypothesis automaton that treats all words over the considered alphabet (of elementary observations) alike; that is, it has one single state and refines this automaton on the basis of query results, iterating the two main steps shown in Figure 11.1: (1) establishing *closedness* and *local consistency* via membership queries and (2) *testing for equivalence* via equivalence queries. As we will see, this procedure successively produces state-minimal deterministic (hypothesis) automata, consistent with all the encountered query results. Key to achieving this result is L^*'s dual characterization of states [36], based on the well-known Nerode congruence, which identifies the states of the minimal language acceptors by means of so-called residual languages [20], that is, the provably finite set of languages that characterize acceptance relative to possible prefixes:

- *from below*, by a set S of *access sequences* (or possible prefixes). This characterization of states is too fine as different words $s_1, s_2 \in S$ may well be Nerode congruent, that is, may accept the same language as possible suffixes. L^* will construct such a set S, containing *access sequences* to all states of the target automaton. It will also maintain a second set $S \cdot \Sigma$, which together with S will cover all transitions of the *SUL*.
- *from above*, by finite projections of the residual languages, that is, of the languages arising as the sets of suffixes completing a given prefix to a word of the considered language. This characterization may be too coarse as

the finite projections may identify two distinct residual languages. It can be shown, however, that it is possible to separate n distinct residual languages by means of at most $n - 1$ potential suffixes. The corresponding construction of such a (even though in general not minimal) finite projection can be considered the heart of L^*. This construction works by dynamically constructing a growing set of (suffix-) words $D = \langle d_1, \ldots, d_k \rangle$ as the target for the projection, where $d_i \in \Sigma^*$. L^* realizes the characterization of states q from above then simply in terms of bit vectors $row(s) = \langle r_1, \ldots, r_k \rangle$ with $r_i \in \{T, \bot\}$, expressing that the corresponding word $d_i \in D$ belongs to the residual language of q or not:

$$r_i \in row(s) = T \Leftrightarrow \langle d_i \in L_q \Leftrightarrow s \cdot d_i \in L \rangle$$

where L denotes the language of the *SUL* and L_q denotes the residual language characterizing q; s is assumed to be a word from S that reaches q from the initial state.

The second characterization is the key to the construction of the (intermediate) hypothesis automata: Each occurring bit vector corresponds to one of its states. It requires some care to ensure that this construction results in a well-defined deterministic automaton.

The initial hypothesis automaton has just one state and is characterized by the outcome of the membership query for the empty observation ε; S and D are both initialized as $\{\varepsilon\}$. It thus accepts any word in case the empty word is in the language and no word otherwise. The learning procedure then proceeds as shown in Figure 11.1 by the following.

Local Exploration. This first step again iterates two phases. The first phase checks whether the constructed automaton is closed under the one-step transitions, that is, whether each transition from each state of the hypothesis automaton ends in a well-defined state of this very automaton, that is, for every $r \in S \cdot \Sigma$ there exists an $s \in S$ with $row(s) = row(r)$. Otherwise, S will be extended by the corresponding r until *closedness* is established. This extension is guaranteed to result in a unique fix point, independent of the order in which the rows are processed.

The second phase then checks whether two access sequences $s_1, s_2 \in S$ with the same bit vector as characterization from above, $row(s_1) = row(s_2)$, have also the same outgoing transitions, a necessary precondition for them to represent the same state. This condition, which is called *consistency*, can be formalized as follows:

$$\forall s_1, s_2 \in S \; \forall a \in \Sigma \,.\, row(s_1) = row(s_2) \overset{?}{\Rightarrow} row(s_1 \cdot a) = row(s_2 \cdot a).$$

It is easy to see that detected inconsistencies can be removed by elaborating the set D of distinguishing futures in a way that makes some of the difference observed on a distinguishing transition visible before that transition: One simply needs to prefix the distinguishing future that separates the two target states on the distinguishing transition by the label of this very transition.

Unfortunately, such additions to D may break the previously achieved completeness, which requires to reiterate the completion procedure. This, in turn, may lead to new violations of consistency. However, successive iteration of these two steps is guaranteed to result in a unique, well-defined, closed, and complete hypothesis automaton whose states are characterized by the bit vectors. In more detail,

- every state $q \in Q$ of the hypothesis automaton is reachable by at least one word $s \in S$, that is, $row(s)$ corresponds to q;
- $q \in Q$ is accepting if it can be reached by a word of L;
- there exists a transition $\delta(q,a) = q'$ iff there exists $s \in S$ (a *witness*) with s reaching q (or with $row(s)$ corresponding to q) and $s \cdot a$ reaching q'.

Checking Equivalence. After closedness and consistency have been established, an equivalence query checks whether the language of the hypothesis automaton coincides with the language of SUL. If this is true, the learning procedure terminates successfully. Otherwise, the equivalence query returns a counterexample, that is, a word that distinguishes the hypothesis from the SUL.

The processing of counterexamples provides new access sequences and new distinguishing suffixes leading to a refined hypothesis automaton (cf. Fig. 11.1): In its basic version, all prefixes of a counterexample will be added to S before a new round of establishing closedness and consistency is started. This is guaranteed to expose at least one inconsistency, whose resolution imposes the introduction of at least one additional state to the hypothesis automaton.

The correctness argument for this approach follows a straightforward pattern, which holds not only for $L*$, but also for all of its known derivatives [39, 41, 42, 50, 51]:

1. The state construction via projections of residual languages guarantees that the number of states of the hypothesis automaton can never exceed the number of states of the smallest deterministic automaton accepting the considered language.
2. The closedness procedure guarantees that each transition of the hypothesis automaton has an access sequence. This means in particular that a hypothesis automaton of the size (in terms of number of states) of the smallest deterministic automaton for the considered language must already be isomorphic to this very automaton.
3. The treatment of counterexamples guarantees that at least one additional state is added to the hypothesis automaton for each counterexample. Thus, due to (1) and (2), such treatments can happen only finitely often.

4. The equivalence checking mechanism, often called equivalence oracle, provides new counterexamples as long as the language of the hypothesis automaton does not match the desired result.

Put together, this guarantees that the learning procedure terminates after at most n equivalence queries with the smallest deterministic acceptor for the considered language, where n is the number of states of this acceptor.

11.2.1 Modeling Behavior Adequately

Active automata learning has originally been introduced for finite-state acceptors [4]. We illustrated the practical relevance of automata learning in the context of the documentation and verification of telecommunication systems [27–28]. However, in contrast to finite-state acceptors, reactive systems do not distinguish between accepting and rejecting states, but produce some output in response to the inputs. To meet this requirement, we transferred automata learning to Mealy machines [42].

Definition 2   A Mealy machine is defined as a tuple

$$S = \langle Q, q_0, \Sigma, \Omega, \delta, \lambda \rangle$$

where

Q is a finite nonempty set of states (be $n = |Q|$ the size of S),
$q_0 \in Q$ is the initial state,
Σ is a finite input alphabet,
Ω is a finite output alphabet,
$\delta\colon Q \times \Sigma \to Q$ is the transition function, and
$\lambda\colon Q \times \Sigma \to \Omega$ is the output function.

Intuitively, a Mealy machine evolves through states $q \in Q$, and whenever one applies an input symbol (or action) $a \in \Sigma$, the machine moves to a new state according to $\delta(q,a)$ and produces an output according to $\lambda(q,a)$. We write $q \xrightarrow{i/o} q'$ to denote that on input symbol i the Mealy machine moves from state q to state q', producing output symbol o.

The transition function $\delta\colon Q \times \Sigma \to Q$ can be extended to $\delta'\colon Q \times \Sigma^* \to Q$ such that for all states $q,q' \in \Sigma$, letters $a \in \Sigma$, and words $w \in \Sigma^*$, the following holds: $\delta'(q,aw) = \delta'(\delta(q,a),w)$. The same holds for the output function. In the remainder of this chapter, by δ and λ we refer to either one, the extended or the original version, of those functions, depending on context.

Mealy machines are widely used models of deterministic reactive systems, and new learning algorithms for Mealy machines are still developed [49, 51]. In fact, Mealy machine learning seems to dominate for practical and larger-scale applications. Examples are the learning of behavioral models for web services [47], communication protocol entities [11], or software components [48, 52]. We will present an example of learning software components in Section 11.4. Conceptually, Mealy machine learning follows the same pattern as described in the previous section. The only difference is that the two-state discriminators, distinguishing acceptance or rejection of reaching words, are replaced by a set of output symbols discriminating transitions. This leads to minor technical modifications at the side of the required data structure, but has no impact on the overall correctness, completeness, and termination argument sketched above.

Recent extensions to inference methods focus on capturing further phenomena that occur in real systems. On the basis of inference algorithms for Mealy machines, inference algorithms for I/O-automata [3], timed automata [26], Petri nets [21], and message sequence charts [12–13] are being developed. With the I/O-automata model, the wide range of systems that comprise quiescence is made accessible for query learning. Timed automata model explicitly time-dependent behavior. With Petri nets, systems with explicit parallel state are addressed. We devote a special section to approaches that address the problem of complex, parameterized interface alphabets (Section 11.7). In Reference 9, active learning is applied to systems with complex actions with parameters over infinite domains comprising an infinite-state space.

Besides the extension of learning algorithms to cover a wider range of phenomena, the application of active learning in model checking (especially in compositional verification) is an active field of research [18, 40, 46], in particular to overcome the so-called state-space explosion problem.

11.3   CHALLENGES IN REGULAR EXTRAPOLATION

Automata learning can be considered as a key technology for dealing with *black box systems*, that is, systems that can be observed, but for which no or little knowledge about the internal structure or even their intent is available. *Active* automata learning is characterized by its specific means of observation, that is, its proactive way of posing membership queries and equivalence queries. Thus, it requires some way to realize this query-based interaction for the considered application contexts. Whereas membership queries may often be realized via testing in practice, equivalence queries are typically unrealistic. The following subsections discuss the challenges according to the various characteristics of application scenarios, and illustrate that "black does not equal black" in real-life black-box scenarios.

A: Interacting with Real Systems
The interaction with a realistic *SUL* comes with two problems: a merely technical problem of establishing an adequate interface that allows one to

apply test cases for realizing membership queries, and a conceptual problem of bridging the gap between the abstract learned model and the concrete runtime scenario.

The first problem is rather simple for systems designed for connectivity (e.g., web services or code libraries), which have a native concept of being invoked from the outside and come with documentation on how to accomplish this. Establishing connectivity may be arbitrarily complicated, however, for, for example, some embedded systems that work within well-concealed environments and are only accessible via some proprietary graphic user interface (GUI).

The second problem is conceptually more challenging. It concerns establishing an adequate abstraction level in terms of a communication alphabet, which on one hand leads to a useful model structure, but on the other hand also allows for an automatic back and forth translation between the abstract model level and the concrete SUL level. Finding adequate abstractions is not easy. For example, one big problem was that they may easily introduce nondeterminism, which spoils the learning process. This problem has recently been overcome by an automatic alphabet abstraction refinement approach [31].

B: Membership Queries

Whereas small learning experiments typically require only a few hundred membership queries, learning realistic systems may easily require several orders of magnitude more. This directly shows that the speed of the SUL when processing membership queries, or as in most practical settings the corresponding test cases, is of utmost importance. For this kind of systems, while simulation environments typically process several thousand of queries per second, real systems may well need many second or sometime even minutes per test case. In such a case, rather than parallelization, minimizing the number of required test cases is the key to success (cf. Section 11.5).

C: Reset

Active learning requires membership queries to be independent. Whereas this is no problem for simulated system, this may be quite problematic in practice. Solutions range here from reset mechanisms via homing sequences [50] or snapshots of the system state to the generation of independent fresh system scenarios. Indeed, in certain situations, executing each membership query with a separate independent user scenario may be the best one can do (see Chapter 8). Besides the overhead of establishing these scenarios, this also requires an adequate aggregation of the query results. For example, the different user password combinations of the various used scenarios must be abstractly identified.

D: Parameters and Value Domains

Active learning is classically based on abstract communication alphabets. Parameters and interpreted values are only treated to an extent expressible within the abstract alphabet. In practice, this is typically not sufficient, not even for systems as simple as communication protocols, where, for example, increasing sequence numbers must be handled, or where authentication requires matching user/password combinations. Due to the complexity of this problem, we do not expect any comprehensive solutions here. We rather think that domain- and problem-specific approaches must be developed in order to produce dedicated solutions.

The following sections will each be devoted to one of these challenges. For each challenge we will provide a brief presentation of corresponding results and a small practical example.

11.3.1   A Remark on Equivalence Queries

A big challenge that we will not discuss in detail in this chapter is the practical realization of equivalence queries. Research in this direction is scarce. Instead of devoting a dedicated section to the topic, we include here references to the attempts that have been taken so far.

Equivalence queries compare a learned hypothesis model with the *SUL* for language equivalence and, in case of failure, return a counterexample exposing a difference. Their realization is rather simple in simulation scenarios: If the *SUL* is a model, equivalence can be tested explicitly. In practice, however, the *SUL* will typically be some kind of black box and equivalence queries will have to be mimicked using membership queries. In general, this can only lead to an approximative solution, as the possibility of having not tested extensively enough will always remain.

Model-based testing methods [14] have been used to simulate equivalence queries. If, for example, an upper bound on the number of states the *SUL* can have is known, the W-method [16] or the Wp-method [22] can be applied. Both methods have an exponential complexity (in the size of the *SUL* and measured in the number of membership queries needed). We have originally discussed the relationship between regular extrapolation and conformance testing methods in Reference 6.

Without introducing any additional assumptions, only approximative solutions exploiting membership queries exist. Here, conformance testing methods may not always be a wise choice. It has turned out that changing the view from "trying to proof equivalence," for example, by using conformance testing techniques, to "finding counterexamples fast" has a strong positive impact. A recent attempt to intensify research in this direction is taken by the Zulu challenge [19] and elaborated in Reference 30.

11.4 INTERACTING WITH REAL SYSTEMS

In this section, we focus on the second problem of system interaction: bridging the gap between the abstract modeling level and the concrete (realistic) SUL level.

An active learning algorithm generates abstract test sequences using its communication alphabet, which need to be converted into concrete test sequences for the SUL. In response, the learning algorithm expects an abstract output sequence, again at the level of the communication alphabet, which is typically an abstraction of the output generated in response to the concrete test sequence. Components realizing this back and forth translation have different names in different contexts, for example, mapper, test driver, or transducer. To emphasize the proximity to conformance testing setups, we will refer to them as the test driver.

Despite the differences in the concrete instrumentation of actual systems, the following general pattern can be observed. A learning algorithm is instantiated with a (abstract) set of input symbols to the SUL. The membership queries (sequences of input symbols), which the algorithm produces in the course of learning, will be passed to the test driver. The test driver then operates the system by

- translating the membership queries into sequences of actions on the real system,
- performing these actions one by one on the SUL,
- recording the reaction each action produces, and
- translating these reactions into symbols of an output alphabet understood by the learning algorithm.

After the execution of a sequence of inputs has finished, the resulting sequence of outputs will be passed back to the learning algorithm. Figure 11.2, already discussed in the introduction as an example for the general topology of learning setups, sketches a corresponding setup for the case of inferring the behavior a web service. In that case, we find the alphabet information in the Web Services Description Language (WSDL) file of the service, and the test driver works with the concrete actions corresponding to the abstract interface symbols used by the algorithms.

Test drivers are a powerful means to handle abstraction (cf. also Section 11.7) or to fully hide parts of the SUL from the learning algorithm [2–3]. Designing a test driver, however, is not an easy task. It requires domain knowledge as it significantly influences the view of the actual system that will be produced by the learning algorithm. Thus, currently most test drivers are hand tailored. To our knowledge, only Reference 37 explicitly addresses the automatic generation of test drivers for active learning.

11.4.1 Test Driver Design by Example

In the following, we briefly describe a real-life system to which automata learning has been applied. A more elaborate discussion of this case study is given in Reference 48. It is a simple router, originally designed in SystemC at the University of Verona as an application of hardware/software codesign. The router provides four ports on which it can send and receive message packets. It essentially consists of a bounded first-in-first-out queue to buffer the messages and a table containing the information about how to route the messages. The messages themselves consist of a sender address, a receiver address, an identification number generated by the sender, the data, and a checksum.

Designing the test driver, we decided to treat equivalently packets, which differ only in their identification number, data, and checksum, and to use a static routing table, which routes destination 0 to port 0, destination 1 to port 1, and so on. Whenever the router receives a message packet on a port, it pushes it to the end of the queue until the queue is full. If the queue is already full when receiving a packet, the message is dropped.

The intricacy of adequate modeling also becomes apparent here. The obvious definition, to take the sending of messages to the router as input alphabet and the corresponding return messages as output alphabet, does not work, at least if one is interested in the boundedness property of the buffer. This modeling would lead to the same model for every nontrivial buffer, as with this choice of modeling the learning algorithm would send an input packet to the router and then wait until it receives a message from the router, before it would send anew.

This problem can be overcome by splitting the input and output actions in order to desynchronize the send and receive operations. More concretely, after splitting the input into two actions receive and route, whenever the receive action is invoked, the router receives a message on a port and tries to store it in the packet queue. This input action is always directly answered by the test driver with a void output, which enables the learner to send additional packets, independently of whether the router could queue the packet or not. The route action, on the other hand, represents taking a message from the queue and routing it to a network port. It is answered by a nop output if the queue was empty or a send output specifying which packet was sent on which port.

Since this router provides four ports, we decided to analyze it using 16 different message packets, covering each combination of source and destination. We applied the automata learning approach to different variants of the router, where we varied the length of the message queue from 1 to 7. Figure 11.3 shows a graphical representation of the smallest model that the learning algorithm created exploring the system with a message queue length of just 1. The transitions are labeled with the observed input/output pairs.

It is easy to see that the models for the routers grow exponentially with the length of the message queue. The largest learned model with queue length of 7 has 21.844 states. To our knowledge, it is one of the largest "realistic" models

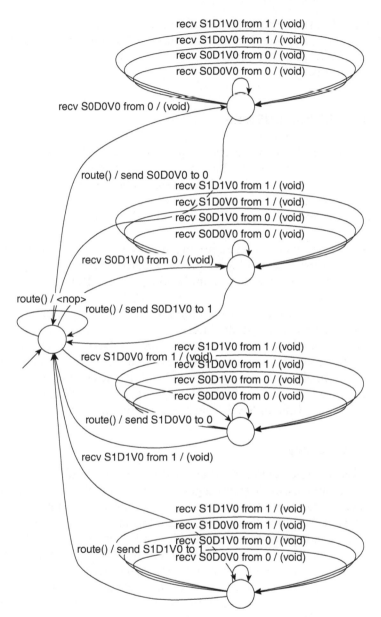

FIGURE 11.3 Model of the router with queue length 1 and 4 ports.

ever learned [48]. The biggest system learned with LearnLib so far is the model of a Plain Old Telephone System with three telephones from the OPEN/ Caesar Tool-Suite [23]. The model has 39.974 states, 51 inputs, and about 2 million transitions.

11.5   MEMBERSHIP QUERIES

Learning algorithms use membership queries extensively to systematically explore a system's behavior, until no more "direct evidence" for inconsistencies between an updated model and the system's behavior is detected.

To reduce the number of queries that is necessary to exploit a system's behavior, some extensions to the original L^* algorithm [4] have been proposed.

The approaches range from removing local consistency checks [41] and optimizing the worst-case number of queries [50] to entirely replacing the data structure [39] or the underlying machine model [3, 35]. In Reference 5, a partial overview is given.

Another approach to reducing the number of tests that have to be executed on a system is application-specific filters. These filters can drastically reduce the number of membership queries and open regular inference to realistic systems. In the following, we briefly discuss some effective though general ideas for filters, in order of increasing specialization. The corresponding experiments were based on a setting with DFAs, but the results similarly apply for the more general setting of Mealy machines as illustrated in Chapter 8.

11.5.1   Redundancy

In the classical implementation, which systematically explores the system's behavioral capabilities, the learning algorithms may generate redundant membership queries, that is, produce different derivations for the same test case. In order to prevent the automated test equipment from executing those test cases twice, a cache can be used to detect doubles and filter them out [42].

Also, in testing-like scenarios, membership queries will return complete traces and not only a single symbol (like acceptance or rejection in the case of finite-state acceptors). Thus, posing a membership query in practice will usually produce the knowledge that, in the theoretical formulation, can only be obtained by posing membership queries for all the prefixes of the questioned word. This additional knowledge can also be kept by means of a cache.

11.5.2   Prefix Closure

If the language to be learned consists of observations of runs of a real-world system, it is obvious that this language is prefix closed, that is, that given a run, every prefix of this run is also in the language (as it is itself also a run of the

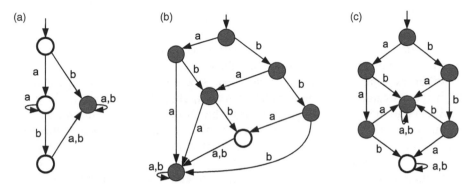

FIGURE 11.4 Deterministic finite-state machines with different characteristics (accepting states have a light color and a thick border). (a) Prefix closed DFA; (b) independent actions a, b; (c) symmetric actions a, b.

system). This observation leads to a very powerful optimization, as the learning algorithm does not need to consider continuations of strings that have already been excluded from the *SUL*'s language by means of a previous membership query. Also, whenever a long string is known to be a run of the system, we can add all the prefixes of this string to the model without further testing effort. Putting it in formally correct terms, a DFA is prefix closed if the set of nonaccepting states $Q \backslash F$ cannot be left:

$$\forall q \in (Q \backslash F) . \forall a \in \Sigma . \delta(q, a) \in (Q \backslash F).$$

Figure 11.4a shows a prefix closed DFA: The bottom state is the only rejecting state, which is a sink. Note that minimized prefix closed DFA can be characterized by having a sink as their only rejecting state.

The theoretical concept of prefix closedness can be transferred to Mealy machines and real systems quite easily. It can be used to skip uninteresting parts of the *SUL*: It is only necessary, for example, in the test driver (cf. Section 11.4), to mask certain outputs to a special error symbol and ensure that an error output will transfer the *SUL* to an artificially defined error sink. Results from the application of a prefix closure filter to real-world models are presented in References 7, 35, 42and .

11.5.3 Independence of Actions

Observable events may be independent in the sense that they can be executed in any order leading to the same system state. Thus, if we have observed (or queried) one execution order, we can deduce that each reordering of independent events results in the same system state. In particular, if one of these execution orders is a run of the system, then so are all the (equivalent) reorderings of the independent actions $a,b \in \Sigma$:

$$\forall q \in Q . \, \delta(\delta(q, a), b) = \delta(\delta(q, b), a).$$

Independence filters exploit this observation by only querying the system for one member of each such equivalence class.

Whereas a prefix closure filter can always be employed, an independence filter requires some additional input from an application expert in the form of an independence relation that specifies which events can be shuffled. As an example, the deterministic finite-state machine in Figure 11.4b contains the pair of independent actions (a, b), highlighted in black. Formally, independence is an irreflexive and symmetric relation on pairs of actions. The used implementation of an independence filter normalized queries according to the independence relation: It calculated the lexicographical smallest equivalent query based on a given ordering on the actions [35, 42].

11.5.4   Input Determinism

For many practical systems, one can distinguish between an input and an output alphabet in the following sense: They are always input enabled, reflecting the fact that a system cannot control its environment, and deterministically respond to input. Thus, whenever one response to a certain input sequence is known, this sequence needs not to be considered any further. This optimization has been proven to be very powerful when modeling such systems as finite-state automata [35] (cf. Fig. 11.4). It turned out, however, that this optimization is much more naturally covered by switching to Mealy machine models.

11.5.5   Symmetry

Hardware and telecommunication systems often contain large numbers of components that cannot be distinguished from each other by observation, that is, without explicitly looking at their identification number. For example, from an observational point of view, it often does not matter which device is performing a certain action (e.g., which memory bank is addressed or which phone calls a certain number), and also the precise identification of the counterpart (the requesting processor or the receiver of the call) in principle is unimportant, as long as we assume a unique and consistent identification, for example, that the called number and the number of the receiver match [42].

This observation provides an enormous potential for optimization, which grows with the number of identical components in a system. We implemented a corresponding filter, which in its essence leads to a symbolic treatment of the devices. Figure 11.4c shows an example of a DFA, where a and b were considered symmetric, that is, fully interchangeable.

11.5.6   Filters by Example

We have carried out model construction experiments on several typical installations of the call center application of Reference 42. For illustration purposes,

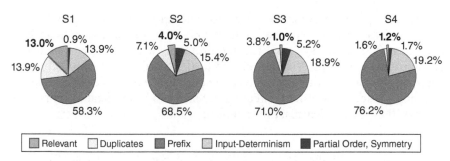

FIGURE 11.5   Percental filtering of membership queries per filter.

we present four simple scenarios, each consisting of a telephone switch connected to a number of telephones. In each of these scenarios, the focus of the learned model was restricted to only include a few actions of the telephones and some responses of the switch. In the simplest scenario (S1), there is just one phone permitted to lift and hang up the receiver; in the last (S4), there are three phones where two may establish a connection. A detailed presentation of the setup is given in Reference 44.

As can be seen in the diagrams of Figure 11.5, a combination of input determinism of the systems, prefix closure of the language, and independence of certain actions allows for significant reductions in the number of tests. The filters were applied in the order that is given in the legend of the figure. Test cases were classified with respect to the first filter that covered the test case. It should be noted that the order in which filters are applied may change their combined effect (cf. Reference 43).

The prefix filter has a similar impact in all considered scenarios. This seems to indicate that it does not depend so much on the nature of the example and on its number of states. The other two filters (input determinism and partial order) vary much more in their effectiveness: the saving factor increases with the number of states. One would expect that the impact of the partial order and symmetry increases with the level of independence. This is indeed confirmed by the experiments: S1 has only one actor, so that there is no independence, which results in a factor of 1. As the number of independent devices increases, the saving factor increases as well, cf. figures for S2 and S3. Compared with S3, the saving factor in S4 decreases. This is due to the fact that the action that has been added in S4 (the initiation of a call) establishes a dependency between two devices, which reduces the potential of the partial order and symmetry optimization.

11.6   RESET

Learning reactive systems in principle requires a means of resetting the *SUL* into its initial state: In order to guarantee meaningful results, all membership queries (or experiments) have to be performed under the same initial conditions. This is a fairly strong requirement and may not be assumed to hold in the case of real-life systems. The requirement of resetting a system into the same state can in practice be relaxed to the requirement of resetting the system into an observationally equivalent state. There are several alternatives to explicitly resetting a system that are more likely to be applicable in practical scenarios than an explicit reset mechanism:

- One way of realizing reset is a globally valid *homing sequence*, a sequence of actions that will always return the *SUL* into its initial state. For most software systems that comprise a complicated control structure, it is not obvious that a globally valid homing sequence exists. However, in hardware systems, this is more common. A globally valid homing sequence is used in Reference 1 as reset mechanism. The inferred distributed software system relies heavily on the message-passing paradigm, and the single components do not comprise a complicated control structure. For this system, a sequence of actions that consume all messages from channels leaves the system in a defined state. Executing this very sequence twice does still lead to the same "empty" state.

  A homing sequence usually has to be designed manually before the actual learning process can start. The possibility of inferring systems with on-the-fly generated homing sequences has been an interest of theoretical considerations [50].

- If one has access to an implementation for off-line experimentation as, for example, in case of the existence of a *SUL* which runs in some kind of test harness, it will usually be possible to simply use a fresh instance of the *SUL* for every experiment. In References 2, 11, and 49, this approach is utilized to infer the behavior of protocol entities. The protocol entities were run in network simulators, and for every experiment, a newly created protocol entity was used.

- If there exists only one instance of a system, it may be possible to use abstraction instead of reset: a system that, for example, to each new connection or user exposes the same behavior, can be learned using an abstract interface alphabet, which in the test driver is translated into concrete experiments exploiting such properties. A case study is presented in Reference 1, in which a behavioral model of a web service was extrapolated without the existence of any means to reset the service. The presented approach relies on the assumption that such services will usually provide the same behavior for every new connection. The existence of concrete transaction identifiers was abstracted from the alphabet that the learning algorithm used, and a new set of transaction identifiers was used for every experiment. This put the concrete service into states that were indistinguishable on the abstract level. This technique was used to learn the global behavior of the OCS as described in Chapter 8.

This short and incomplete list of ideas for relaxing the requirement of an explicit reset mechanism indicates that there are manifold ways to circumvent literally resetting the *SUL*.

11.6.1 Reset by Example

We here present excerpts of a case study that exemplifies the third discussed approach to realizing a reset mechanism. The case study is discussed in detail in Reference 1. Basis for this case study was the "Pay on the Move" (PoTM) service, which provides the functionality to manage payments between customers and owners of web shops. Users of PoTM can begin transactions providing thereby wiring details for a payment and credentials for the used account. They may also suggest a transaction ID. The service exposes two additional primitives: one to check the status of a transaction and one to let a bank confirm a transaction (in case the planned withdrawal is possible). An excerpt of the WSDL document defining the interface of the web service is shown in Figure 11.6.

Resetting the system was realized by abstraction: The differences between the individually used instantiations, each with their own "fresh" transaction IDs, became unobservable. Fresh here means transaction IDs that have not been used in the system so far. Freshness was tested using the checkTransactionStatus primitive that returns differently for used and unused transaction IDs and does not change the state of the system.

```
...
<xs:complexType name="BeginTransaction">
 <xs:sequence>
  <xs:element minOccurs="0" name="transactionId" type="xs:string"/>
  ...
 </xs:sequence>
</xs:complexType>

<xs:complexType name="CheckTransactionStatus">
 <xs:sequence>
  <xs:element minOccurs="0" name="transactionId" type="xs:string"/>
 </xs:sequence>
</xs:complexType>

<xs:complexType name="AknowledgeTransaction">
 <xs:sequence>
  <xs:element minOccurs="0" name="transactionId" type="xs:string"/>
  ...
 </xs:sequence>
</xs:complexType>
...
```

FIGURE 11.6   WSDL of the PoTM web service (excerpt).

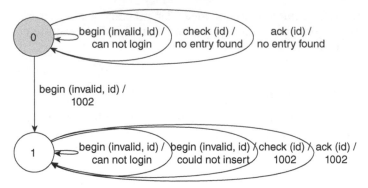

FIGURE 11.7   Extrapolated model of the PoTM web service.

Figure 11.7 shows a graphical representation of the model the learning algorithm created exploring the payment service using only fresh transaction IDs. The transitions are labeled with the according input and output symbols. The shown output symbols are the return values of the primitives' invocations. A return value of "1002" denotes a successful return. In the case of an error or exception, the cause given by the web service is shown as output symbol.

As can be seen in Figure 11.7, only a new transaction using an unused transaction ID leads to a new state of the system. The learned model approves the assumption that allowed the relaxation of the reset requirement: The service's behavior is independently the same for all concurrent transactions.

11.7   PARAMETERS AND VALUE DOMAINS

As discussed in Section 11.4, learning models of real systems requires a test driver, which provides a bridge between the learning algorithm and the *SUL*. The test driver can, as discussed, also be used to take care of abstraction, for example, by hiding certain parameters. In this section, however, we will consider methods that deal with interface alphabets, which comprise actions with parameters (like, e.g., method calls) automatically. For these systems in general, it is not possible to infer the behavior for all possible instantiations with concrete data values of every alphabet symbol. But, to certain subclasses of such systems, regular extrapolation methods can be applied. It becomes possible, for example, if the parameters influence the behavior of the *SUL* only in a way that can be modeled by Boolean expressions over the parameters.

Definition 3   A parameterized Mealy machine is defined as a tuple

$$S_P = \langle Q, q_0, \mathcal{A}, \Omega, \Gamma \rangle$$

where

Q is a finite nonempty set of states (be $n = |Q|$ the size of S_P),

$q_0 \in Q$ is the initial state,

$\mathcal{A}$ is a finite set of parameterized actions,

Ω is a finite output alphabet,

Γ is a finite set of transitions. Each transition is a tuple $\langle q, a(\bar{z}), g, q' \rangle$, where $q, q' \in Q$, and $(a(\bar{z}), g)$ are guarded actions.

Like a Mealy machine, a parameterized Mealy machine will evolve through states consuming input and producing output symbols. Be $a(\bar{z}) \in \mathcal{A}$ an action and $\bar{z}$ a vector of abstract parameters for a. By $\bar{c}$ we denote a concrete valuation of $\bar{z}$. A guard g for $a(\bar{z})$ is a conjunction of atomic Boolean propositions over single components of $\bar{z}$. A guarded action is a pair $(a(\bar{z}), g)$ of action and guard; it is an abstract representation of all concrete $a(\bar{z})$ with $\bar{c} \vDash g$. We require Γ to be a well-defined function.

Learning algorithms for parameterized Mealy machines will be typically initialized only with some concrete input symbols and the most general guard resembling the Boolean value *true*. The alphabet will be extended dynamically and the guards will be refined accordingly. Basis for the refinement of the guards is the adoption of combined inference methods: Active learning becomes a frame for inferring the state space that has to be combined with strategies for inferring a correct abstract interface alphabet, that is, construction of guard formulas in this case. The general pattern of this technique for *automatic alphabet abstraction refinement* has been presented in Reference 32: Basis for the extension of the alphabet are the counterexamples obtained in equivalence queries, which either indicate that

- the current hypothesis misses at least one state or
- one of the hypothetical guards is too general.

Alphabet refinement comes into play when a counterexample reveals that a hypothetical guard/alphabet symbol is still too general. In this case, the too general guard/alphabet symbol is split into two and the learning continues with the refined alphabet. This leads to the extension of the classical learning pattern as highlighted in the left-hand side of Figure 11.8.

References 8 and 24 present two concrete realizations of this pattern: In Reference 8, a method is proposed for inferring behavioral models for systems that are parameterized through input actions with Boolean parameters. The guards in this scenario are formulas in disjunctive normal forms (DNFs) over those parameters: All concrete parameter valuations for one symbol that are covered by one guard satisfy a particular DNF. For alphabet refinement, that is, to construct refined guards, a technique for learning DNFs is used that follows the lines of Reference 10.

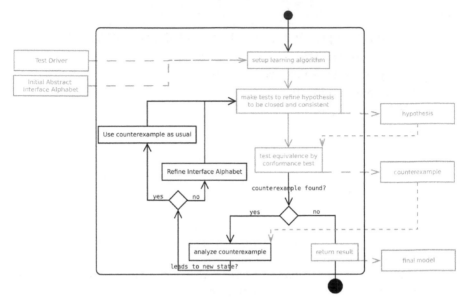

FIGURE 11.8 Structure of combined extrapolation algorithms (modeled in XPDD [38]).

In Reference 24, the general pattern is used to incrementally extend a given alphabet during the learning process. However, in the proposed white-box scenario (model checking), there are no guards and no abstraction is refined. Rather, previously ignored input alphabet symbols are added when the currently considered alphabet is not distinctive enough.

11.7.1 Parameters by Example

Reference 29 considers actions with multiple integer parameters, and develops a method for alphabet refinement based on the technique proposed in Reference 25 for learning unions of axis-parallel boxes in the d-dimensional space. Key to this implementation was the clear separation of two intertwined analyses, one in which the structure of the automaton is revealed using $L*$, and a second one in which the threshold concerning the integer parameters is determined following Reference 25.

In this setting, abstract input symbols can be represented by the linear equations that describe these unions of axis-parallel boxes as Figure 11.9 shows schematically. In the following, we only briefly present some experimental results without going into the implementation details of the employed alphabet refinement method. For a detailed discussion of the employed methods and results, we refer to Reference 29.

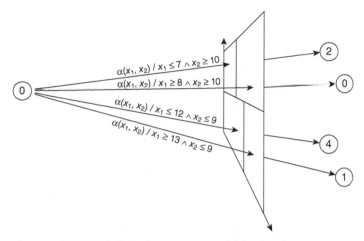

FIGURE 11.9   Integer parameterized actions.

To estimate how changes in the properties of parameterized Mealy machines will affect the behavior of the learning algorithms with respect to membership queries, we conducted four series of experiments on randomly generated machines with varying properties. In each of the four series of learning experiments, the black-box systems varies in exactly one of the following properties: arity of actions, number of transitions, size of parameter domain, and complexity of guards. All generated automata had six states, one abstract action, and an output alphabet of size two. For each resulting class, 60 models were generated with varying frequencies for the output symbols.

The models were learned in a naive way, treating every possible valuation of parameters as separate input symbol (dark), and then using the above-mentioned method for refining the abstract set of actions only on demand (bright). We assumed that the system to be learned is deterministic at the concrete level, and took the occurrence of nondeterminism as the sole sign for a too coarse abstraction. Figure 11.10 shows the average number of membership queries used for the different series in logarithmic scale:

- Figure 11.10a shows the results for the series in which the number of parameters was increased. It is easy to see that increasing the number of parameters for the naive algorithm leads to an exponential increase in the number of membership queries, while for the refinement algorithm, this has no significant impact.
- The increase of the size of the parameter domains (Fig. 11.10b) results in an akin effect.
- Increasing the number of transitions (i.e., the number of guards) on the other hand has no effect on the naive version of the algorithm, which is hardly surprising (Fig. 11.10c).

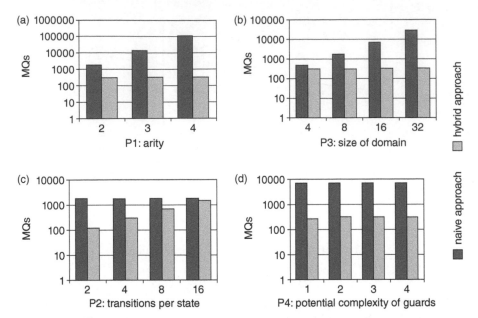

FIGURE 11.10 Average number of membership queries (MQs) per series of experiments.

- In the fourth series, the potential complexity of guards was increased stepwisely. Figure 11.10d shows that increasing the potential complexity had no significant impact on the actual complexity.

11.8 THE NGLL

The practical knowledge we gained during the last 6 years has been made available to users in the *LearnLib* tool [49]. In spite of being configurable and offering a rich library of algorithms and filters, creating fitting learning setups is still laborious. In part, this is because available learning methods are not engineered to be versatile in practice, and they are often hard coded for specific use cases and thus show limited potential for adaptability toward new fields of application.

The NGLL [45] is designed to ease this task by supporting model-based construction of dedicated learning solutions on the basis of extensible component libraries. These libraries comprise various methods and tools to deal with realistic systems including test drivers, reset mechanisms, and abstraction/refinement techniques. Being Internet enabled, NGLL supports the usage of remote components. Thus, learning solutions can be composed of mixtures of components running locally or anywhere in the world, a feature that turned out to be particularly useful for learning remote systems, or to flexibly distribute the learning effort on distributed resources.

11.8.1 Base Technology

The NGLL is based on jABC [53], our service-oriented framework for modeling, development, and execution of complex applications and processes. NGLL is an extension of the LearnLib, which was originally designed to systematically build finite-state machine models of unknown real-world systems (telecommunications systems, web services, etc.). The experience with the LearnLib soon led to the construction of a platform for experimentation with different learning algorithms and for statistical analyses of their characteristics in terms of learning effort, runtime, and memory consumption. NGLL provides implementations of the learning algorithms presented in References 4, 35, 39, 41, 50, and 51. However, (re-)implementing well-known algorithms is not its primary focus.

One of the main obstacles in practical learning is the implementation of the idealized form of interrogation in terms of membership and equivalence queries proposed by Angluin. This requires an application-specific interplay of testing and abstraction technology, which is well known to be a hard task in practice. Improving this aspect led to a complete redesign of the LearnLib, that eventually resulted in the NGLL. NGLL provides here a new degree of flexibility, as well as improved means for profile analysis and abstraction handling. The key aspect is a new and simple way of composing learning processes that directly describe the learning setup.

11.8.2 Modeling Learning Setups

A complete learning setup is usually composed of several types of components: learning algorithms for various model types, test drivers, query filters, caches, model exporters, statistical probes, abstraction providers, handlers for counterexamples, and more. Some of them are optional while others are not, and many of these components are reusable in nature and should easily be employable in varying application contexts. The NGLL provides collections of such components and exposes them as easy-to-use building blocks. This enables learning process engineers to graphically compose application-fit learning setups.

Figure 11.11 illustrates the graphical modeling style typical for NGLL along a very basic learning scenario. As shown in the canvas on the right that reports a typical learning setup, one easily identifies a common three-phase pattern recurring in most learning setups:

- The learning process starts with a *configuration phase*, in which in particular the considered alphabet and the test driver are selected, before the learner itself is created and started.

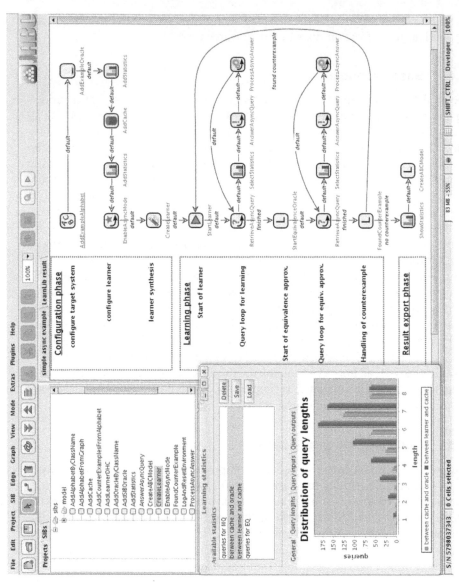

FIGURE 11.11 Executable Service Logic Graph (SLG) of a simple learning setup in jABC.

- The subsequent central *learning phase* is characterized by the L^*-typical iterations, which organize the test-based interrogation of the *SUL*. These iterations are structured in phases of exploration, which end with the construction of a hypothesis automaton, and the (approximate) realization of the so-called equivalence query, which in practice searches for counterexamples separating the hypothesis automaton from the *SUL*. If this search is successful, a new phase of exploration is started in order to take care of all the consequences implied by the counterexample.

- Otherwise, the learning process terminates after some *postprocessing* in the third phase, for example, to produce statistical data.

Basically, all learning setups follow this pattern, often enriched by application-specific refinements. Our graphical modeling environment is designed for developing such kind of refinements by supporting, for example, component reuse, versioning, and evaluation.

The learning setup is composed in the right canvas of single components that are organized in thematic collections and presented in the upper left of Figure 11.11. The setups designed this way are executable. In the window at the bottom left, NGLL presents a selection of statistics on the execution of the learning setup, in this case the distribution of query lengths.

11.9 CONCLUSION AND PERSPECTIVES

We have reviewed the essence of practical automata learning, its major challenges, its variants, possible solutions, and illustrative case studies, in order to indicate how active learning can be an application specifically enhanced to become a powerful tool for practical system development. Indeed, real-life case studies, where behavioral models with several ten thousand states have been extrapolated, illustrate that the technology has the potential to scale to sizes that allow for a better runtime-oriented control of emerging behavior.

Our initiative to establish a flexible experimentation environment for the systematic investigation and treatment of different application scenarios, technologies, and tools led to the development of the NGLL. Using NGLL, it is possible to combine technologies from different solutions (e.g., References 4, 35, 39, 41, 50, and 51) into executable heterogenous tool compositions in order to better understand the impact and interplay of the various design decisions and optimizations. This way, users are enabled to study the impact of problem-specific model structures including various types of parameters and abstraction technologies, different treatments of counterexamples, and alternative approximations of equivalence queries. In order to encourage people to participate in this kind of experimental research, we started lowering the initial threshold by initiating the RERS platform [15]. The acronym RERS for Regular Extrapolation of Reactive Systems is meant to emphasize the practicality of this enterprise, and the NGLL is meant to provide the corresponding technological backbone.

REFERENCES

1. F. Aarts, J. Blom, T. Bohlin, Y.-F. Chen, F. Howar, B. Jonsson, M. Merten, R. Nagel, A. Sabetta, S. Soleimanifard, B. Steffen, J. Uijen, T. Wilk, and S. Windmuller. Establishing Basis for Learning Algorithms, 2010. Available at: http://hal.archives-ouvertes.fr/inria00464671/en/

2. F. Aarts, B. Jonsson, and J. Uijen. Generating models of infinite-state communication protocols using regular inference with abstraction. In *ICTSS*, pp. 188–204, 2010.

3. F. Aarts and F. Vaandrager. Learning I/O automata. In P. Gastin and F. Laroussinie, eds., *CONCUR 2010—Concurrency Theory, Volume 6269 of Lecture Notes in Computer Science*, pp. 71–85. Springer Berlin/Heidelberg, 2010.

4. D. Angluin. Learning regular sets from queries and counterexamples. *Information and Computation*, 75(2):87–106, 1987.

5. J. L. Balcázar, J. Díaz, and R. Gavaldà. Algorithms for learning finite automata from queries: A unified view. In *Advances in Algorithms, Languages, and Complexity*, pp. 53–72, 1997.

6. T. Berg, O. Grinchtein, B. Jonsson, M. Leucker, H. Raffelt, and B. Steffen. On the correspondence between conformance testing and regular inference. In M. Cerioli, ed., *Proceedings of the FASE '05, 8th International Conference on Fundamental Approaches to Software Engineering, Volume 3442 of Lecture Notes in Computer Science*, pp. 175–189. Springer Verlag, April 4–8, 2005.

7. T. Berg, B. Jonsson, M. Leucker, and M. Saksena. Insights to Angluin's learning. Technical Report 2003-039, Department of Information Technology, Uppsala University, August 2003.

8. T. Berg, B. Jonsson, and H. Raffelt. Regular inference for state machines with parameters. In L. Baresi and R. Heckel, eds., *Proceedings of the FASE '10, 13th International Conference on Fundamental Approaches to Software Engineering, Volume 3922 of Lecture Notes in Computer Science*, pp. 107–121. Springer Verlag, 2006.

9. T. Berg, B. Jonsson, and H. Raffelt. Regular inference for state machines using domains with equality tests. In J. L. Fiadeiro and P. Inverardi, eds., *Proceedings of the FASE '08, 11th International Conference on Fundamental Approaches to Software Engineering, Volume 4961 of Lecture Notes in Computer Science*, pp. 317–331. Springer Verlag, 2008.

10. A. Blum and S. Rudich. Fast learning of k-term DNF formulas with queries. In *Proceedings of the 24th ACM Symposium on Theory of Computing*, pp. 382–389. ACM, New York, 1992.

11. T. Bohlin and B. Jonsson. Regular inference for communication protocol entities. Technical Report, Department of Information Technology, Uppsala University, Sweden, 2009.

12. B. Bollig, J.-P. Katoen, C. Kern, and M. Leucker. Replaying play in and play out: Synthesis of design models from scenarios by learning. In O. Grumberg and M. Huth, eds., *Proceeding of 13th International Conference on Tools and Algorithms for the Construction and Analysis of Systems (TACAS '07), Held as Part of the Joint European Conferences on Theory and Practice of Software (ETAPS '07) Braga, Portugal, Volume 4424 of Lecture Notes in Computer Science*, pp. 435–450. Springer, 2007.

13. B. Bollig, J.-P. Katoen, C. Kern, and M. Leucker. Smyle: A tool for synthesizing distributed models from scenarios by learning. In F. van Breugel and M. Chechik, eds., *Proceedings of 19th International Conference on Concurrency Theory (CONCUR '08), Toronto, Canada, August 19–22, 2008, Volume 5201 of Lecture Notes in Computer Science*, pp. 162–166. Springer, 2008.

14. M. Broy, B. Jonsson, J.-P. Katoen, M. Leucker, and A. Pretschner. *Model-Based Testing of Reactive Systems, Volume 3472 of Lecture Notes in Computer Science*. Springer-Verlag New York, Secaucus, NJ, 2005.

15. Chair of Programming Systems, TU Dortmund, Department of Computer Science. RERS—A Challenge in Active Learning, 2010. http://leo.cs.tu-dortmund.de:8100/. Version from 20.06.2010.

16. T. S. Chow. Testing software design modeled by finite-state machines. *IEEE Transactions on Software Engineering*, 4(3):178–187, 1978.

17. E. M. Clarke, O. Grumberg, and D. A. Peled. *Model Checking*. The MIT Press, 1999.

18. J. M. Cobleigh, D. Giannakopoulou, and C. S. Pasareanu. Learning assumptions for compositional verification. In *Proceedings of the TACAS '03, 9th International Conference on Tools and Algorithms for the Construction and Analysis of Systems, Volume 2619 of Lecture Notes in Computer Science*, pp. 331–346. Springer Verlag, 2003.

19. D. Combe, C. de la Higuera, and J.-C. Janodet. Zulu: An interactive learning competition. In *Proceedings of FSMNLP 2009*, 2010 (to appear).

20. F. Denis, A. Lemay, and A. Terlutte. Residual finite state automata. *Fundamenta Informaticae*, 51(4):339–368, 2002.

21. J. Esparza, M. Leucker, and M. Schlund. Learning workflow petri nets. In *Proceedings of the 31st International Conference on Application and Theory of Petri Nets and Other Models of Concurrency (Petri Nets'10), Lecture Notes in Computer Science*. Springer, 2010.

22. S. Fujiwara, G. von Bochmann, F. Khendek, M. Amalou, and A. Ghedamsi. Test Selection based on finite state models. *IEEE Transactions on Software Engineering*, 17(6):591–603, 1991.

23. H. Garavel. Open/caesar: An open software architecture for verification, simulation, and testing. In *Proceedings of the 4th International Conference on Tools and Algorithms for Construction and Analysis of Systems*, pp. 68–84. Springer-Verlag, London, UK, 1998.

24. M. Gheorghiu, D. Giannakopoulou, and C. S. Pasareanu. Refining interface alphabets for compositional verification. In *TACAS*, pp. 292–307, 2007.

25. P. W. Goldberg, S. A. Goldman, and H. D. Mathias. Learning unions of boxes with membership and equivalence queries. In *Proceedings of COLT '94, 7th Annual Conference on Computational Learning Theory*, pp. 198–207, ACM, New York, 1994.

26. O. Grinchtein, B. Jonsson, and P. Pettersson. Inference of event-recording automata using timed decision trees. In *Proceedings of CONCUR 2006, 17th International Conference on Concurrency Theory*, pp. 435–449, 2006.

27. A. Hagerer, H. Hungar, O. Niese, and B. Steffen. Model generation by moderated regular extrapolation. *Lecture Notes in Computer Science*, pp. 80–95, 2002.

28. A. Hagerer, T. Margaria, O. Niese, B. Steffen, G. Brune, and H.-D. Ide. Efficient regression testing of CTI-systems: Testing a complex call-center solution. Annual review of communication. *International Engineering Consortium (IEC)*, 55:1033–1040, 2001.

29. F. Howar. Inferenz parametrisierter moore-automaten. Master's thesis, Technische Universität Dortmund, Fakultät für Informatik, Lehrstuhl für Programmiersysteme, 2009.

30. F. Howar, B. Steffen, and M. Merten. From ZULU to RERS—Lessons learned in the ZULU challenge. In T. Margaria and B. Steffen, eds., *ISoLA (1), Volume 6415 of Lecture Notes in Computer Science*, pp. 687–704. Springer, 2010.

31. F. Howar, B. Steffen, and M. Merten. Automata learning with automated alphabet abstraction refinement. In R. Jhala and D. A. Schmidt, eds., *VMCAI, Volume 6538 of Lecture Notes in Computer Science*, pp. 263–277. Springer, 2011.

32. F. Howar, B. Steffen, and M. Merten. Automata learning with automated alphabet abstraction refinement. In *Twelfth International Conference on Verification, Model Checking, and Abstract Interpretation*, 2011.

33. H. Hungar, T. Margaria, and B. Steffen. Model generation for legacy systems. In M. Wirsing, A. Knapp, and S. Balsamo, eds., *RISSEF, Volume 2941 of Lecture Notes in Computer Science*, pp. 167–183. Springer, 2002.

34. H. Hungar, T. Margaria, and B. Steffen. Test-based model generation for legacy systems. In *Test Conference, 2003. Proceedings. ITC 2003. International, Volume 1*, pp. 971–980. September 30–October 2, 2003.

35. H. Hungar, O. Niese, and B. Steffen. Domain-specific optimization in automata learning. In W. A. Hunt, Jr. and F. Somenzi, eds., *Proceedings of the 15th International Conference on Computer Aided Verification, Volume 2725 of Lecture Notes in Computer Science*, pp. 315–327. Springer Verlag, July 2003.

36. H. Hungar and B. Steffen. Behavior-based model construction. *International Journal on Software Tools for Technology Transfer*, 6(1):4–14, 2004.

37. V. Issarny, B. Steffen, B. Jonsson, G. S. Blair, P. Grace, M. Z. Kwiatkowska, R. Calinescu, P. Inverardi, M. Tivoli, A. Bertolino, and A. Sabetta. CONNECT challenges: Towards emergent connectors for eternal networked systems. In *ICECCS*, pp. 154–161, 2009.

38. G. Jung, T. Margaria, C. Wagner, and M. Bakera. Formalizing a methodology for design- and runtime self-healing. In *Engineering of Autonomic and Autonomous Systems, IEEE International Workshop*, 0:106–115, 2010.

39. M. J. Kearns and U. V. Vazirani. *An Introduction to Computational Learning Theory*. MIT Press, Cambridge, MA, 1994.

40. M. Z. Kwiatkowska, G. Norman, D. Parker, and H. Qu. Assume-guarantee verification for probabilistic systems. In *TACAS*, pp. 23–37, 2010.

41. O. Maler and A. Pnueli. On the learnability of infinitary regular sets. *Information and Computation*, 118(2):316–326, 1995.

42. T. Margaria, O. Niese, H. Raffelt, and B. Steffen. Efficient test-based model generation for legacy reactive systems. In *HLDVT '04: Proceedings of the High-Level Design Validation and Test Workshop, 2004. Ninth IEEE International*, pp. 95–100. IEEE Computer Society, Washington, DC, 2004.

43. T. Margaria, H. Raffelt, and B. Steffen. Analyzing second-order effects between optimizations for system-level test-based model generation. In *Test Conference, 2005. Proceedings. ITC 2005. IEEE International*. IEEE Computer Society, November 2005.

44. T. Margaria, H. Raffelt, and B. Steffen. Knowledge-based relevance filtering for efficient system-level test-based model generation. *Innovations in Systems and Software Engineering*, 1(2):147–156, 2005.

45. M. Merten, B. Steffen, F. Howar, and T. Margaria. Next Generation LearnLib. In *Seventeenth International Conference on Tools and Al-Gorithms for the Construction and Analysis of Systems*, 2011.

46. C. S. Pasareanu, D. Giannakopoulou, M. G. Bobaru, J. M. Cobleigh, and H. Barringer. Learning to divide and conquer: Applying the L* algorithm to automate assume-guarantee reasoning. *Formal Methods in System Design*, 32(3):175–205, 2008.

47. H. Raffelt, T. Margaria, B. Steffen, and M. Merten. Hybrid test of web applications with webtest. In *TAV-WEB '08: Proceedings of the 2008 Workshop on Testing, Analysis, and Verification of Web Services and Applications*, pp. 1–7. ACM, New York, 2008.

48. H. Raffelt, M. Merten, B. Steffen, and T. Margaria. Dynamic testing via automata learning. *International Journal on Software Tools for Technology Transfer*, 11(4):307–324, 2009.

49. H. Raffelt, B. Steffen, T. Berg, and T. Margaria. LearnLib: A framework for extrapolating behavioral models. *International Journal on Software Tools for Technology Transfer*, 11(5):393–407, 2009.

50. R. L. Rivest and R. E. Schapire. Inference of finite automata using homing sequences. *Information and Computation*, 103(2):299–347, 1993.

51. M. Shahbaz and R. Groz. Inferring mealy machines. In *FM '09: Proceedings of the 2nd World Congress on Formal Methods*, pp. 207–222. Springer Verlag, Berlin, Heidelberg, 2009.

52. M. Shahbaz, K. Li, and R. Groz. Learning parameterized state machine model for integration testing. In *Proceedings of the 31st Annual International Computer Software and Applications Conference, Volume 2*, pp. 755–760. IEEE Computer Society, Washington, DC, 2007.

53. B. Steffen, T. Margaria, R. Nagel, S. Jörges, and C. Kubczak. *Model-Driven Development with the jABC, Volume 4383 of LNCS*, pp. 92–108. Springer Berlin/Heidelberg, 2006.

INDEX

Lightning Source UK Ltd.
Milton Keynes UK
UKHW022129300419

341879UK00002B/77/P